CW00531146

Retirement Migration

Routledge Research in Population & Migration

SERIES EDITOR: PAUL BOYLE, *University of St. Andrews*

Retirement Migration

Paradoxes of Ageing

Caroline Oliver

Routledge
Taylor & Francis Group
New York   London

Routledge
Taylor & Francis Group
270 Madison Avenue
New York, NY 10016

Routledge
Taylor & Francis Group
2 Park Square
Milton Park, Abingdon
Oxon OX14 4RN

© 2008 by Taylor & Francis Group, LLC
Routledge is an imprint of Taylor & Francis Group, an Informa business

Printed in the United States of America on acid-free paper
10 9 8 7 6 5 4 3 2 1

International Standard Book Number-13: 978-0-415-37271-8 (Hardcover)

Except as permitted under U.S. Copyright Law, no part of this book may be reprinted, reproduced, trans-
mitted, or utilized in any form by any electronic, mechanical, or other means, now known or hereafter
invented, including photocopying, microfilming, and recording, or in any information storage or retrieval
system, without written permission from the publishers.

Trademark Notice: Product or corporate names may be trademarks or registered trademarks, and are
used only for identification and explanation without intent to infringe.

Library of Congress Cataloging-in-Publication Data

Oliver, Caroline, 1976-
    Retirement migration : paradoxes of ageing / Caroline Oliver.
        p. cm. -- (Routledge research in population & migration ; 9)
    Includes bibliographical references and index.
    ISBN 978-0-415-37271-8 (hardback : alk. paper)
    1. Retirement, Places of--Foreign countries. 2. Retirement, Places of--Spain. 3.
Aging. I. Title.

HQ1063.O45 2007
306.3'80869120946--dc22   2006102912

Visit the Taylor & Francis Web site at
http://www.taylorandfrancis.com

and the Routledge Web site at
http://www.routledge.com

Contents

Illustrations

Acknowledgements

In 1998 I began to approach the task of researching the stories of retired migrants in Spain presented here. Some of this material appeared in a first incarnation in a PhD submitted in 2002 at Hull University. Since then, the work has been developed through further research and reflection. Over this long period, innumerable people have supported, encouraged and challenged me. I count myself fortunate that despite the few social anthropologists actively research ageing in European contexts, a number were at Hull University. In particular, I cannot thank enough Andy Dawson, Jenny Hockey and Judith Okely for their time and encouragement for both my doctorate and the book and I would especially like to thank Jenny, for her advice when writing the book. I would also like to thank the staff and postgraduates in Sociology and Social Anthropology at Hull (1998–2002) for their feedback and friendship. Allison James and Nigel Rapport have also helped through their engagement with the research, and I would particularly like to thank Peter Phillimore, Karen O'Reilly and Mike Hepworth for their attention to parts of an earlier draft. I must also extend gratitude to the referees of the proposal and the editors at Routledge, Terry Clague and Benjamin Holtzman for their patient support and guidance. I owe all these people a debt of gratitude for their time and help, which is particularly appreciated in the early stages of an academic career. However, despite their insights I acknowledge the weaknesses as entirely my own.

Papers based on some of the material were presented at seminars at York, Kent, Newcastle and Oxford Universities and at Queens University Belfast. I am grateful to the organisers of these events, as well as those colleagues attending for their comments. I would also like to thank the British Academy for funding later follow-up research in 2005, and special thanks are also due to Esther Jimenez for her rapid turnaround of transcriptions of large volumes of interview data, which was extremely helpful. Of course, immense thanks goes to those in Spain who opened their homes and lives to me. I feel privileged to have worked in such an interesting place. There are too many people to mention by name, but the people participating in the study and their kindnesses are not forgotten. I use pseudonyms to disguise people in the book, but I must mention the help of some individuals, including Dorothy Price for her interest and invaluable help and both Brenda Haddon and Marta Taylor Whitehead for their support and friendship. Thanks also to Jim and Herta Ellerbe, George and Sylvia Brooks, David Earle, Erik Tönsberg, Sarah Oliver and Chris and Ann Stewart for their help and hospitality in the fieldwork stage. In particular, thanks to Erik and Brenda for kind permission to reproduce their work in Chapters 3 and 7. And above all, I wish to thank Eduardo Navas Fernandez and Ana Marí Martin Lomas and their families for their hospitality, help with the research and continued friendship.

Finally, much of the writing of this book was undertaken between jobs and in weekends. I must thank my family for their support, although I feel that 'thanks' is too weak a word for Marc Verlot, my partner, who patiently shared the pleasures and pains of this endeavour, particularly in the arduous final stages when a number of delays hindered the book's completion. This coincided with a period where I was both expecting our first child and I saw the illness and death of my own dear grandad, Leslie Grout, an inspiration throughout my life; it is to them both that this book is dedicated.

1 Introduction
Flirting with Freedom

On the expatriate radio in Southern Spain, advertisers urge listeners to 'buy a dream home' in a nearby corner of paradise. They respond to the aspirations of growing numbers of people, who, as retirement approaches, face questions about when, where and how they will spend the time 'off'. The possibilities are diverse for many people in an increasingly mobile, transnational and globalising world. Castles and Miller (1998) point out how the last half of the twentieth century has been 'an age of migration', with unprecedented movements of people across the globe and yet whilst this has been a topic of increasing study in contemporary social sciences, 'retirement as a key contemporary "mobility"' is less well explored (Katz 2005: 211). This book hopes to address that gap. Written from an anthropological perspective and based on ethnographic research, it considers the cultural and age-based identities of British (and some other Northern European) older people in Southern Spain, who have retired abroad in the hope of finding warmth, good health, enjoyment, company and friendship. Their migration offers a passport to a new leisured identity following working lives,[1] in sociological and anthropological terms, the process represents something of a modern day rite of passage.

The book describes the stories of the people who go through this process. A central concern however, is the way these individuals' identity negotiations are sharpened by existential and biological factors of ageing. It considers the degree to which the possibilities of people moulding identities in new surroundings are circumscribed by the reality of getting older. The march of the clock means that year on year, people who have retired to Spain face questions of how to maintain their chosen lifestyle whilst simultaneously negotiating challenges wrought by ageing: How much longer can they live in their *tipico* 'Spanish' house at the top of a steep, cobbled street? Does the esteem and pleasure gained from organising community activities justify their sometime feelings of tiredness? Whilst the freedom from family responsibilities may be liberating, who will look after them if they fall? The book explores how such tensions presented in aspirational retirement migration are managed on an individual basis.

The stories in this book are underpinned by wider cultural questions, not least because many of the tensions in retirement migration lifestyles arise from the ambivalent and ill-defined messages and expectations of ageing in Western societies today. Even the term 'retirement' is somewhat of a misnomer, capturing little of the experience of the later life period in the current era. Far from retiring or withdrawing, for many older people, life after sixty-five is experienced as a period of activity, social connection, good health and financial security (Jerrome 1992). Blaikie describes a 'transformation of retirement' (1999: Chapter 3) related to demographic changes, developmental shifts in medical technology as well as the emergence of consumer culture. Notions of 'the third age' suggest rather different experiences in mid to later life periods than in the past (Laslett 1989, Blaikie 1999) and have led to discussions of 'positive' or 'successful' ageing' as alternatives to previous gloomy depictions of old age (Featherstone and Hepworth 1991). Blaikie explains, 'older citizens are encouraged not just to dress 'young' and look youthful, but to exercise, have sex, diet, take holidays, and socialise in ways indistinguishable from those of their children's generation' (Blaikie 1999: 73–74). Yet the optimistic fluidity this shift enables in interpreting the life course coexists uneasily with the continued significance of material, bodily ageing, as modernist models of the life course continue to retain hegemonic dominance in instating the significance of bodily ageing (Vincent 1995, Hockey and James 2003). These persist in part through state policies on employment, which legislate for when retirement occurs (Hazan 1994, although see Chapter 2). They also resonate with wider cultural values that continue to affirm the potency and social significance of biological ageing of the body.[2] But, as this book shows, it is at the personal level too that the effects of unpredictable biological ageing and the uncertain knowledge of certain mortality may disrupt many of the best laid plans for this time of life.

As such, if cultural messages around ageing are ambivalent in contemporary society, there is a need to investigate how individuals manage these tensions. The research aimed to explore how the contradictions are lived through and dealt with by individuals. The book shows in particular how migrants' lifestyles are framed by uncertainty concerning how long the hard-earned retirement abroad will continue. With the fetters of work shed and the migrant context offering possibilities for the construction of desired lives, the only certainty of the aspired lifestyle is that it is finite; it will not go on for ever. The awareness of the indeterminate nature of this point manifests itself in two opposing drives which shape behaviours and identities. One is a spontaneous orientation to the present, evident in the assertions by migrants that they want 'to make the most of the time we have left'. Yet knowledge of the uncertain but finite nature of this leisure time also exerts an extremely powerful countervailing pull for time to be spent wisely and not frittered away in less than meaningful encounters. In this way, feelings of freedom from former expectations battle against opposing concerns for time-discipline and productivity. The tension around this time of life influences many other wider choices to do with behaviour, activities and relationships. Therefore, whilst migrating abroad is pursued according to the spirit of living in the 'here and now', people also pursue conflicting desires for endurance, permanence, trust and stability. And whilst retirement may involve relaxing from work in a leisured existence, the morality of structured time-use that has governed the years before is not so easily forgotten, and retirees' 'free' time thereby becomes subject to new regulations and expectations.

Based on investigation of the day to day practices of retirement migrants, the book centrally shows how individuals reintroduce certain constraints (voluntarily and as a response to others) when faced with the freedoms imagined in the experience of retiring abroad. As such, the account hopes to avoid entering into evaluations of whether their experience is 'successful' (see Chapter 2). It is rather a story that exposes individuals' vigilance and self-management in their straddling of the contradictory messages of ageing: their commitment to respect one's own space at the same time as needing others, their hopes to continue individual self-growth without being too demanding of themselves and their requirement to balance the desires for consumption with care for their body. It is a story about the possibilities for people to explore their identities outside of a lifetime's definition without losing their security and moorings, about enjoying unscheduled free time without wasting the time 'left' and the ways in which their activity is balanced with 'retiring'. It is a story about finding the way between innumerable paradoxes in ageing that these people 'living the dream' are confronting as pioneering 'new' old agers.

Although travellers in a physical sense, it is as much the case therefore that the individuals in this study are also exploring new cultural territories. They are, like others of their generation, pioneering new approaches to ageing (see also Warnes, Friedrich, Kellaher and Torres 2004, Warnes 2004). With no script to follow they confront the 'possibility of exploring alternative pathways to those followed during earlier parts of the life course, laid down by a particular culture or expected by other generations' (Daatland and Biggs 2004: 5). The analysis shows that as these people discard irrelevant presumptions about ageing but have no precedent themselves to follow, their negotiations of the tensions inherent in their chosen lifestyles mark a 'flirting with freedom'. In flirting with new possibilities, but yet not abandoning their previous modes of being, they engage in a process that is not without risk, but nevertheless enables the playful and optimistic contemplation of different ways of living, and opens up spaces in the stories they can tell about themselves (Phillips 1996).

RETIREMENT MIGRATION: AN
ETHNOGRAPHIC APPROACH

Although the book focuses on British retired migrants' experiences of ageing, it is important to consider the phenomenon as an example of wider contemporary experiences of ageing, especially given demographic projections of an ageing population. The second world assembly of the UN forum on ageing anticipates that by 2050, an estimated 2 billion people will be over sixty, comprising 20% of the entire world population (International Labour Organisation 2002). Whilst the majority will be in the developing world, there will also be an enormous relative and absolute growth in the numbers of older people in the developed world. And, although care should be taken to avoid portraying Western retirement as a period of leisure particularly as unpaid work often continues (Mason 1988) and the UK pensions' crisis undermines guarantees of financial security in later life, it is without doubt the case that the nature of current life course transitions has made possible qualitatively different experiences of retirement for growing numbers of people in the West than before.

In particular, there is clear evidence of increasing mobility in retirement. Law and Warnes show how retirement migration in Britain has escalated in the post war period (1982). This has commonly been to domestic seaside resorts, as people exploit prior connections made through previous holiday experiences. Yet the ease and affordability of long-distance travel has also facilitated the growth of retirement migration on an international scale. Destinations in other areas of Europe and beyond are marketed as feasible new homes (King, Warnes and Williams 2000: 23–26) and recent estimates suggest that there are around 840,000 British pensioners living overseas (Fixsen, *The Independent* 1999).[3] With many older people already familiar with regular overseas tourism, the continuation or extension of travel in retirement is hardly surprising. Many migrant experiences are preceded by tourist journeys (Rodríguez, 2001) and certainly in the Mediterranean, retirement migration can be seen as something of 'a natural progression' (King, Warnes and Williams 1998: 97) from the patterns of tourism established during the mass tourism boom of the 1960s.

However, this creates difficulties for analysing the phenomenon, particularly as migration from Northern to Southern Europe blurs tourism and migration (Williams and Hall 2002, Gustafson 2002, O'Reilly 2003). Indeed, the range of types of movement mean the migrant experience is better understood as a range of experiences of displacement (Warnes 1991) in which migrants fall somewhere along a continuum ranging from the status of tourist to permanent migrant (O'Reilly 2000a). However, this ambiguity has meant that even defining the extent of the phenomenon of retirement migration, both in Spain and elsewhere, has proven difficult, leading to a variety of widely varying estimates of the actual numbers of British residents in Spain (ibid.). Many migrants are not officially registered because their movement is fluid, they do not realise they must register, they wish to avoid bureaucracy or do not want to relinquish ties with Britain (Williams, King and Warnes 1997, O'Reilly 2000a and see discussions in Warnes 1991 and King et al 2000: 36–39 on the wider difficulties of ascertaining the scale and scope of international retirement migration). Certainly, one must bear in mind O'Reilly's caution that in Spain, the 'official records of "residency" are an unreliable reflection of what should be a clearly defined group' (2000a: 46). Nevertheless, discussing the numbers of UK pensioners in Spain, King et al (2000: 25) refer to 34,225 UK pensioners in Spain in 1997 based on figures from the Department of Social Security Benefits Agency.[4] Certainly Spanish (non age-specific) statistics also show that the British are the largest national group of EU nationals living in Spain (*Instituto de Estadística de Andalucía*, 2002) and of these, there are a particular concentration in Andalucía and more particularly Málaga province (King et al 2000: 40–41).

Those migrating tend to be of a particular social makeup; King, Warnes and Williams' study of British international retirement migrants shows that almost two-thirds of migrants engaging in retirement migration were from social classes 1 and 2 (ibid.: 76). Whilst this suggests that like other experiences of 'successful ageing', it is dependent on the availability of a sufficient income[5] (Featherstone and Hepworth 1991, Thompson, Itzin, Abendstern, 1991) other research shows that retirement migration may also be employed by the less wealthy, who use it as an economic survival strategy made possible by the intensification of globalising trends. As Huber and O'Reilly (2004: 329) suggest, there are therefore many retired people who move to Spain in order to 'get more for their money'.

In response to the growth of international retirement migration in the latter period of the twentieth century (ibid.) there has been a growing body of academic work on the phenomenon, particularly from geographical and sociological perspectives. King, Warnes and Williams' (2000) comprehensive study of Northern European International Retirement Migration, *Sunset Lives. British Retirement Migration to the Mediterranean*, documents the backgrounds, motivations, levels of social integration, health and welfare for British retirees living in various destinations, including the Costa del Sol.[6] Survey research by Rodriguez, Fernandez Mayoralas and Rojo (1998) also offers a cross-national comparison of Northern European retirees' reasons for moving to Spain, their experiences of life there and impacts on the local region. The latter is also considered by Rodríguez, Casado Díaz and Huber (2000) whilst interdisciplinary research presented by Echezarreta Ferrer (2005) considers demographic, political and social aspects of the phenomenon in towns in the Costa del Sol. Betty (1997) considers language difficulties of retired migrants in Spain, their enhanced quality of life (Betty 2001) and documents their experiences of health and social services (Betty and Cahill 1999) whilst Ackers and Dwyer (2002, 2004) examine policy implications in their analysis of retired migrants' citizenship rights and social entitlements when moving to a host member State. Qualitative research by Gustafson (2001, 2002) on Swedish seasonal migrants explores some cultural implications of transnational living for older people. However, the only ethnographic work on foreign residents in general is O'Reilly's work on the British on the Costa del Sol (2000a, 2000b, 2004), Lund's research on incomers in the Alpujarras (2005, 2006) and Waldren's (1996, 1997) work on incomers in Mallorca. These offer pertinent insights but nonetheless intentionally depart from a specific focus on migrants of retirement age (apart from Huber and O'Reilly 2004).

This study of retirement migration offers an ethnographic perspective on the phenomenon, and is based on fifteen months of fieldwork and intermittent field visits spanning eight years in a town and village to the east of Málaga (described in more detail in Chapter 3). In 2001, the town in which I conducted the research had a population of nearly 17,000 people of which 17% were officially from another country, whilst 10% of the village's 2100 population were foreign residents (municipal padrón, *Instituto de Estadística* 2001). Although, as suggested earlier, these figures are likely to be vastly underestimated,[7] this is still relatively low in comparison to other settlements, particularly in the western Costa del Sol, where some 33% of the registered population are European foreigners (O'Reilly 2004). However, the municipalities present an interesting case because of the recent spurt of 'rapacious development' associated with migration from EU countries that is occurring in these areas (Barke and Towner 2003). For example, the municipalities in question have seen a substantial boom in real estate contracts for land purchase and construction in 2000, and in the first three months of 2001, 95% of these contracts were signed by non-Spanish buyers (mainly British and Scandinavian people (ibid.). This may lead to the impression formed by one Spanish retiree I talked to, who stated, 'here there are times that you go out on the street and the ones who seem foreigners are the Spaniards' (*'aquí hay veces que sales a la calle y lo que nos hacemos extranjeros somos los españoles'*).

EXPLORING AGEING AND MIGRATION IN GLOBALIZATION

In exploring the experiences of ageing of Northern European people moving to Spain, the ethnography is inspired by anthropological research on ageing in Western contexts. Anthropologists have not been particularly forthcoming in studying ageing experiences in Western contexts. Yet the few studies, based on the premise that 'natural' processes such as ageing, are always culturally shaped and interpreted, offer significant insights into ageing as a cultural experience. The studies have chiefly documented older people's resistance to social marginalization (Keith Ross 1977, Myerhoff 1978, Hazan 1980, Okely 1990, Hockey 1990, Hockey and James, 1993,

Jerrome 1992, and Dawson 1990, 1998, 2002) and testified to how older people, on an individual basis, are engaged in intense work to reassert self-hood, visibility and continuity in the face of the social subversion they face in old age (Cohen 1994).

The research is also inspired by ethnographic research on migrant subjectivities in globalization (Rapport and Dawson 1998). This growing body of research responds to the critique that social anthropologists have inadvertently marginalised movement and privileged the experiences of people who reside *in situ* through their research focus, methods and presentation (Appadurai 1991, Clifford 1992, Hannerz 1992, Featherstone 1995, Malkki 1995, 1997, Gupta and Ferguson 1997a and b, Rapport and Dawson 1998). Addressing these issues has engendered a shift of sorts within the discipline, towards exploring 'ethnoscapes', transnational 'landscapes of group identity' (Appadurai 1991: 191) and the 'routes' rather than 'roots' of cultural identities (Clifford 1992). A growing number of studies explore how migrant identities are constructed in 'transnational spaces of belonging' (Xavier and Rosaldo 2002: 12, e.g. Rouse 1991, Fog Olwig 1993, Malkki 1995, Paerregaard 1997, Linger 2001) and aim to capture the fluid, processual nature of the cultural as 'liquid, emergent and open-ended' rather than exploring 'culture' as necessarily territorially circumscribed (Hannerz 1992: 17 and see also Kahn 1989, Abu-Lughod 1991,[8] Hannerz 1996 for critiques of the anthropological concept of culture).

This book also considers mobility a central topic of inquiry, but is especially mindful of the need to consider how life course experiences relate to mobility, particularly through more consideration of older people's experiences of migration in the contexts of globalization. Sociological and anthropological studies of migration have often been based on specific types of analyses, in which the dominant migrant figure studied is a young, male, economic migrant[9] (Anthias and Lazaridis 2000, Kofman, Phizaclea, Raghuram and Sales 2000). There are signs of widening scope in the range of experiences that are studied, especially in considering gender (Anthias and Lazaridis 2000, Kofman, Phizacklea, Raghuram and Sales 2000) ethnicity and class (Anthias 1992). Moreover, the mobilities of those engaging in privileged travel such as foreign news correspondents, business travellers and other expatriates have recently received some attention (see Hannerz 2004 and Amit 2007). And there is some consideration of the life course in studies of migration strategies in peasant households (Brettel 2000 and see Paerregaard 1997). To date however, social scientists interested in transnationalism have paid little attention to the international mobility of older people (Gustafson 2001) and whilst there is an established body of research on the overlaps between migration studies and gerontology, the significance of international migration and its influence on ageing processes has not been widely considered (Blakemore 1999, Warnes and Williams 2006).

The book is built on the premise that in considering migrants' identities, there is much to be gained from a confluence of perspectives which considers the intersection of ageing and migrant/cultural subjectivities. As others have argued, cultural aspects of older people's lives, including their traditions, beliefs, customs and (where relevant) migration trajectories could be given more central consideration in gerontological understandings (see Keith et al 1994, Torres 1999, 2001, 2004, Blakemore 1999 and Phillipson and Ahmed 2004) whose prevalent focus is on the material conditions of ageing. As Torres (1999: 34) argues:

> as gerontologists, we have allowed our ways of thinking, and in particular a focus on social inequality, to overshadow the objective of understanding the cultural backgrounds and present realities of the older people whose conceptualisations and experiences we have attempted to study.

Furthermore, considering ageing and the life course is also important for understanding migrant identities. For example, Gardner's rare study of first generation Bengali migrants' experiences of ageing in London exposes how migrants' orientations to the traditions of their homeland are not stable, but change over the life course. She also points out the risks of overlooking how generational perspectives and life course histories shape migrant identity. She suggests in particular that the overwhelming interest in younger South Asians (and other ethnic groups) as the domain of cultural fusion in Britain is misleading, and asks convincingly:

> Where are the voices of their parents and grandparents? Are they subconsciously assumed to be less 'hybrid' and culturally creative, guardians of the 'traditions' whose study will lead to less interesting theoretical insights into the nature of cultural identity? (Gardner 2002: 13)

As ethnographies of migration have shown, transnational influences or relationships beyond immediate proximity bear influence on people's experiences generally (Brewer 2007), and this is likely to also be the case in ageing experiences (Phillipson and Ahmed 2004). This opens up an exciting arena of research which allows for a consideration of how dominant received ideals of ageing may come under revision in contexts of globalization[10] and considers how cultural belongings, hybridity, or degrees of cultural bifocality may operate in the choices, behaviours and orientations of older people (ibid.). It may well be the case that, as Gardner contemplates, older people are less amenable to hybrid identities. For example, Škrbiš' (1999) research amongst Slovenian and Croatians in Australia suggests long-distance nationalism persists because there is a transmission of cultural and nationalist persuasions from first to second generation migrants. And as Gelfand (1994) also shows (see Torres 2004) later life migrants may be less likely to be able to incorporate new customs, languages and ways of life than younger ones. Yet more empirical consideration of how migrant experience fragments according to the life course promises interesting insights into topical questions of motivations, belonging, cultural re/construction and integration. And there are multiple experiences barely explored in Europe, where older migrants range from poor and excluded minorities, to others such as those considered here who possess the capital to be able to pioneer innovative approaches to growing older (Warnes, Friedrich, Kellaher and Torres 2004, Warnes and Williams 2006).

However, the application of contemporary anthropological perspectives on globalization and identity to the study of ageing mobilizes scholars to think less in terms of 'different' orientations to ageing as dictated by 'a' culture. It behoves us rather to consider the way in which individuals' approach to ageing is shaped by the *cultural* as a fluid process, in a focus on individuals 'not as robots programmed with 'cultural' rules, but as people going through life' (Abu-Lughod 1991: 158). This means attention to both the direct cultural contexts (see Chapter 2) but also how, as Appadurai suggests, specific individuals increasingly *imaginatively* comprehend their lives 'through the prisms of the possible lives offered by the mass media in all their forms' (1991: 198). It requires consideration of how the inundation of dominant cultural expectations and images may impinge on how individuals imagine and experience ageing. And it means close consideration of the ways that these particular cultural mores might be re-evaluated, modified or confirmed following observations and knowledge of 'other' cultural forms of ageing. As Torres argues, for older migrants, international migration not only challenges migrants' behavioural repertoires, but 'it questions the very essence that gives their preferred behavioural patterns their meaning' (2004: 127).

Certainly for this book on migration in later life, these insights shed light on the meaning that place, mobility and confrontation with other ways of life and ageing may have for people growing older. Movement influences wider identity-making processes for people as they grow older (Torres 1999, 2001, 2004) particularly as the experience of migrancy engenders a sharpening self-awareness through the confrontation of difference between oneself and the 'other' (Chambers 1994). The migrant experiences 'a constantly challenged identity....perpetually required to make herself at home in an interminable discussion between a scattered historical inheritance and a heterogeneous present' (ibid.: 6). The experiences of migration documented in this book more particularly demonstrate how the act of moving from the UK to Spain is employed cognitively by migrants to rethink and rewrite the common scripts of dehumanisation, invisibility and marginality associated with old age. As I will show, migrants creatively engage with ideas and images associated with place, travel, culture and age in order to realise certain aspirations about time-use, the body and ageing, sociability and cultural identity. In doing so, they also however socially, spatially and temporally displace negative fears/stereotypes associated with ageing in other geographical locations, whilst concentrating 'positive' aspects of an ageing lifestyle in Spain. Before expanding on how this occurs, I explain how the research was conducted.

THE RESEARCH APPROACH

A cultural outlook on ageing requires adopting a position that starts from the subjectivity of older people and attempts to explore the meanings of ageing to them. The research therefore adopts a social constructionist position, exploring the subjective experiences of ageing rather than researching through 'definitional rigour, hypothesis testing and quantification' (Jerrome 1992: 4). The interpretive and inductive approach I use is one that considers social phenomena less as facts than as experiences which give rise to emergent meanings. Inspired by the notion that the analysis of culture should 'not [be] an experimental science in search of law but an interpretive one in search of meaning' (Geertz 1973: 5) my research aimed to understand the themes, symbols and metaphors by which people feel, understand and express themselves as they grow older in this context. In order to try to understand these issues, I immersed myself in the daily lives of older migrants in the town and village for two periods in 1998 and 1999, in a total of fifteen months' fieldwork. There, I frequented the associations run by and for foreign residents, attending group meetings of the Royal British Legion, International Club, American club, Labour Club, History Club, Spanish classes for expatriates, and other ad hoc meetings such as the Embroidery Club. I also engaged myself in their social networks, and participated in their lives through attending trips, sharing meals and drinks, and informally visiting people in their homes.

Grounded study remains anthropology's great strength, but new styles of research are being used to capture the fluidity of cultural processes and non-local influences discussed previously. Ethnography may now be multi-sited (Marcus 1995, Hannerz 2003) based on the use of historical records (Olwig 1993, Paerregaard 1997), engage in research through the internet (Miller and Slater 2000) or entail extended contact with informants through email or telephone. In the light of these developments, my research approach seems quite traditional; I spent my research periods in a defined geographical site of a village and a town some way to the East of Málaga on the Costa del Sol. I walked with Malinowskian[11] shoes when I arrived in the village. Lodging with a Spanish family and limited by the poverty of youth, I was more or less physically restricted to the village and the local town, where I attended a variety of the clubs, associations, trips and events frequented by retirees. I had no car, no mobile telephone and beyond a few bus trips here and there, I had a fairly sedentarised experience of fieldwork.

However, whilst this is no doubt a community-study, it is one which has mobility, transience and cultural complexity at its heart. Although situated in one place, the field site could be conceived as 'several sites in one' (Hannerz 2003: 18) to be explored through 'multi-levelled single-site fieldwork' (Eriksen 2003: 15). This includes, 'studying the same setting from the perspective of different social groups participating in it, or studying a site at several levels of abstraction from ongoing social processes' (ibid.). Whilst the cities, airports or hotels are often explored as the province of culturally complex cultures, the town and village I studied here was equally a context of heightened mobility, as Clifford (1992) would describe, a 'place of travelling' or nexus of flows of different people. Retirement migrants are seasonal visitors, some live there permanently and others are in between those extremes (see O'Reilly 2000a). They coexist in this area with other permanent residents, other migrants from within and outside of Spain, second-home owners, people on sabbatical and those seeking work in building, gardening, teaching or the tourist industry.

Such complexity renders any simple 'village' or 'town' ethnography a complicated affair. The site becomes the unique 'point of intersection in a wider network of relations' (Morley 1999: 157) in which the emphasis is on the 'indeterminacy of infinitely overlapping tangles of personal relationships' (Amit 2002: 16). These are not simply negotiated between easily definable groups of foreign residents and Spaniards but amongst migrants themselves, where differences are evident in terms of lifestyle, attitudes, background, class, economic situation, motivations and longevity in the site. The analysis therefore pays attention to how attachments are newly constructed in situ as much as are maintained in transnational ties, which is the common focus of much ethnographic research on migration. In any case, as Amit and Rapport suggest, for many, movement is associated with 'disjunction, compartmentalization and escape' rather than sustained connections (Amit and Rapport 2002: 4). Whilst this does not mean neglecting evidence of transnational collectivity, it nevertheless alters the scope to uncover the particular circumstances of *how*, *when* and *why* ties are mobilised (Chapter 5 and 7).

Furthermore, this ethnographic investigation, although focusing on British retired migrants, is more a study into a category of experience: ageing,[12] than purely of 'a' cultural or national group. Globalization has enabled the possibility for people to choose to live in 'lifestyle enclaves' in which places are inhabited with likeminded people (Bellah et al 1984) whether they are retired people who like golf, or young, childless professionals (Griswold 1994). This raises the question of whether other shared preferences, characteristics, or experiences — such as ageing — offer the basis for associations that transcend (or perhaps intersect with) identity categories of national difference in these emerging social formations (see Chapter 7). To some extent therefore, the study of 'ageing' although approached through the lens of a focus mainly on 'British retired people' is also an exploration of emerging postnational communities. This means that references to individuals of other nationalities are made where these have emerged in the ethnographic context.

Moreover, the focus on older people is a choice elected upon consciously, whilst mindful of the fact that moving to Spain is undoubtedly an attractive option for those of working age. However, others' working experiences arguably present different issues to those facing older people considered here. Of course, there are overlaps in lifestyles between retired and working migrants (and indeed it is, in practice, difficult to strictly separate the two) but the focus in the book is on qualitatively documenting experiences of *retirement* and *ageing* (see O'Reilly's 2000a, 2000b, 2002, 2003, 2004 work for alternative perspectives). And the attention to 'experience' means that there is less emphasis or consideration of strict definitions or categorisations of retired migrants. Thus, when considering the social negotiations of ageing as witnessed in my ethnographic work, I include reference to older foreign residents regardless of whether they have recently intentionally moved upon retirement to Spain, or have lived for some time in Spain and now face older age there. Such longer term migrants are perhaps, in other works, not strictly 'retirement migrants' but their presence was so enmeshed in the ethnographic contexts I researched and their stories prove important for understanding ageing as a category of experience in this context. In particular, longer term migrants show cohort effects, and their views are significant in influencing other migrants' values and moralities around ageing (see Chapter 5).

PRACTICAL DETAILS OF THE RESEARCH

The practicalities of my research also need some mention. In the first period in 1998, I lodged with a Spanish couple and their two young boys in the heart of Freila village. This choice was on one hand simply a pragmatic option, as my teaching-related research grant[13] was insufficient for me to afford to pay for rental at the regular tourist prices. However there were also unforeseen benefits that living in the village allowed, as it enabled me to research the experiences of less visible migrants who do not necessarily participate in the well-established social scene on the coast. It also enabled me to gain some experience of Spanish society, which, as I show in Chapter 7, is morally valued amongst certain segments of the foreign community. The main advantage however was that living with a Spanish family offered a linguistic learning experience which enabled me later on (in 2005) to access multiple points of view on the phenomenon of retirement migration. The continuing contact with the family gave me insight into arenas that remain distant for some migrants. Thus, as much as I was always considered an *extranjera* (foreigner) in the village, I was also familiar to many Spaniards in the village as *la niña* (girl) of the family. The association with their extended family and friends enabled a fuller contextual understanding of the place of foreign residents (myself included) in the locality and allowed a critical interrogation of retirees' claims of integration in Spain. It also allowed me to ascertain how local Andalucían daily routines, beliefs and approaches to life merged or differed with other people that I spent my time with and offered a reference point for thinking about the veracity of migrants' images of Andalucían villagers. The ethnography therefore includes some insights from ethnography and interviews into how Northern European incomers relate to and are received by the local population in the areas studied,[14] although the Spanish perspective is a limited aspect of the project used insofar as to how it relates to retirement and ageing abroad.

During the second period of research in 1999, through my informants' networks I was able to rent a property on my own at an affordable price, which helped me to experience a life more similar to those I was studying. In both periods, I tried to be visible in the community, so in addition to attending as many of the clubs and associations frequented by older migrants as possible in the town (see Chapter 3) I also aimed to be out and about often, visiting people and meeting up with them on an informal basis. However, whilst participant observation was the main method, I used loosely structured interviews (based on Mason 1996) to explore the narratives of retired migrants. They enabled me to access the particular circumstances and life stories of migrants in their own words, enabling me to probe aspects of the shorter, rehearsed narratives that were presented in the public domain. These details are unlikely to have been revealed in pure observation, whilst the process also enabled inclusion of those who do not necessarily participate in the public 'scene'.

As Hockey (2002a) argues, interviews can, in any case, offer a useful dimension of ethnographic research as they can be intimate encounters which correspond with many of the core means of social interaction in the West. When migrants allowed me into their private home spaces, the informal talk is, as Hockey suggests, 'a practice that conforms closely to Western categories of experience' (ibid.: 220). Furthermore, conducting interviews were not only useful means of data-collection, but had the social effect of making explicit my role as 'researcher' and constructed my reputation as someone with a legitimate 'job'. As I discuss in Chapter 4, there is an expectation amongst retirees that one must deserve to live in Spain and that it is a privilege earned by working hard. Particularly as a younger woman there on my own, the 'hanging-out' associated with some ethnographic practice (Dingwall 1997) may have opened no doors in the long run and hindered my wider intentions to engage with people's activities and share their ways of life. Using an initial 'clipboard stance' therefore helped instigate first encounters, which then led to friendship through further visits and personal correspondence. I conducted sixty-seven interviews/actor-led conversations with migrants and fifteen interviews with Spanish people, using a snowball strategy starting from key figures in club life and from Spanish acquaintances respectively, although I also participated in countless other informal social conversations which followed similar lines of inquiry.

Selecting interviewees through snowball sampling involves the exploitation of existing social networks to access respondents (Atkinson and Flint 2001). The use of contacts in this way was particularly beneficial as it enabled me to introduce myself to others through association with and by recommendation of, trusted individuals in the wider community (which, as I discuss in Chapter 6 is important in the transient context). Downsides of this approach are that in following the recommendations of certain individuals, others who participate less in social networks may be missed out (ibid.) and a rather too cohesive appearance of community may be assumed. The danger was mitigated by my accompanying long-term participant observation, which allowed me to observe from my own experience, how, when and why people moved in and out of social networks. It meant that as more and more individuals became alert to my interests, they were often able to point me towards less visible cases that might otherwise be missed in my participation in public events.

In the main study, I interviewed fifty-three people who were retired (ranging in ages from mid-fifties to late-eighties) six people who were semi-retired[15] (working part-time in Britain or in Spain) and eight other people (ranging from an English Spanish teacher to the owner of a cafe) who were related to the community and had opinions pertinent to my interest. Fourteen people I interviewed lived in coastal urbanisations, twenty-three lived in flats or houses in the town, one person was in a residential home, fifteen people lived in houses in the village and fourteen people lived in the *campo* (country) away from the town, village and coast. Thirty-nine people interviewed were married, of whom one man was separated from his wife. Twelve were widowed women, two were widowed men. Twelve women were unmarried, six of whom were divorced whilst two men were unmarried of whom one was divorced. The interviewees came from a range of professional backgrounds and included a former journalist, some Royal Air Force professionals, a number of expatriate executives, two academics, a number of teachers, a legal secretary, a nurse, a social worker, a number of accountants and members of the police force. Respondents reflected the very limited racial differentiation in the expatriate society; migrants are overwhelmingly white and Northern-European in origin. The larger proportion of women (63 per cent) interviewed reflected the networks on which the snowball sample was drawn. It is unclear exactly what the real gender divide of retired British migrants is, because of the difficulty of obtaining reliable statistics, although O'Reilly (2005) suggests there are more women than men registered. Previous surveys have been based on a 50% divide (Rodríguez et al 2000) whilst King et al's (2000) research had slightly more male respondents than women. In some ways inadvertently perhaps because of my own gender, this study has turned out to be, like Jerrome's, 'about old women, and a few old men' (1992: 4).

THE SAME YET DIFFERENT: THE SELF
IN THE RESEARCH PROCESS

Although researchers are keen and obliged to reflect the 'facts' as accurately as they can (Scheper Hughes 1992) it is nevertheless well documented how the research enterprise is fundamentally researcher-specific (Okely and Callaway 1992). Obviously, my research and interpretive reflection on the data are coloured by my position. On one hand, I was 'part-native', as a British young woman researching British migrants. Like my informants, I had moved away from 'home' and as a woman, I shared the gender of the majority I researched. Similar to other British migrants, I struggled with ongoing attempts and setbacks involved in learning the language and negotiating structural and symbolic barriers for integration. Like them, I felt at various times enthralled by the environment, excited and keen to create meaningful relationships, whilst on other occasions I, like them, felt similarly less enamoured with life in Southern Spain, and felt lonely or homesick. And these similarities brought benefits, as Rapport (2002: 7) observes of anthropology in Britain,

> an anthropologist thoroughly at home in linguistic denotation, and familiar with behavioural form, is more able to appreciate the connotative: to pick up on those niceties of interaction and ambivalences and ambiguities of exchange, where the most intricate (and interesting) aspects of sociocultural worlds are constructed, negotiated, contested and disseminated.

On the other hand, a special insight of native researchers cannot necessarily be assumed. This claims an epistemological privilege, which as Ong (1995) observes, can obscure more subtle differences along lines of status, education and outlook. And clearly despite the similarities to the migrants I studied, my age set me dramatically apart from those I researched. Many migrants, through their shared history were a cultural group of sorts that I, a young woman (at the time in her twenties) could never be part of. It is not uncommon for anthropologists of ageing to be younger than their subjects (see Keith-Ross 1977 and Myerhoff 1978) but it does bring obvious implications; I did not and could not experience processes of physical and mental change that my informants were going through and I could only empathize with, rather than share the same emotions around dealing with later life (see Hepworth 1998). More practically, discussions of shared history, such as of life in the war, drew silence on my part and my lack of 'know-how' in skills such as ballroom dancing and embroidery meant that more than once, I could only sit and watch. These differences are only some of the limitations which explain calls for the use of older people to research older people (see Bytheway 1995).

However, whilst the insider perspective is clearly valuable (see for instance Betty 2001 on retirement migration) cultural gulfs can themselves be used to one's advantage. It no doubt influenced some initial problems with access, but these ultimately proved useful lessons. For instance, I ventured in to one club early on in fieldwork and explained to the chairman, Tony, who I was and what I was doing. Rather naïvely, I had anticipated his interest, but he responded abruptly, 'No thank you, we don't want your sort around here'. I was startled and asked him to explain why he objected to me conducting research. 'People here keep themselves to themselves', he said. 'They've had students doing this sort of thing before and they don't like it'. When I pointed out that I was visiting other well-established clubs in the area, Tony's manner altered and he said that he was prepared to discuss the situation with other club members. The problem remedied itself after Judy, a 'leading light' with much social capital, acted as my advocate. Although I attended the club again later that week with trepidation, after Judy had 'put a word in' for me, Tony was friendly and welcoming and explained that his initial reluctance was purely intended to protect the members. He explained, 'people don't want to feel like Big Brother is watching them' (see O'Reilly 2000a on the problems of asking about personal details of tax and residency status). As I show in Chapter 6, these experiences informed my understanding of issues of trustworthiness in the transient society.

More positively, in other situations, my marginal position as a younger person meant I was often welcomed, fussed over and taken care of by retired migrants, located as I was by my age into comparisons with their own children or grandchildren. Hockey and James (1993) also point out that old and young are often grouped together and are projected with similar characteristics. They share a cultural evaluation as marginal through their positions at the beginning and end of the Western life course. This suggests that whilst there is difference, there is also sameness between young researcher and older participant which can stimulate a particularly fruitful and intimate research encounter, based on models of older teacher/student and guardian/child relationships. The fact that I was not in the same age-cohort as my subjects also meant that, as some informants told me, there was a lesser need to 'keep up appearances'. In this respect, the research process can be useful for informants too, as the researcher is someone who they can recount their reflections to (Hastrup 1992) without repercussions for their esteem by others. Myerhoff (1978: 36 in Hastrup 1992: 121), studying an elderly Jewish population in the United States, points out aptly of her own similar experiences, 'they were the teachers and I, surrogate grandchild, was the student. I was deeply moved and saddened when people blessed me for merely listening'.

Despite the differences of age, my research activities were extremely similar to those regularly undertaken by informants. Sitting over lunch, a coffee or a glass of wine, I would ask questions about the locality, how things work there and would find out about people's histories and current lives. These social activities were helpful for creating intimacy, although, as I develop more fully in Chapter 6, there was little at face value that separated my research pursuits from the regular socialising and information sharing within expatriate society. The situation raises ethical dilemmas, particularly when some people do not fully understand what an anthropologist does (Hammersley and Atkinson 1995) and whilst transcending a subject/researcher divide fosters warmth, I regularly struggled with doubts that this was exploitative of genuine friendships made within these parameters. Thus whilst I was anxious to avoid a 'one-night-stand' approach to research (Rossman and Rallis 1998), I had to consider whether continued friendships beyond fieldwork simply extended exploitation? Years of troubling reflection have led me to conclude however that intimacy in research encounters should not be interpreted as sacrifice by the researched for the researcher. These interpretations lead only to paralysing guilt and ultimately risk distorted representation, as the researcher censors anything that may present participant-friends in anything but the very best light. Rather, in awareness of respecting those involved, I chose to write the book with a vision of my friends' eyes, as the closest critics I have, surveying the words I write. And Rapport's suggestion that, 'the competent fieldworker is he or she who learns to live with an uneasy conscience but continues to be worried by it' (1993: 74) enabled me to move beyond potential paralysis in representation towards an ethnography that aims to reflect critically but compassionately about the lives of those I have come to know.

Finally, laying open the partial and power-laden nature of research (Clifford and Marcus 1986, Marcus and Fischer 1986) requires some appraisal of the literary techniques and constructions used to represent anthropological research (Geertz 1988, Denzin 1997). The text here is constructed using direct quotations from participants and a blend of first and third person in reports from fieldnotes. I attempted a dialogical engagement through presenting my research on expatriate radio and provided written summaries of my earlier thesis to some interested parties, although I acknowledge this is *my* account of what I saw. It is also one that is quite self-consciously constructed using novelistic description at times, to evoke as much as represent other lives (Tyler 1986). Clifford and Marcus (1986) rightly expose the use of travel and literature tropes in anthropological writing, yet my attempts to evoke the pleasant environment is less a technique to claim authenticity than fundamental to understandings of migrants' experiences, particularly as for most, the environmental attractions are a key reason as to why they live there at all. It reflects a Geertzian tradition in anthropology, which impresses the importance of depictions of context to understand meanings.

Finally, the epistemology of the research, in exploring the contextual and relational construction of cultural meaning means that much of the analysis interprets themes voiced in narrative and dialogue. These produce research results that are more messy, contradictory and ambiguous than other styles of research, and do not lend themselves easily to categorisation. The ability of ethnography to question and go beyond categorisation is however its strength, and thus despite the inconsistencies and messiness that ensue, like Scheper-Hughes, I 'suppress the urge to smooth over the bumps with a lathe' (1992: 30). This is even more appropriate in this case, because as I will show, the contradictions, discrepancies and ruptures in practice are shown by the people in this study to be necessary and fundamental in their negotiations of ageing, and indeed form the basis of the book's central argument.

A final note is required on provisions undertaken to ensure participants' anonymity. I have not coded interview respondents, and all names,[16] locations and significant details have been changed in both text and visual records to avoid locating any individual. The exception to this rule is when I have taken photographs, at which point I explicitly reminded people of my research purpose, and when people have asked to be identified when they have given me their own work. The place names of the town and village are also disguised in pseudonyms (Tocina and Freila respectively) although the broader region is not. The names of the town and village have no significance; they were selected at random using the process by which one migrant, Mary came to live in the area — by sticking a pin in a map to identify alternative place names. I have considered whether practices intended to disguise places and people are still useful, as with even a limited knowledge of the region it is possible to identify the sites in which I researched. However, I still feel it important to cling to the tradition, as the use of a pseudonym alerts readers to its function: to respect the anonymity of the participants. It also respects the agreement established with participants that I would assure confidentiality when I sought their informed consent (as recommended by the British Sociological Association's *Statement of Ethical Practice* 2002, point 18). Ultimately however, whilst the book emerges from close relationships with specific individuals in particular places, it is not written in a spirit to reveal, applaud, judge or condemn the activities of any one of those. It is rather to learn from insights gained in relationships with these close informants to speak more widely about experiences of ageing in the contemporary world.

A BRIEF OUTLINE

The book in summary develops as follows. The next chapter situates the analysis through an account of theoretical work on the cultural contexts of ageing and migration. Chapter 3 gives a more descriptive introduction to the specific contexts of the research. It is in Chapters 4, 5, 6 and 7 that the reader will find the staple ethnographic account. The analysis is thematically organised around examining how certain aspirations for retirement are experienced, and these are explored in relation to four themes: 1) time (Chapter 4), 2) space, place and body (Chapter 5), 3) social relation-ships (Chapter 6), and 4) cultural identity (Chapter 7). I reveal systemati-cally through exploration of these four thematic domains how migration is associated with freedoms but show how these freedoms are paradoxical, ambiguous and regularly re-evaluated.

In more detail, the following two chapters are concerned with exploring the theoretical and practical contextualisation of the ethnographic work. In Chapter 2, I outline the cultural contexts of growing older in Britain today, especially in discussing themes of 'successful' or 'positive' ageing. Furthermore, the chapter considers how these are related to individualism, consumption and travel. The discussion continues with a consideration of how this form of migration can be theorised, and ends with a brief his-torical contextualisation of Northern European migration in the region. Following this, Chapter 3 introduces some of the individual migrants fea-turing in the study and explores their outlooks and opinions. It also offers a description of the social and physical infrastructures they inhabit.

Chapter 4 considers the first theme arising in the ethnography, by explor-ing how migrants' positive articulations of moving involve the adoption of an alternative approach to time and time use. It shows how on one hand, individuals celebrate how migration fosters feelings of 'starting afresh', a leap into a liminal, stretched, relaxed and spontaneous experience of time, a notion aided through cultural imagery of Spain. Migrants' time is asso-ciated with certain qualities linked to their later stage of life; it is seen as 'free' and 'me-time', or time for themselves. On the other hand, the research reveals other contradictory and conflicting motifs of time, in which time has the status of a precious and scarce resource to be used wisely. These themes are no doubt related to and influenced by many people's experi-ences of work-capitalism that have enabled people to be there in the first place. But it also relates to their awareness of the value of unknown time remaining. This tension encourages paradoxical orientations to both seize the day, throw caution to the wind, yet still to plan for time well-used. I explore how such contradictory ideals of time compete in the daily lives of migrants, and show how ideas of time as value, measured, not to be wasted and structured are upheld as much as the aspiration of leisurely, unhurried and spontaneous time-use.

In Chapter 5, I explore how migration is understood by people as a cata-lyst for experimenting with desired visions of how to age well. Movement to the new place encourages more positive orientations towards active, leisured and independent experiences of growing older compared with the homeland. Age is more fluidly interpreted amongst retired migrants, where old age is seen as a lesser barrier to social participation. Moving away is also associated with feelings of personal autonomy through dis-tance with kin, coupled with feelings of continued familial intimacy. In documenting the obvious benefits that these positive orientations bring, I also show how some of the freedoms aspired to in this approach to ageing can be contradictory, or even paradoxically become expectations in themselves. Williams found in his study of older people in Aberdeen that, 'the idea of relaxation kept running into contradiction with the activist tenor of most nostrums for retirement' (1990: 66). Here, those same pressures exist between activity, body maintenance and relaxation and enjoyment. Furthermore, societal expectations impinge, which stress the individual's responsibility to prepare for dependency.

Comparable tensions are explored in Chapter 6 through negotiations of self and community. On one hand, retirement migration encourages the creation of sociable relations amongst others who tread similar paths. It is suggested that individuals' pasts are less important and everyone is equal under the Spanish sun (see Fitzgerald 1986 on retirement communities and O'Reilly 2000a). However, a commonality between retired migrants is their concern to maintain independence and show a healthy disregard for what others think. And there is a limit to the extent to which previous identities and successes are discarded. I show how as a result, the celebrated egalitarian ethos of the community is not secure or easy to maintain, and becomes managed through techniques of social control, including gossip and reputation construction. These activities deal with the paradoxes of a community of strong individuals. They establish a web of communal belonging, impart some expectations about appropriate behaviour, and deal with disruptive elements of the egalitarian ethos of society whilst they simultaneously facilitate the expressions of individual personalities.

Finally, in Chapter 7, I explore how migrants' cultural and national identification are negotiated as they grow older. I show how a range of attitudes to nationality is articulated. Some feel strong attachment to certain rituals, home comforts and language, yet many others vaunt desired aspects of self — particularly of excitement and exploration — through claiming non-national, 'cosmopolitan' identities. Overt associations with the British are rejected and demonstrated through negative reactions to tourists and other 'Brits' who are depicted as engaging in behaviours that are antithetical to the retiree's own ageing identities. Yet again, the chapter shows how such ideals are not easy to maintain, because there is comfort in succumbing to the temptations of culturally specific habits, such as buying familiar foodstuffs or using well-established English-speaking businesses. Furthermore, whilst many claim to wish to remain in Spain (and a substantial number do so), nevertheless, others return because of home-comforts, family and healthcare provisions when illness occurs. The chapter also shows the salience of the cultural in influencing how death is dealt with in migration, particularly when confronting different disposal and memorialisation practices in Spain (such as niche interment rather than burial). The analysis shows how cultural attitudes may influence whether migrant's commitment to Spain extends to include cremation or niche interment in foreign soil.

In the concluding chapter, I return to consider the general aims of the book. In interrogating the Western cultural phenomenon of upping sticks to move elsewhere in retirement, I consider the realities beyond the retirement 'dream'. Campbell (1987) argues that fantasies omit elements of real life, and as a result, pleasure lies in the longing for goods and not their achievement. This book explores the day-to-day reality of a fantasy shared by many in the Western world today. It considers the reality of the culturally informed aspirations to move away to sunnier climes in retirement and the experiences of leaving behind the structures of one's life to enter a social milieu in which one's past is — in theory at least — erased. In the ethnographic exploration, it shows how the contradictions and paradoxes that ageing in the current era bring invoke less a wholesale change of life through migration than a flirtation with freedom in a number of domains. It reveals retiring abroad as involving a careful balancing act negotiated along the path of ageing, in a 'projected journey through unknown territory with an unknown end' (Gibson 2000: 778) by today's older travellers.

2 Cultural Contexts
Positive Ageing, Migration and Place

My initial interest in retirement migration was stimulated by a visit in March 1995 to visit family who lived in the Andalucían hills by the Costa del Sol. During my time there, I met a number of retired people who had moved nearby. They seemed to me living exemplars of those who are, as Blaikie identifies, 'shedding both the retirement uniform and the work uniform, formal suit for track suit and shell suit, escaping the straitjacket of old age as our parents or grandparents knew it' (1999: 98). Those Northern European retired migrants I met appeared *prima facie,* to embody 'vigour and resilience' (Jerrrome 1992: 4) and countered dominant associations of older age as a time of passivity and marginality. And when I came to research their experiences, I found our conversations replete with their powerful articulations of feelings of independence and agency. Studies confirm the satisfaction felt by international retirement migrants (King et al 2000; Rodríguez, Casado Díaz and Huber 2000; Betty 2001) showing that most migrants feel they have a better quality of life following their move to Spain. Much of this is surely explicable when considering the multiple motivations for moving abroad in retirement, of which the core reasons cited in King et al's study of retirement migration refer to the climate, landscape, clean air, the health benefits of the pace of life and lower living costs[1] (see ibid.: 93–96 for further analysis of motivations). These decisions about relocation to Spain I suggest are also made in a framework of reference to wider cultural aspirations for ageing and retirement, which are explored in this chapter, alongside a consideration of the geographical context of the research.

The chapter offers an exploration of the wider cultural and geographical contexts that shape the individuals' experiences of moving abroad in retirement documented in this book. It begins by situating the process of retirement migration in the wider contemporary cultural contexts of becoming old in Europe, by analyzing transformations in the nature of retirement in recent decades and critically exploring emerging discourses of 'positive' or 'successful' ageing. It also considers how these trends are related to corresponding cultural shifts in individualism, consumption practices and experiences of travel, which arguably shape the contemporary aspiration for retirement migration. The second part of the chapter outlines the specific geographical and historical contexts of this form of migration, because the appreciation of retiree's post-migration experiences requires some contextualisation of this migration flow in the particular locality. The chapter ends with a brief historical consideration of the cultural encounters and transformations in the region of Andalucía to situate the ethnographic account that follows in the remainder of the book.

AGEING IN CONTEXT: CULTURAL
AGEING IN NORTHERN EUROPE

The study of ageing is dominated by the adoption of medicalised perspectives on later life (Katz 2005) and, whilst ageing can be understood by these means, sociological and anthropological research points out how far from a 'natural' process, ageing is one that is interpreted, shaped and negotiated within certain social-structural and cultural contexts. Attention to how people of different ages are socially categorised in particular ways has shown that over the last few decades, the Western life course and understandings of old age have come under fundamental revision because of a number of factors. Crucially, advances in healthcare have led to increasing population longevity. Coupled with other social trends towards early retirement, this means that retirement may now constitute a large part of some people's lifespan (Jerrome 1992). If good health is enjoyed, the experience of that period of life is also altered, especially when expectations may be shaped by previous educational experiences (King et al 2000). Other changes in family structures — and particularly the increasing rates of divorce — have altered patterns of family relationships and responsibilities. And finally, many of today's older people also benefit from increasing affluence. A combination of higher real earnings, personal and occupational pensions, home-ownership and participation by women in the labour force have increasingly placed some older people in positions of financial security (Evandrou 1997, King et al 2000). Their disposable income makes achievable certain aspirations in retirement.

Associated with this changing social makeup of fitter, healthier and wealthier older people, scholars in gerontology have departed from a primary focus on ageing which pathologised old age and associated it with ill-health (Jerrome 1992). Advanced old age used to be often overwhelmingly identified as 'a condition of dependency and deterioration' (Hareven 1982: 12), a picture shaped by a 'persistent preoccupation with disability, disease, and chronological age, rather than with the positive aspects of ageing' (Rowe and Kahn 1998: foreword). The increasing longevity of the population was seen as a cause for concern, especially given the prevalent cultural valuation of work that consigns those not active in the economic sphere as a 'problem' (Phillipson 1990, Arber and Ginn 1995). In the 1980s, critical social gerontological research sought therefore to expose the interpretation of older people as a 'burden' as a social construction, which stems from society's admiration for youth and independence (Phillipson, 1982, Jeffrys 1989, Tinker 1992). And retirement was shown to be the result of state ideologies which enforce the withdrawal of older people from the workforce through welfare and employment policies (Walker and Phillipson 1986) and sustain their 'structured dependency' (Townsend 1986). The moral panic that ideologically capitalised on the growing numbers of older people in post-industrial countries however ill-reflects the reality of an overwhelmingly self-sufficient cohort of older, active people (Jeffrys 1989, Bytheway 1995).

More recently, some studies of ageing from a sociological perspective have moved towards theorising how ageing experiences are diverse and varied, through explanations of the life course (Featherstone and Hepworth, 1991, Hockey and James 2003). A life course perspective explores individual 'pathways' through life (Elder 1978). According to Hareven,

> Underlying a life course approach is the assumption that the family status and position that people experience in later years of life is molded by their cumulative life history and by the specific historical conditions affecting their lives at earlier times. (1982: 1)

The perspective entails attention to how personal experiences interact with wider family shifts as well as how they are interconnected with current and cumulative demographic, societal, economical and cultural influences (ibid.). The use of life course analyses enables us to be, 'more appreciative of difference and variation' as well as to be able to link, 'historical time with individual biography' (Morgan 1985: 178).

Employing a life course perspective enables the deconstruction of standardised expectations of age-appropriate behaviours, in which individuals are expected to proceed through several isolated stages of a 'life cycle' — including old age — sequentially. This standard understanding was founded upon a 'taken-for-granted shift from childhood dependence to adult independence, with the prospect of an eventual slide into "old age" dependency' (Hockey and James 2003: 100). Yet this model has been exposed as a historically recent construction which emerged in the late nineteenth century. Institutional processes, such as the formal registration of births, were established in response to the fact people were living predictably longer lives (ibid.) and these practices helped to chronologise the life course (Bytheway 1995). However, in the twentieth century, expectations of ageing according to a standard pattern have been dislodged, 'with less emphasis than in the past being placed upon age-specific role transitions and scheduled identity-development' (Featherstone and Hepworth 1991: 372).

The analysis of the life course as a social institution shows therefore how the shape of the life course has been subject to profound change in the late twentieth century (Hockey and James 2003). Not only has the increased longevity of the population initiated a fragmentation of the category of 'older people' into the 'young-old' and 'old-old' (Neugarten, 1974) but there is also emerging evidence that some boundaries based on age are dismantled altogether, 'as grandmothers start to dress as their daughters do and grandfathers jog with their sons' (Blaikie 1999: 73). And there are also signs that this fluid postmodern cultural conceptualisation of the life course is beginning to be mirrored by structural developments. For example, in Britain, legislation designed to tackle age-discrimination came into force in October 2006. Although it still includes regulations for a national default age of sixty-five for retirement, this legal cut-off point is now, for the first time, open to challenge[2] (Department for Work and Pensions 2005). Indeed, this move, in conjunction with existing possibilities (in some occupations) for early retirement, signals possibilities for a more flexible retirement, in which cutting down work may be negotiated over a phase and combined with part-time work (see also Schuller 1989). It is a move which corresponds with Blaikie's (1999: Chapter 3) observations of a 'transformation of retirement' since post-war society, in which retirement has become an increasingly fragmented experience both in terms of when it occurs, but also in how the time is spent.

Certainly the cultural expectations associated with retirement have significantly changed as negative expectations of ill health and dependency have yielded to notions of the 'Third Age' (Laslett 1989). Laslett's theory of the Third Age emerged in response to the demographic transitions discussed previously which necessitated a rethinking of prevailing expectations of ageing. It heralds later life as a time of productive fulfilment achievable through mental and physical activity, education and leisure (Walker and Maltby 1997) seen, for example, in the activities of the University of the Third Age (Laslett 1989). The Third Age is contrasted to the Fourth Age (of seventy-five years and above), which is a period inevitably characterised by the transition towards eventual dependency. The theory converts early experiences of old age into a time in which ageing should be 'active' or can be negotiated 'successfully' or 'positively'. It is a theme evident in wider societal and state encouragement of older people 'to achieve a "good" old age' (Tulle Winton 1999:282) and maintain their employability (see Chapter 3 on 'Active Ageing' in the UK Department for Work and Pensions' 2005 strategy report *Opportunity Age*). In this cultural shift, old age becomes more a continuation or prolongation of a 'mid life' period, described by Featherstone and Hepworth (1991: 384) as, 'a rather loosely arranged collection of ideals which intersect around the concept of youthfulness and its capacity for social change and the irrelevance of chronologically determined age-related statuses'.

LIMINALITY AND THE 'NEW' OLD AGE

In trying to analyse life course moments such as retirement, some scholars have found the concept of liminality helpful. It comes from *the rites of passage*, which is a schema developed by Arnold Van Gennep to understand how societies deal with life-transitions. He argued that, 'The life of an individual in any society is a series of passages from one age to another and from one occupation to another' ([1909] 1960: 2–3). Van Gennep and later Victor Turner (1967, 1969, 1974) explored how life course transitions are marked by rituals which bestow age-based identities upon individuals, thereby socially marking the biological processes of ageing[3] (Hockey and James 2003). Turner, for example, explored how circumcision and puberty rituals marked changes from child to adult status in Ndembu society and showed that the rituals reflect a common tripartite structure. First, there is an initial period of disengagement, in which the individual is separated from a fixed social structure, for instance, through being removed to a different place. This marks entry into the second phase, a period of 'liminality' in which the individual is ambiguously 'betwixt and between' two statuses. The phase is a timeless state, characterised by the dissolution of status hierarchies, role reversals, transgressive behaviours and comradeship between others undergoing the same ritual process. It precedes the final phase, which involves re-entry into social structure in a different status.

The analysis proves particularly useful for understanding 'in-between' or 'liminal' periods of life in life course transitions, including retirement or adolescence (Spencer 1990). In such periods, individuals are understood to inhabit a zone 'betwixt and between' one status or identity and another (for instance, 'child' and 'adult' for the adolescent). Retirement is therefore explored as a significant threshold which marks a person's entry into a distinct liminal period of the life course which falls between working life and extreme old age (Myerhoff 1984). Of course, in the light of the previous discussion, some questions have understandably been raised about the utility of the schema, particularly because the rigidly sequential nature of the rites of passage. Notions of passing through a series of relatively fixed stages appear at odds with the current fluid experiences of ageing today that I have previously explored, in which retirement is not sharply defined and may involve a gradual transition.

Nevertheless, for many, retirement still represents a moment of symbolic importance in the life course (Long 1989) and the language of rites of passage is still applied to contemporary ageing processes. For example, Blaikie refers to the emergence of mid-life 'middlescence', a period, which, much like adolescence, 'is characterised by liminality and identity crises' (1999: 25). Furthermore, retirement has been reinvented in consumer society as a 'time of transition to a new life' (Hockey and James 2003: 102) marked by liminality. The transition is aided by a proliferation of cultural industries that help disguise one's advancing years and sustain fantasies of timelessness in old age (Katz 2005). Featherstone and Hepworth also point out the number of 'heroes and heroines' who through their youthful and healthy demeanour, 'vigorously deny the relevance of age-graded statuses' (1991: 373) and attempt to halt the irreversibility of time in an enduring liminality.

Certainly orientations towards liminal revitalisation, transgression or renewal are evident in some of the new approaches towards 'active' or 'positive' ageing, which are based on different norms of age-related behaviour than those expected for past generations (Featherstone and Hepworth 1995). A recent newspaper account, for instance, profiles a number of 'over-seventies for whom "retirement" is a dirty word' (Bedell, *the Guardian Review* 2005: 1). It is cast instead as a turning point or transitional moment to create new roles outside of work, through taking up volunteering or sporting endeavours, for instance. One extreme example is that of Fauja Singh, a marathon runner who began running at eighty-one years old, and at the age of ninety-two was signed up for the Adidas 'Impossible is Nothing' campaign. This followed his participation in the 'Sikhs in the City' running team (whose youngest member was seventy) in the 2005 Edinburgh marathon (*Senior Journal*: June 13, 2005). Other examples include the *'Young at Heart'* chorus, a group of North American singers, whose youngest member is seventy-five years old. They have received international critical acclaim for their world tours, which feature the groups' interpretation of songs by bands such as *Radiohead* and *the Rolling Stones*.[4]

Other social groups have also been formed which are ideologically based on the resistance and repudiation of ageist stereotypes. In the United States, there has been a recent growth of grassroots subcultural movements which ritually celebrate older women as 'crones' through croning rituals, that consciously recast negative and contemptuous images of ageing women (see Arber and Ginn 1991: Chapter 3) into positive ones as 'active wise women' (Bower 2001 from http://www.croning.org and see discussion in Cruikshank 2003: 197–198). Furthermore, the 'Hen co-op' was a group of older women in Britain who celebrated retirement as a time where the motif is, 'it is my turn now' (The Hen Co-op 1993: 111). On the basis of the success of their meetings, they subsequently published (in 1993) a collection of their life-stories, poems and discussions entitled *Growing Old Disgracefully: New Ideas for Getting the Most Out of Life*. Such examples demonstrate aptly how a new morality of ageing (Blaikie 1999: 74) is often associated with principles of transgression or resistance. This is increasingly reflected in newly emerging terms in popular culture equating old age with adolescence, which refer variously to older people as 'recycled teenagers', or even, as I heard from one woman, 'saga louts',[5] a tongue-in-cheek referral to people, like her, who spent much of their retirement on holiday.

RELOCATION IN RETIREMENT

The latter reference hints to how travel is increasingly becoming a way of life for some people in retirement. This is evident in Counts and Counts' (1996) study of seniors who travel around the United States in recreational vehicles/camper vans and identify positively with the freedom of their mobile life. And tabloid headlines of the 'Gran Tours' (Morgan, *the Mirror* 2006) speaks of the readiness of many older people in the UK, with the means at their disposal, to holiday, sojourn or overwinter in warmer destinations. Urry observes that, 'for many reasonably wealthy retired people life may indeed be akin to a continuous nomadic existence' (2002: 32). Such practices can be understood as related to the historical association in Western cultures between travel and improved health. Victorians toured to the spas or the Mediterranean and 'getting away from it all' continues to be associated with restoration and rejuvenation (Rojek 1993, Rojek and Urry 1997). Recent years have therefore seen an increasing tethering of leisure experiences to old age and many tourist zones are now also constructed as appropriate places for more permanent relocation in retirement; Blaikie, for example, explores the 'conflation of positive ageing and seaside living' (1999: 150) through longstanding mythologies connecting older people with the spiritual and moral virtues of the coast.

The trend of lifestyle change through retirement migration is particularly evident in the United States, where many people have moved to retirement enclaves in retirement (see Warnes 1991 which includes a review of research on US seasonal elderly migration and see research by Longino 1982, van den Hoonaard 1994, McHugh 2000, 2003 and Katz 2005). Fitzgerald's study of retirement in Sun-City, Arizona, refers to one respondent who described the experience there as 'the long vacation we wished we'd always had' (1986: 229). Other research by social geographers into various forms of 'retirement migration' in the United States and Northern Europe (including urban-rural, sunbelt and International Retirement Migration) has paid attention to how migration affects intergenerational relationships, kin-support as well as 'the complex interrelationships between an individual's personality, competences, living arrangements and residential location, and the material and psychological satisfactions that they gain from their environment or place of residence' (Warnes 1982: 6).

Although some enclaves are designed especially for retirement living, Longino also suggests that when people commonly move to an area in retirement, this can lead to the construction of a *de facto* form of 'retirement community' (*'any living environment to which most residents have moved since they retired'*, Longino 1982: 239, author's italics). These communities are not planned with provisions of specially provided services, but they nevertheless emerge as communities of sorts simply in attracting older people and then developing services to cater for them[6] (ibid.).

Longino explores the Ozark Lakes County (in Missouri, Arkansas and Oklahoma in the United States), a mountainous region of fishing lakes and freshwater reservoirs which has seen a substantial influx of older people. His respondents stress the positive aspects of the new destination against negative aspects of the former environment[7] (see also Cribier 1982 on older Parisian migrants moving to natal rural areas) and much of their satisfaction is articulated with reference to the benefits of 'community':

> The pluses of their new community had to do with their positive feelings of being accepted, being secure, or being a useful member of the community. It had to do also with being able to do those things that were enjoyed and which fulfilled fantasies of the good life, such as being associated with a place of beauty, strength and occasionally even purpose, being nearer to people and things that were loved and desired, and being in a more controllable and convenient environment where their needs could be met without frustration, worry, or delay. (Longino 1982: 251–252)

This concurs with Blaikie's (1999: 160–163) observations of UK seaside destinations for retirement migration, where he shows how older people recreate a nostalgic 'community' away from younger generations and modernity's more negative excesses. Other research on planned retirement communities also reveals how residential segregation in older age similarly offer benefits of 'communality' and peer support (van den Hoonaard 1994, Biggs, Bernard, Kingston and Nettleton 2000[8]). In both RCs and de facto retirement communities, age-segregation occurs as older peers form the majority of the community. And, as Longino (1982) documents, age-homogeneity can lead to the development of age-consciousness or a subculture for those people living together, who experience improved morale and increased interaction.

From an anthropological point of view, this 'community feeling' documented amongst retirement migrants could be interpreted as the articulation of a form of 'communitas' emerging in the new destination. Emerging in liminal conditions, this is a transient condition of an egalitarian 'communion of equal individuals' (Turner 1974: 49). Communitas involves the breakdown and irrelevance of previous social distinctions, in which the individual arrives as a 'tabula rasa' or 'blank slate' ready to be inscribed with group knowledge. Positive feelings of genuine comradeship and egalitarian social relations emerge spontaneously in these liminal moments, particularly amongst individuals undergoing the same transition.

In this light, as I suggested in Chapter 1, retirement travel and migration can be understood as a rite of passage, which fosters a kind of liminality, through retirees 'opting out' (Turner 1969) of mainstream living to move to marginal geographical spaces. McHugh's (2003) analysis of retirement living in Arizona in the United States shows, for instance, how advertisements regularly feature themes of 'escape' to a near-perfect utopia. This corresponds with anthropological analyses of tourism, in which travel is depicted as an escape or 'sacred journey' away from normal social conventions (Graburn 1978, Crick 1989). Cultural geographers such as Rob Shields (1991) have also explored how certain 'places on the margin' are associated with freedom from constraints and hierarchical obligations of 'normal' life. Shields' analysis of the British coastal town of Brighton could equally be extended to the Costa del Sol where the marginality of space gives rise to consequences for identities and experiences of those who inhabit them (see Chapter 3). O'Reilly suggests that British migrants in Spain are in a liminal position, and feel 'that life in Spain is about freedom and escape rather than supervision, documentation and control' (2000: 156).[9] Yet these appeals to freedom, transgression and resistance rather than control or categorical identities seem to be particularly pertinent cultural motifs for those in the later stages of the life course, when those ideals may come under threat (see Chapter 5 and cf. Oliver 1999).

This said, the extent to which 'opting out' in practice involves a radical break with former values and processes is debatable. Indeed, McHugh's study of the marketing of retirement destinations in the United States shows how agencies replicate dominant cultural values in their promotion of images of 'successful ageing' in retirement communities. He shows how older people are targeted as a homogeneous and aggregate market by the retirement industry and reveals that promotion of Sun Belt retirement communities are addressed only to particular older people (who are the 'right' sort, 2003: 173). Moreover, the companies sustain ageist attitudes through using images that propagate a myth of 'the ageless self', encouraging a societal mantra of activity that is directed towards keeping old age at bay (2000: 106). Not only are the dominant values of capitalism confirmed (ibid.) but the images used are wholly unrealistic and 'parade an impossible ideal' (2003: 180). These concerns highlight wider doubts about the recently emerging cultural expectations of 'positive' ageing (or 'successful' ageing, which is used interchangeably) which inform retirement migration. These require further critical consideration.

DEBATING POSITIVE AGEING

The notion of 'positive' or 'successful' ageing has recently emerged as a composite of professional and popular knowledge elaborating the sorts of behaviours and activities that are appropriate for ageing (Katz and Laliberte-Rudman 2005). On one hand, they build on notions of ageing well which are found throughout history (Torres 1999); for example, Thompson et al (1991) refer to Francis Bacon's exhortations of attention to diet, sleep and exercise as means of delaying physical ageing in the seventeenth century. However, it was only following the development of geriatric medicine from the 1900s in the United States that a more scientific vision of a 'positive' way to age began to emerge in earnest, and attempts to define and explain positive or successful ageing as a specific topic of academic inquiry have grown from the middle of the twentieth century onwards (ibid.). For some gerontologists, however, 'successful ageing' is proving highly contentious and subject to much debate (Torres 1999).

It is not my intention to offer an exhaustive review of the gerontological studies of successful ageing (see Torres 2004) but it is worth considering some examples of what is advocated. Whilst initial definitions of successful ageing focused upon it as an outcome, this has been countered by a shift towards its consideration as a process achievable through certain strategies (Torres 2004). Gerontologists have focused attention on how individuals come to terms with the challenges of ageing and maintain continuity of identity in the face of a series of social, physiological and psychological changes wrought by growing older (ibid.). In 1990, Baltes and Baltes developed an assessment model to consider how individuals deal with ageing as an adaptive process of 'selection, optimization and compensation' to maintain productivity with respect to an individual's limits. This process-oriented focus explores 'change as adaptation in the service of maintaining self-esteem' (Daatland and Biggs 2004: 224). Fisher and Specht also envisage successful ageing as a developmental process in which continuity is paramount, demonstrated in an ability to adapt and 'cope with present circumstances by drawing on past experiences and maintaining a positive sense of future' (1999: 458–459).

Rowe and Kahn (1998), drawing on evidence from the MacArthur Foundation study in the United States, consider 'what successful aging consists of, and what each of us can do to achieve it' (ibid.: 37). They emphasize the duty that older individuals have to enhance their own physiological and psychological capabilities. They suggest that successful ageing involves the ability to maintain a low risk of disease and disease-related disability, a good mental and physical function and active engagement with life. According to Rowe and Kahn, everyone can influence their ageing, as demonstrated by a case-study of Anne, an older woman who was diagnosed with painful osteoarthritis thirty years previously, but who swims one mile three times a week, uses an exercise bike, weight trains and does yoga once a week for an hour, with stretching, balance, breathing and relaxation exercises (ibid.: 120). Their analysis points to scientific evidence showing how mental and physical exercise and social relationships enhance older people's wellbeing, but a key point of their argument is that the process of physical ageing can be altered through the adoption of a particular lifestyle. A positive experience of age, is, Rowe and Kahn (1998: 37) argue, a choice:

> To succeed in something requires more than falling into it; it means having desired it, planned it, worked for it. All these factors are critical to our view of aging which, even in this era of human genetics, we

regard as largely under the control of the individual. In short, successful aging is dependent upon individual choices and behaviours. It can
be attained through individual choice and effort.

Despite the obvious advantages of these developments, there are a number of reservations from critical gerontologists and sociologists around
notions of 'successful' or 'positive' ageing and the theory of the third age.
Scholars object to the problematic cultural implications of these discourses
for older people, particularly when utilised for commercial and political
interest. Hazan considers successful ageing, 'the patronising instruction of
aged persons for better or fuller lives' (1994: 15) and Bury argues with
reference to the theory of the third age that it is normative, 'more an exhortation than a calculation' (1995: 22) in which the 'emphasis on the creative
aspects of the third age too readily conveys a thinly disguised set of élitist
middle-class values' (ibid.: 23). Cruikshank also argues successful ageing
is a concept in which, 'a white, male, middle-class professional outlook is
taken for granted' (2003: 2). It is fundamentally flawed, she suggests, in
the application of a template of success more usually applied to competi-
tive businesses than to complex human processes. She argues provocatively,
'perhaps the concept of successful aging is popular with gerontologists
because of its positive connotations, but it is simplistic and its promise of
mastery is false' (2003: 3).

Critical gerontologists also suggest that notions of successful ageing are
pernicious because of their emphasis on individual capacities to manage
ageing. This misleadingly credits 'success' as due to the efforts of the individual rather than exploring the wider contexts and structural conditions
in which an individual's ageing experience is moulded (Tulle-Winton 1999,
Cruikshank 2003). Related to this is the way positive ageing is increasingly tied to individual wealth, as not everyone has the resources available to purchase products touted as encouraging successful ageing, such as
gym memberships and dietary supplements. It is, somewhat of a bourgeois
option, unattainable for those with poor health and insufficient income
(Ginn and Arber 1995) and as such, may be particularly problematic for
older women who are more likely to live longer but yet possess less of the
material resources needed to fulfil such expectations of good ageing (Bury
1995). Featherstone and Hepworth (1990, 1995) indeed show convincingly
how ideals of 'positive ageing' are created and sustained by consumer culture, as agencies target the affluent niche market of baby-boomers (see also
Blaikie 1999). In their (1995) analysis of Choice, a magazine addressed to
'young-old' consumers, they show how health advice is regularly combined
with advertisements for solutions to the discomforts of old age. Many of
the products designed for this niche market are specifically addressed at the
maintenance of older bodies, upholding entrenched ideals of bodily perfec-
tion and maintenance (Featherstone 1991).

Interpretations of 'successful ageing' by the lay public and their exploitation by businesses thus ironically reinstate the determining role chronology and the body plays in conceptualisations of ageing, despite the apparent trend away from it in allusions towards a fluid 'mid-life'. As Hockey and James sum up, notions of freedom and choice exist alongside the 'considerable evidence that the chronologised body continues to be a source of constraints' (2003: 116) by which the increasing limits of the ageing body render it more difficult to change one's identity at will (Biggs 1999). Indeed, given that physical appearance continues to be the key marker of social identity (Shilling 1993) ageing bodies are afforded lesser status as they fail to embody the efficiency and capacity for production required in Western capitalist societies (Shilling 2005, Cruikshank 2003). In this privileging of 'the tyranny of the flesh' (Hockey and James 2003: 109) it falls upon individuals themselves to invest in means by which they can delay the impacts of ageing and ultimately, the fourth age. And individuals' attempts to modify the body and disguise the visible changes of ageing through diet, clothing, exercise can now be aided by the more radical means of surgery through liposuction, breast enhancement and face lifts, whilst the transition to later-life sexuality can be deferred through the use of drugs, such as HRT and Viagra (ibid.).

In this light, the liberating and anti-ageist possibilities of successful ageing are questioned as being rather more ironically anti-ageing, and ultimately failing to challenge the obsession with youth in Western society at all. Despite the fact that gerontological depictions of successful ageing acknowledge adjustments to losses as part of its remit, the means by which ageing successfully are lived in practice forbid identification with the realities of growing older (Tulle Winton 1999). As Andrews argues, 'ageing well' is often code for minimalisation of the ageing process' (1999: 309). Thus the critical deconstruction of the gerontological 'gaze' (Katz 2005) has unmasked the political consequences of 'successful ageing' in shifting the responsibility for ageing onto the individual (Tulle-Winton 1999). Aided by a gamut of cultural products and services older people must, 'adopt instrumental strategies to combat deterioration and decay (applauded too by state bureaucracies who seek to reduce health costs by educating the public against bodily neglect)' (Featherstone 1991: 180). This drive towards individual responsibility for one's experience in old age is replicated in wider institutional shifts, the current crisis around pension provision a timely reminder of how the imperative to be responsible for saving for a worthwhile retirement has passed on to the individual (Ginn and Arber 1999).

Moreover, successful ageing risks stigmatising a number of older people who cannot age 'positively' (Wray 2003). As McHugh suggests, it provokes a deep-seated fear that is 'projected outward in the form of disdain and disgust for "old" people who do not "measure up" and who tumble down the spiral of "bad" old age' (2003: 181). It is less a fabled means of ageing healthily than an imperative loaded with moral connotations around behaviours and activities, constituting old age, as Katz describes as an 'ethical domain' (2005: 124). And when emphasis in the third age is placed on personal achievement and 'success', the fourth age — embodied by those whose older bodies do not fit these ideals — is pushed into a more sequestered, and de facto more ominous and feared future. Blaikie (1999: 75) suggests that the focus on youth in 'mid-life' ultimately fosters a taboo on deep old age and argues,

> The 'positive' ageing discourse effectively eclipses consideration of illness and decline, yet final decay and death take on a heightened hideousness since these will happen, regardless of whatever cultural, economic or body capital one might possess...

Successful ageing is also questioned as a result of the theoretical foundations on which the gerontological concept is based. In particular, Torres argues that successful ageing is a universalising and ethnocentric concept, rooted as it is in a 'culturally-specific, American concept of success and failure' (1999: 36). Wray (2003) also argues that, similar for other gerontological concepts such as 'quality of life' and empowerment, little is done in the way of investigating the different meanings attached to those concepts. She states that they 'are often used uncritically despite their cultural specificity' (Wray 2003: 512). For example, in the United States, ageing well involves self-autonomy, yet for the !Kung of Botswana, older people are expected and entitled to complain and shame their adult children into supporting them (Keith et al 1994). In Hong Kong, positive ageing is evidenced through family willingness to help (Torres 1999) and for people of different ethnicities in Wray's (2003) study in Britain (which include African Caribbean, West Indian, Pakistani, British-Polish and Indian participants) successful ageing is as much linked to religious belief, spiritual fulfilment and a sense of belonging in religious activities than the criteria outlined previously. Such differences in constitutions of successful ageing are important to consider, not least because there is practical application of the gerontological discourse. This is demonstrated in Gardner's ethnography of Bengali migrants in London, which reveals how ideals of active ageing in British state discourses clash with Bengali migrants' expectations. Gardner (2002: 165) states that,

> pressure is put on old people by their professional English carers to be as active and independent as possible. For their clients, however, embracing the independence that the professionals often urge upon them is a negation of what is seen as their due, as elderly relatives and as citizens.

As such, Torres' demonstrations of how 'understandings of ageing–related constructs are therefore inevitably shaped by the culture in which these are constituted' (1999: 39) are timely in an increasingly globalizing society. It encourages insight into problems of 'fit' between minority and dominant cultural perspectives on ageing, but also shows how confrontation with other modes of ageing may lead to revisions in notions of successful ageing. Torres (2001, 2004) shows, for example, that some Iranian older migrants in Sweden abandoned their 'surrendering' approach to ageing in favour of a 'master-oriented approach' they saw in Sweden, which was less passive, more active and more future-oriented. And yet awareness of 'other' ideas of successful ageing point to how people may be judged as ageing 'unsuc-cessfully' according to given yardsticks in Western contexts, but still dem-onstrate other (disregarded) capacities (Cruikshank 2003). This suggests that careful consideration is required, not only of the particular contexts in which individuals age (ibid. 2003) but also of how people negotiate cul-turally specific ideals of positive ageing in practice, as this ethnographic account hopes to provide.

TESTING OUT OTHER LIFESTYLES: INDIVIDUALISM AND CONSUMPTION

Despite the reservations around successful ageing, we can be left in little doubt that its premise is increasingly reflected in many experiences of and beliefs about ageing in Western societies. It is articulated, for example, in older people's clubs in concern for 'good' ageing or 'ageing well' (as Dawson 1990 and Jerrome 1992 show). It also underpins the increasingly personalised retirement paths carved out by many older people today, of which those in this study provide an example. This shift however demon-strates a wider move that sees more emphasis on individualism arising in late modernity. Giddens (1991) argues that there has been an increased concern with self-identity in the face of structural economic, political and social changes of the last century. Such orientations have loosened the pull of other moralities experienced in the past, as Hockey and James (2003: 107) point out,

> Within this changed environment, individuals, necessarily therefore, become anchored to the project of the self....Rather than economic obli-gations or community involvement, individual fulfilment is the guiding rationale — or vocabulary of motive — for choice and decision making.

The ramifications of these cultural shifts for ageing are profound as ageing also becomes an increasingly individualised experience (Cruikshank 2003, Andersson and Öberg 2004, Katz 2005). Indeed, notions of 'independ-ence', 'choice' and 'autonomy' become almost synonymous in the Western cultural vocabulary with 'good' ageing. Cruikshank (2003), referring to older people in the United States, points out how bodily old age itself is constructed as a challenge to be fought through demonstrations of 'rugged individualism'. Advertising groups are quick to confirm these ideals through targeting older people, who have grown up in a more permissive era and possess a disposable income whose, 'values are of the "me" generation: from the conformist to the individualistic; from the ascetic to the hedonistic' (Sawchuk 1995: 184). In this way, individualistic self-development becomes the hallmark of a good retirement, and increasingly tethered to consumption. This is perhaps no surprise, as non-essential consumption has been closely associated with romantic individualism throughout British and European history, as I briefly explore in what follows.

According to Rapport and Overing, individualism is a particular cultural norm professing self-development, respect for privacy and self-determination (Rapport and Overing 2000). Studies have shown it to be a particularly prevalent trait in English society and although it is often identified as a product of modern society, MacFarlane (1978) traces back the origins of English individualism to at least the thirteenth century (but with evidence of elements even earlier). He demonstrates how English society was particularly predisposed towards the development of individualism and capitalism because of specific features of English kinship, inheritance rules and property relations. Strathern's (1992) fascinating account of English kinship relations also documents the history behind the contemporary hyper-individualism apparent in late twentieth century England. She shows, for instance, how in early nationalistic presentations in the eighteenth and nineteenth century, England was presented as a land of rugged individualists, each with their own private life-plans. Civilised existence was demonstrated in ostensive displays of independence, self-sufficiency and choice as daily life was spent in improving personal skills and talents through a range of pursuits. Individuals were perceived as 'individual dwelling places' (ibid.: 104) to be enhanced, worked upon and improved. A person grew through the awareness of inner, emotional development and the improvement of their intellect and personal talents.

Campbell argues however that the romantic conception of the individual in the eighteenth century coincided with an acceleration of consumption. The growing efficiency of the economy at this time meant that pleasure was no longer met simply through satisfying basic needs, but became an object for pursuit in its own right, and the growth of non-essential consumption was intimately tied to a shift in concern away from sensations to emotions (Campbell 1987). Ideologies of Puritanism had already encouraged a self-regulation of emotional experience, a split between feeling and action, leading to the possibilities for self-determining of emotional experience and the use of the faculty of the imagination. According to Campbell, this was an essential ingredient for 'modern autonomous imaginative hedonism' (1987: 77) a state of pleasurable *anticipation* of the possible fulfilment of mental images which precedes consumption. However, the satisfaction of these desires,

....is thus a necessarily disillusioning experience for the modern hedonist as it constitutes the 'testing' of his day dream against reality, with the resultant recognition that something is missing. The real experience in question may yield considerable pleasure, some of which may not have been anticipated, but despite this, much of the quality of the dream-pleasure is bound to be absent. (ibid.: 86)

According to Campbell, the object or focus of desire is, he argues, less essential to modern consumerism than the pleasure generated through its anticipation. This imaginative basis transforms modern consumerism into the pursuit of novelty, as any desired, imagined object or experience once achieved, will fall short of how it was imagined, and is soon replaced by another to be attained (ibid.). In this analysis, consumption is not envisaged purely as a marker of social prestige (although undoubtedly this is a strong motivation for it, see Veblen 1899 and Bourdieu 1984) but is identified as driven by a romantic ethic, in which consumption contributes to an individual's self creation. As Friedman explains, 'One is what one makes oneself to be' (1994a: 10) or as Turner has put it, 'I consume therefore I am' (1996: 7). This is helpful to understand the striving to try 'other' lifestyles and pursue novel alternative existences, which are so much a condition of modern times. And it frames individual consumption practices as romantic pursuits directed to help discover the distinctiveness of the individual.

Travel, one form of non-essential consumption, is therefore culturally vested with promises of aiding individualistic processes of reflexive self-making. In this way, buying a new house abroad or pursuing a 'different' lifestyle as undertaken by those within this study can be understood both as a means of seeking novelty and 'discovering' one's self. This is certainly reflected in the narratives of this study, where for many retirees, migration abroad in this stage of their lives is associated with enhanced opportunities for the sort of self-development increasingly believed to be an essential ingredient for a good old age. The aspirational mobility explored here is interpreted as a period of 'me-time': a time and space for self-development through various pursuits of sports, arts and cultural activities, which are both pleasurable ways of passing the time, but yet also articulated as forms of self-improvement. Ideals of living a cosmopolitan existence in the company of others of different nationalities also support similar stories (see Chapter 7). Influenced by wider cultural imperatives to age positively, individualistic fulfilment through travelling to live in a community of like-minded individuals is a key aspiration to be met through retiring abroad.

THE FOREIGN COMMUNITY IN THE LOCALITY

In interrogating the nature of a 'community' of retirement migrants, it is nevertheless equally important to consider its development in a specific context, and how the new arrivals relate to others living in their chosen destinations. In this section, I explore the specific contexts that influence retirees' experiences, through considering how they fit into the locality in this particular part of Spain. However, most research on retirement migration focuses mainly on the experiences of retirees themselves, and the case of Spain is no exception; analyses of Northern European migrant and Spanish host relationships are few. However, those studies considering this aspect depict a story of limited integration, suggesting that foreigners orientate inwards to peers, rather than create meaningful relationships with others in the locality. Rodríguez et al argue, 'an expatriate society has been created parallel to the Spanish society, in which most of the retirees' social relations are with people of their own nationality, whereas their relations with the local population are very limited' (1998: 195). O'Reilly's (2004) latest study on the integration of European migrants in Spanish society also shows that although there is some interaction with Spanish people, it is minimal, as many foreign residents spend significant amounts of their time with their own compatriots. Rozenberg (1995) also points out the 'parallel worlds' in which locals and foreigners live in Ibiza.

One of the most considerable barriers to integration facing foreign residents is the problem of speaking different languages, which leads to many foreigners and Spanish living separate lives (Conde and Palaez 1998). In the region of this study, many foreign residents attempt to learn Spanish but struggle with the Andaluz dialect (Betty 1997). As my own Spanish teachers pointed out, foreign residents may also hold unrealistic expectations of the time-span involved in learning a language, have a low belief in their ability to learn at an advanced age[10] (Huber and O'Reilly 2004) and fight a '*Land of Lotus* syndrome', in which the spirit of relaxation contradicts the demands of learning the language (Hawkin and Rouse 1999). Migrants also struggle against the constraints preventing immersion, in a space where there are limited opportunities for non-commercial relations with Spaniards and the sheer number of other English speaking tourists and migrants means that English is widely spoken and heard (O'Reilly 2003). But as O'Reilly (2003, 2004) argues, even when people do speak reasonable Spanish, the tourist-oriented infrastructure renders it likely that Spanish service-staff respond to Spanish questions in English.

This situation has provoked various interpretations. Some have problematised the arrival of the many new arrivals, likening the migration process to imperialism because of the economic and cultural dominance of foreign privileged migrants, as seen in the title of the books *España en Venta* (*Spain for sale*) (Jurdao 1990) and *España, Asilo de Europa* (*Spain, Asylum of Europe*) (Jurdao and Sánchez 1990). Indeed, in the 1970s, under the Franco regime, this reaction was widespread amongst locals, as noted by Suárez-Navaz:

> By contrast [to other Mediterranean immigrants], Andalusians clearly perceived as "invader" the large numbers of Europeans who were visiting Andalusia's Mediterranean coasts as tourists or building homes and hotels there. In 1974, a well-known jurist wrote about the "European invasion" with a nationalist rhetoric typical of the Francoist regime: "In addition to the invasions Spain has suffered historically, we are now suffering an invasion led by tourists, foreigners who are negotiating contracts for the peripheral and island areas of our territories....It is difficult to find another country that accords [foreigners] so many advantages while imposing so few obligations on them.... The foreign 'invader' arrives in our territory as a key player and not as an 'invited artist'; he arrives to conquer, it seems, given how part of our territory has been sold off to them". (Aznar Sánchez 1974: 7–8, in Suárez-Navaz 2004: 63–64)

However, there are dangers in adopting this point of view as an analytical perspective, and rather than support negative media stereotypes constructing the British as colonisers, O'Reilly's account of the British on the Costa del Sol paints a rather more complex picture. She explores how migrants feel that they are 'marginalised by the Spanish...' (2000a: 152) because their integration is not encouraged or enabled by the host society. Their marginality is one however that is sustained by British migrants' complicity in these processes, as, '...they do not seem to object' (ibid.) particularly as they feel they belong in Spain through their engagement with other expatriates (O'Reilly 2004). This depiction is particularly appropriate for those of an older age, whose limited possibilities for integration are compounded by an absence of integration channels through common avenues of work and schooling (King, Warnes and Williams 2000). In the light of these factors, King, Warnes and Williams comment, '...the question must also be posed as to whether integration is a useful normative concept in the south of Spain...' (1998: 102). Huber and O'Reilly also maintain that for British and Swiss retired migrants, 'integration with the Spanish makes little sense in their situation' (2004: 347).

Such discussions point to the particular difficulties in analyzing retirement migration using existing analytical frameworks on migration, and certainly provoke appraisal of the scope and limits of the existing intellectual apparatus to account for such migration processes. King et al (2000) point out that it is inappropriate to apply templates usually applied in cases of economic migration, because retirement migrants, who are generally of mid to high socio-economic status, certainly cannot be analysed as 'immigrants', as the term implies marginalisation or powerlessness in relation to the host society (ibid.). In this phenomenon, even when economic motivations underpin migration, movement is not for work or higher earnings but governed by aspirations towards living a desirable lifestyle more cheaply. On the other hand, as O'Reilly (2003) argues, descriptions of these migrants by Spanish agencies and academics as 'residential tourists' are not quite satisfactory either as they lead to the conflation of tourists with resident foreigners.

The dilemma is particularly acute for anthropologists, whose typical stance of representing 'the voice of the underdog' is difficult to reconcile with the privileged migration evidenced in this case. Mindful of the fact that as Werbner argues 'the class dimensions of a theory of global subjectivity have remained mostly unexamined' (1999: 18) and the need to be attuned to the power dynamics in movement experiences (Oliver, Jansen and Heller 2000) the phenomenon presents a conundrum. How can the relative power of migrants be addressed within an ethnographic analysis in which migrants' views are adequately represented, yet that still reflects upon how their material privilege and feelings of marginalisation may impact subsequent relations and experiences in the migrant context? In considering the place of retirement migrants in their geographical context, one needs to factor in how 'linguistic colonialism' in the dominance of English (King, Warnes and Williams 2000: 132), expatriates' monopolisation of space (see Sibley 1995) or their relative power as consumers within local economies (Betty and Cahill 1999) have arisen, and therefore consider the degree to which perceived marginalisation may impinge — or not — on the lives, material conditions and possibilities of well-being for migrants of different statuses and histories.[11]

A useful way to proceed, I suggest, is to acknowledge and interrogate the present day relations of foreign resident and Spanish relations through the context of historical encounter. Karen Fog-Olwig (1993) utilises an historical approach in her research on the global nature of a Nevisian identity. She shows how it developed since the 1600s through African and European influences, colonial encounters and migration. Although the scope for a deep analysis is much less here, given the comparatively recent growth of the process, historical contextualisation, nonetheless, aids recognition of the relations that have shaped migrants' reception in the past, but, arguably still have resonance in the present. I suggest this is important to build into an anthropological account, because although limited integration is, on one hand, a reality for most retired migrants, there are nevertheless other risks through underestimating the significance of indirect cultural influences that living in Spain, and having relations (however limited) with other Spanish people may have for some of them. The remainder of the chapter therefore documents the history of Northern European migration to Southern Spain and the presence of the British in Andalucía (which is more personally considered through migrants' narratives in Chapter 3).

Contextualising the process this way leads to an understanding of the complex dynamics that influence both the perspectives of, and the reception of incomers in this part of Spain. This helpfully moves us to an analysis which does not simply castigate, critique or defend the subjects of the study intertwined in such processes, but equally acknowledges retired migrants' combined economic clout they hold in the region. It also considers the ways in which the clear links to tourism of this form of migration (O'Reilly 2003) bear important ramifications for current day cultural encounters, particularly through the pervasiveness of a historically constituted Northern European tourist 'gaze' (Urry 2002) which still influences the relationships between foreign residents and the Spanish people amongst who they live. I show later in the book (Chapter 7) that this is important for understanding migrants' current day cultural identifications in Spain.

THE BRITISH IN SPAIN

Although mass tourism in Spain is a fairly recent phenomenon, Northern Europeans, including the British, have a history of fascination with Spain as 'the outsider within'. There is a long history of contact; commercial activity by the British in Spain dates back at least to the fourteenth century, but the last two hundred years in particular have seen a steady flow of British people to Spain, as workers or travellers. In the region of Andalucía, by the 1850s, the port of Málaga was a regular stop for British seamen. There was also a small number of permanent British artisans and miners, whilst around three hundred English travellers visited every year, some staying for the winter period (Grice Hutchinson, 1964). At this time, there was a hotel in Málaga, *la Fonda de la Alameda*, run by an Englishman, which served, according to Grice-Hutchinson, 'Harvey's sauce, pale ale, and Stilton cheese' (1964: 36). However, one delicate issue plagued the mainly Protestant residents and visitors: until the 1830s, there was no means of burial available to them. In Catholic Spanish territory, they faced rather a gruesome form of burial, in which the corpses were buried upright in the sand, to be washed away (ibid.: 10). The British consul of the time, William Mark, repulsed at this practice, campaigned until a plot of land for underground burial was finally granted, which remains today as the English cemetery in Málaga. In 1850, a permanent chaplain was appointed to preside over the English residents and visitors, and by 1891, the lodge-temple in the cemetery grounds was converted to the chapel of St George's Church. Elsewhere in the region, the port of Cádiz was a thriving base for ship-building and sherry and fruit exports (Grayson, 2001) and in 1873, a British led consortium bought the Riotinto mines in Huelva. Yet there, the relations between locals and British workers were distant, as the latter lived apart in *'la colonia Inglesa'* (ibid.: 43) (the English colony) an estate of Victorian villas built around a clubhouse and protestant chapel.

The nineteenth and early twentieth centuries also brought a number of travellers and explorers, fascinated by Spain, its people and its customs, who helped construct a particular literary portrait of the region and its people. Notable amongst these were George Borrow and Richard Ford, who analysed the 'Spanish way of life' in their mid-nineteenth century accounts, *the Bible in Spain* (1843) and *Handbook for Travelers in Spain* (1845) respectively. Later, the literary gaze at Andalucía and Spain developed through writers such as Gerald Brenan (1980), Ernest Hemingway (1932, 1940) and Laurie Lee (1955, 1970). The publication details of Brenan's (1980) *South from Granada* summarise how Brenan, famed for establishing himself in the *Alpujarras* in 1919, 'needed to break free and find room to breathe, so to speak, in a country where he could acquire what he felt he so badly needed: self knowledge through a true education of mind'. Brenan's book discloses village customs, folklore and events which occurred during his time there, revealing close relationships with villagers. During Brenan's stay, he was visited by elite literary figures of the Bloomsbury group, such as Lytton Strachey, Virginia Woolf and Bertrand Russell. At this time, Málaga city was fast becoming a cosmopolitan watering hole for elite travellers. According to Marjorie Grice-Hutchinson, a Málaga-born informant and scholar, in the 1910s and 20s there was a well-established English scene in Málaga, revolving around events such as tennis, tea and cocktail parties.

To this day, despite (or even because of) major tourist development, Andalucía continues to provoke fascination and the region plays muse to a number of contemporary novelists and artists as being quintessentially Spanish and exemplifying the spirit of the nation (see Fernandez 1988). Recent years have seen a proliferation of 'good life abroad' books, such as *The Bottlebrush Tree* (Seymour-Davis, 1996), *Driving over Lemons: An Optimist in Andalucía* (Stewart, 1999) and *A Parrot in the Pepper Tree* (Stewart, 2002) based on the adaptation to a different life in the region by British foreigners. Lund's research on outsiders moving to a village in the *Alpujarra* at the present time also reveals how Andalucían figures are still sometimes interpreted by foreigners as demonstrating 'anti-rational' features (and see Chapter 7). She shows how newcomers moving to the village see themselves moving back in time (see also Oliver 2002 and Chapter 4). They are attracted to a type of 'historical nature', interpreted through an intellectual stance of knowledge and interest in the surroundings, whilst (Spanish) 'locals' relate to the environment less as scenery 'but rather as people who live in it, engage with it and create it' (2007, unpaginated). These different understandings are not always compatible; on one occasion when environmental protective measures were broken, Lund reports how some incomers assumed that one of the local 'savages' was the culprit.

Despite these romantic images (which may even be detected in early anthropological accounts,[12] as suggested by Llobera 1986, Pina de Cabral 1989, Pink 1997), Collier (1997) shows that Andalucían villages are far from the pristine and 'traditional' sites they have often been portrayed as.[13] The region has experienced unprecedented social and economic transformation following the period of Franco's dictatorship, and when Spain entered the (then) European Community in 1983, it was forced into a new market orientation whilst becoming a recipient of aid that redressed some regional inequalities (Dunphy 1995). The rapid change depended on the continuing growth of the service sector, and most notably tourism; in 1985, Andalucía played host to an estimated 5 million tourists (Valenzuela 1988). This reliance is still evident; currently in Málaga province, two-thirds of the employed population work in the service sector (Salmon 1991) whilst in the town and village in which this ethnography is based, 91% and 92% (respectively) of the employed population work in either construction or services[14] (*Instituto de Estadistica de Andalucia* 2001). The region has also witnessed vast immigration, as the last twenty years of the twentieth century have seen the foreign population in the region almost triple (265% increase) compared to an overall population increase in Spain of 13.6% (*Instituto de Estadística de Andalucía*, 2002: 15). This period has initiated a radical shift in consciousness of Andalucíans; far from being poor émigrés shown in Brandes' (1975) anthropological study in the 1970s, the social class distinctions between foreigners and Spaniards have been broken down (see also Waldren 1997) and Andalucíans are now 'privileged citizens of the southernmost borders of the EU' (Suárez-Navaz 2004: 2). Their reception of migrants has shifted because of their experiences of related processes of tourism, which have considerably altered their economic situation and lifestyles.

The account suggests that the tourist gaze, developed between foreign migrants and Spaniards over many years, may still likely influence, shape and inform mutual perceptions of migrants and Spaniards. As the remainder of the book shows, an important theme in migrants' narratives is their subtle employment of historically constructed ideals of 'Spanish people' and 'Spanishness' (particularly around time, age and community; see Chapters 4, 5 and 6). The gaze continues to influence social interactions between expatriates and Spanish, which are enacted in a framework of perceptions of cultural difference on both 'sides' (see Chapter 5 and 7). However, as Waldren (1996) cautions, the degree of distance between migrants and locals varies greatly according to individuals and situations. As such, only in-depth introductions to specific migrants, their migration histories and the specific contexts in which they live can capture the range and complexity evident in relationships amongst foreign residents and Spaniards. I consider these further in the next chapter's introduction to particular individuals, which explores different migrants, and how their experiences and reception in the locality have changed over recent decades.

SUMMARY

The chapter has provided an account of both the theoretical debates and the historical circumstances that situate the experiences of retired migrants in Southern Spain. First, I have argued that retirees' perspectives are informed by wider societal, demographic and economic shifts which have transformed retirement possibilities in the current era (Daatland and Biggs 2004) and particularly led to the emergence of ideals of 'successful ageing'. I also explored how migrants' imagining of lifestyles of leisured travel as 'good' for individual self-development in this book are related to historically produced cultural ideals. In other words, interrogating the cultural linking of individualism and consumption shows the practice of retirement migration, a form of non-essential consumption, as cognate with aspirations for individualistic 'projects' of retirement. Second, in using ethnography to explore how these experiences are lived in practice, care must be taken in considering how to analyse this form of migration. I argue that attention must be paid to the historical particularities of the development of migration in the region and should attempt to situate retired migrants within cultural relationships — however limited — with others in the region. Building in this rich and layered cultural context within this introduction allows a fuller understanding of how retirees' experiences of ageing are influenced by wider dynamics of particular places, histories, cultural relationships and images in globalization.

Having explored the cultural contexts informing migration to Spain, the following ethnography of experiences of retirement abroad is offered as a way of lending substance to debates on 'successful ageing'. Explorations at an ethnographic level allow close consideration of how different individuals live out aspirations for particular ageing experiences in a specific Spanish town and village. The next chapter first presents an introduction to the diversity of individuals who are currently experiencing retirement in Spain, some of whom have moved recently and others who have been there much longer. Moving beyond categorisation, it gives an in-depth description of the worlds these different people inhabit in their experiences of retirement in this part of Spain.

3   Location, Location, Location
Retiring in Spain

And yet...and yet...what had originally enthralled us, from our first day here, had been the discovery where the juggernaut of time had creaked almost to a halt. Except for the arrival of television, the twentieth century had not yet made its way up the hill. It was Dalmácija's immutability which had made it precious to us, and to those of our friends who had visited it. But that immutability was now crumbling. Moreover its erosion had coincided with our presence here. Was that a coincidence, or were we in some way responsible for what was happening? Perhaps our arrival here, like that of the conquistadors in the Caribbean or of Cook in the Pacific, had tainted the very culture we admired. The fatal impact. (*The Bottlebrush Tree. A Village in Andalusia,* Hugh Seymour Davis 1996: 283)

...I noted the features of this silent world: the memory-erasing white architecture; the enforced leisure that fossilised the nervous system; the almost Africanised aspect, but a North Africa invented by someone who had never visited the Maghreb; the apparent absence of any social structure; the timelessness of a world beyond boredom, with no past, no future, and a diminishing present. Perhaps this was what a leisure-dominated future would resemble? Nothing could ever happen in this affectless realm where entrophic drift calmed the surfaces of a thousand swimming pools. (*Cocaine Nights,* J.G.Ballard 1996: 34–35)

Two descriptions: two worlds. These accounts, one autobiographical, one fictional reflect contrasting idioms through which Andalucía and the Costa del Sol are constructed (see also O'Reilly 2000a). The first is based on ideals of 'traditional' Spain as a rural idyll of peace and tranquility, whilst Ballard's description is the non-place of the Costa del Sol, an unreal, liminal and disembedded leisure world beyond the 'normal' realm of work. Both representations collide in the ethnographic context of this research. This chapter, departing from such images, introduces a range of migrants who inhabit those places in reality. It shows how they experience place in varying ways and form different attachments with the foreign 'community' and the Spanish people amongst who they live. Demonstrating the diversity of migrant experiences both highlights the contingent nature of categorisation and ultimately takes us beyond it to look at how individuals create meaning in the particular contexts in which they live. Rapport demonstrates eloquently the variance in world-views amongst a farming village-community in the North of England (1993) and similarly in this ethnographic context, differences range in terms of age, background, region, class, life-experience, history and, as Rapport would probably concur, in terms of the particular consciousnesses of individuals themselves. Some of the older migrants I introduce came to seek companionship, others to escape it; some came to exploit financial advantages of living abroad, others moved rather to simplify and 'downgrade' their lives.

The chapter, in giving a general depiction of the ethnographic context, begins with a consideration of some individuals who arrived forty years ago. These people are now growing older in a place transformed beyond recognition from the underdeveloped region of peasant farming they moved into. It ends with others who have arrived recently, attracted by ready-made luxury apartment-complexes complete with facilities such as shops, bars and swimming pools. For some people, imaginings of 'Spain', 'Spanishness' and the particularity of atmosphere, smells, noises, and sense-experience of the villages or towns feature strongly in decisions to move and in subsequent depictions of their experience. For others, this is less important. The examples show the range of involvement and attachments to the place depends rather on a whole host of individual factors that include but do not in themselves explain them, including: longevity in the area, age, health, geographical location of dwelling, aptitude for language, motivation and interests. As the remainder of the book show, the diversity of migrants in background, motivation and experience is ultimately highly important in shaping their experiences of growing older.

THE VILLAGE

> We weren't looking for fancy living, none of urban man's frills and follies. We could do without that. We just wanted a basic back-to-nature existence in the sunshine. The simple life. (Baird 2004: 1)

Freila, in the Axarquía, is a village with a population of around 2200 people. It has changed from an undeveloped settlement into a highly publicised *pueblo blanco* (white village), known as a 'must-see' location in any tourist itinerary to this part of Spain. The village is perched at an altitude of 435 metres in the foothills of the *Sierras* (mountains), clinging tightly to a steep hill on one side and backed by a deep and vast gorge carved out by the river on the far side (see artist, Erik Tönsberg's representation of the area of study, Figure 3.1). The village has received considerable investment in

Figure 3.1 Artist's depiction of the area. Thanks to Erik Tönsberg.

order to 'prettify' it: the streets have been repaved, the overhanging pipes have been re-laid underground and landmarks are illuminated at night. It is established as part of the inland *ruta del vino* (wine route) for tourists. The village has benefited from the construction of a public swimming pool, an international language school, an outdoor sports stadium and a covered stadium, which attracts nationally popular bands in the summer. It is a very cosmopolitan place, particularly because it is home to many Northern European migrants, some of whom are retired. Elizabeth, in 1965, was the first of many foreigners to settle into Freila permanently but, like other original settlers, now faces ageing in her long-term home, which is very different to the place she moved to when seeking the 'simple life'.

Elizabeth is an elegant woman, now in her eighties, who lives alone in the tower, a historic old building in the centre of the village where she has lived for the past forty years. Elizabeth's balcony is carved into the rocky outcrop on which the village sits. Provided a chair can be wrestled free from Elizabeth's cats, it is a place blessed with a magnificent view over the hills. The vision of the landscape she observes from there changes regularly; the plots are sometimes rich with subtropical fruit-trees that are heavy with avocados and mangos, yet at other times they are dry and barren. The plots are laboured over in a daily grind by *campesinos* (peasant farmers) accompanied by their *mulos* (mules). Every year on these plots, the scattered white renovated *cortijos* (farmhouses) and grander palatial houses proliferate, sprawling upwards in a steady growth from the sea. On my first meeting with Elizabeth, we sat outside on her tiny patio overlooking these hills, taking in this beautiful view that I was to become very familiar with over the years. She mentioned at the time that we might be interrupted by someone calling in to read her blood pressure, although explained, 'I don't want to know...I mean if I did, what could I do about it? It's the same with my weight, there's no point weighing myself and finding out I'm too thin'. She mentioned that she usually avoids sitting in the sun, so people often ask her why she is so pale. 'I didn't come to Spain to lie in the sun, I came to *live* here', she explained.

When Elizabeth first came to the village, she was the first foreign inhabitant (although this is a matter of dispute with Mary, another woman a mile or so away, who arrived around the same time). Whilst born in Luxembourg, she married an English man and spent twenty years in England where she had worked as a model (some rumours suggest it was for famous fashion houses, like Dior). She moved to the village on her own following her divorce, when the nearby town of Tocina was merely a small fishing village that she had seen advertised in a brochure in Madrid. Freila is now easily reached by a smart new *autovía* (motorway) which interrupts some people's former countryside views, much to their annoyance. A constant sight on this road is the local bus running people to and from the town, as well as the tourist buses that relentlessly bring tourists for a stroll through the village, a beer and a couple of *tapas*. They follow a trail of decorative tiles explaining the history of the expulsion of the *moriscos* (moors) in the sixteenth century. Now the village is being marketed on the basis of its history as a place where in the twelfth century, Jews, Muslims and Christians lived together in harmony. This new branding of the town has emerged over the last couple of years, much to the annoyance of Elizabeth because the brand is indicated by a symbol that was on one of the whitewashed pots that Elizabeth found in her house years before. Walking through the village the tourists may call by the entrance patio to see the pot, before discovering the plaza, the busy meeting point for the men and women of the village which sits under the imposing white church. It is surrounded by a number of bars in the streets nearby which exude scents of garlic, fish, potatoes, beer and the sickly sweet smell of the potent *vino del terreno* (locally produced wine).

Elizabeth's cool house, comfortably furnished with ornate antique furniture, paintings and sculptures, is scattered with books. She has the company of some seasonal lodger-friends, who stay in the small annex upstairs. This arrangement gives her guests privacy but also offers her security and companionship, particularly important for her now, following a number of operations on her leg which make it difficult for her to get around. Elizabeth is fluent in Spanish and converses comfortably with Alicia, a Spanish woman who comes in to help. When I call in to Elizabeth, Alicia is pottering around the kitchen, frying up some fish for lunch or making us coffee. Elizabeth has known Alicia from when she was a child, because Alicia's mother and grandmother worked for Elizabeth before. This close family connection is observed by Alicia as she described Elizabeth as, 'well, it's like she's my mother or grandmother. People say to me here, 'bring your gran!'... [or] ask me 'how's your gran?'[1] Notwithstanding Alicia's daily presence in her house, Elizabeth considers herself a very private woman. She avoids going to the town of Tocina, visible in the distance from her balcony, and especially the associations there apart from occasionally visits to the cinema or art club. She complains about other expatriates' inability to speak Spanish well and the difficulties that result when they are ill. Elizabeth, intends to stay in Spain forever: 'I'll be the last one on the shelf', she maintained firmly, although she was perturbed by the building work and development in the village (see Figure 2.2). Elizabeth sadly pointed out that many of her friends have left or have died over the years.

One of those friends was Derek, who died during the course of my fieldwork. He was a former British spy who had spent his early childhood in Spain and had returned to the village in the 1960s. At this time, he had bought an old ruin before moving on to another village because 'there were too many bloody Brits' in Freila. He recalled how when he arrived, his belongings were taken up to his house on a donkey, because there was no road to his house, then a ruin at the top of the hill. He described life as 'cheap and easy' then. Other long-term residents described themselves as 'pioneers' and adventurers, and this was particularly true for the women, like Elizabeth and Kate, another English woman, who came on their own. Kate ended up moving to the town following her divorce in 1963. She

Figure 3.2 Construction work. Photograph by author.

impulsively bought a cheap flight to Spain and visited Tocina, where she met and fell in love with a Spaniard, who died some time ago, before she remarried an English man. Mary, on the other hand, was an actress on the London stage who accompanied her husband Peter on periodic working visits to Spain. She described herself as being enchanted by Spain, and spent her time whilst Peter worked, 'hunting down romantic ruins'. On her original visits, she was introduced to 'the set' in Málaga, and told me, 'they were *interesting* though, not like the ones you get now'. To arrive in the area she stuck a pin in a map, and when she and her husband drove there, they unexpectedly ended up buying an old ruin. She recalled, 'we weren't really serious about buying a house, but we went to see some old ruins, and that was it', referring to how she felt seduced by the beauty of the area. She has lived in the *campo* around Freila ever since and struggles to keep up her isolated existence as she grows older, particularly since Peter died many years ago.

According to Derek, when larger numbers of migrants swelled, 'a ghetto syndrome' started to develop in the area, with British people settling in Tocina and later Freila, and Germans settling in another town further up the coast. In the 1960s in the town, Kate recalls there were only around half a dozen permanent foreigners, some tourists and two small hotels. Most of the early migrants coming at this time were of a certain ilk; they were well educated and wealthy. Thus in the early days of migrant settlement, the village of Freila counted amongst its inhabitants a former British spy, a model, a well known Danish painter, an English travel writer and an American poet. The comparatively low cost of housing for the incomers also meant that they could buy or rent housing cheaply, giving an impression of affluence. Alicia, Elizabeth's housekeeper, confirms this, as she describes those who came in the past as 'another sort' (*otra clase*) who socialised in a small network, compared with the present:

> But it's not like in the past. In the past - I'm telling you - I used to know lots of them and they were all part of a circle. There was a villager who was a friend of Elizabeth [over there], another one over there, and they all partied together, but not any longer...[2]

This helps explain Elizabeth's occasional feelings of loneliness, as she told me numerous times, 'I thought about going home...but where would I go?'

It is unsurprising to note that initially there was a large economic disparity between the new migrants and established Spanish population, although the distance was bridged by a sense of cultural fascination from both. María, my landlady and Maite, her friend, recalled to me how they were impressed by the initial arrival of Elizabeth in the village. They were particularly struck by her glamorous clothes and shoes and recounted how they all rushed to touch the luxurious material of her coat. Alicia was only a small child when Elizabeth arrived, but recalled the sense of fascination that the foreigners provoked in their behaviours: their hiring of mules to go for trips out to the country, the goods they brought such as natural yoghurt and avocados that Alicia had never seen. They were accommodated as local patrons (see also Waldren 1997), and referred to in respectful terms as Dons and Doñas. Alicia remembers some of the interest in the foreigners:

> I was so impressed because of her [Elizabeth's] shoes... I'd have a pair of shoes and when they broke I'd get another pair. But she had one pair, another, another ... and more and more! And these kinds of things really shocked me. I've lived all this from the inside, because I've been with her since when she used to bring friends here. Oh, everything... the way of eating, the strange things... as people here said: 'uh, what a weird way of eating the foreigners have!'[3]

Alicia explained that particularly in the early days she was envied because of the material benefits gained in her association with Elizabeth. She said, 'people used to tell me, "Alicia, when Doña Elizabeth gets fed up with you, my daughter will go and work for her!"'[4] This is because many migrants, keen to escape the 'rat race' of Northern Europe also donated the accoutrements of their former lives to villagers. Mary told me that when she had arrived, her husband had told her to wear the same practical smocks as the local women, so she gave away her cocktail dresses and high-heeled shoes that she had brought over from London to some of the villagers. As such, relations were far more than simple business transactions. Mary referred to how her husband Peter had helped many Spaniards 'with pensions and things like that which they didn't know they were entitled to'. And whilst Spaniards tended the land of migrants, cleaned their houses, cooked and did their washing, the involvement of Spaniards in migrants' lives transcended the roles expected in formal (business) relationships, and they gained prestige from being associated with the foreigners (see also Waldren 1997).

This blurring of relationships has particular implications for foreign residents, now ageing, whose 'employees' take on wider care responsibilities (see Chapter 5). Mary recalled her long relationship with Sebastián, whom she has known since he was a child, whose official registration for insurance purposes is a *mayordomo* (butler). In reality, he does a range of jobs for her, from running errands to looking after her land. Proudly showing me a picture of his children that he had given her for Christmas she describes her affection for Sebastián as 'the closest I've been to maternal feelings'. And those in the village recounted how their lives had also been changed through the contact with such foreigners; Dolores explained how when they first arrived, a woman in the village had 'only her house, her children, her husband... that was life' (*'sólo su casa, sus niños, su marido... esa era la vida'*) but the more liberal attitudes held by early migrants influenced them. She recounted, 'I think that many people wanted to imitate some things, like the freedom, because we were very over-protected...They [foreigners] came and we saw that "this foreign girl is more free than me, I want to be like her"'.[5]

Following the early migrants, a number of 'hippies' and bohemians in the 1970s moved into the area, inspired by a counter-culture and attracted by 'going back to nature' envisaged in the relative simplicity of life in the area (see Rozenberg (1995) on 1970s Ibiza). Some of these still reside there, as can be seen from the odd painted VW van by the side of the road. In the village, there are fewer now as they move increasingly inland, fleeing the areas following the perceived despoiling of the coast and hinterland. There also remain a number of artists, sculptors and writers of various nationalities who live in the village and surrounding environs. Other people moved in retirement to the village in the 1980s, such as Dorthe and Frederik, two Danes and Jean, Jenny and Sarah from Britain. More recently still, there are growing numbers of younger people who arrive to work, inspired by recent popular TV programmes of relocation abroad, such as Channel 4's *A Place in the Sun*. For reasons of economy and clarity, little more will be added about them although for further ethnographic analyses of other migrants in Spain, refer to Waldren (1996), O'Reilly, (2000a) and Lund (2005, 2006).

THE TOWN

From Elizabeth's balcony, if you cast your eyes towards the expanse of the Mediterranean, Africa beckoning beyond, there lies Tocina, some six kilometres away. It is a larger hive of tourist activity, but still, some say, one that retains a pleasant 'Spanish' atmosphere. There is growing expanse of hotels built around the rocky coves, sandy bays and the main expanse of beach at the extremes of the town, which can just about be made out in the distance from the village. The town has grown since the 1970s not only through tourism, but also through the relative explosion in migrant numbers in the early-mid 1980s, precipitated by a favourable exchange rate and inexpensive prices (King et al 2000). Some earlier residents, such as Elizabeth, interpret this growth negatively, suggesting it marks a gradual intellectual drain, corresponding with King et al's (ibid.) observations that show migrants in the 1970s as more highly educated than those in the 1980s.

Perhaps the longer established migrants also object to the carnivalesque ambience used in the promotion of mass tourism in the town. The carnivalesque is a tongue-in-cheek manner that inflates, exaggerates, inverts or symbolically parodies official, mainstream culture and conventions (Dentith 1995, Shields 1991, Hetherington 1998). It is evident everywhere in promotions of the region; such as in the advertisements for properties and tourist services found in the expatriate magazines, whose descriptions excessively glorify the area through superlative descriptions.[6] For instance, a typical advert of a new housing complex describes the 'wonderful views as far as the eye can see' and continues, 'it's difficult to attempt to describe the beauty of the area — some say it's the closest to paradise on earth: The azure sky, the glittering sea'. The luxury homes on sale, 'are most people's dream of the perfect place to live...far from the hustle and bustle of the cities of Northern Europe' (*the Marketplace*: August 1999). Many of the articles in the expatriate press are also written in a tongue-in-cheek fashion and commentaries are often loaded with frankness or innuendo (see examples in Chapter 6). Similarly, ironical comic twists are also given to imitations of English services: the English bookshop is named *W H Smiffs*, a parody of the chain, *W H Smiths*, whilst the *Balti Towers* Indian restaurant refers to the 1970s English comedy TV show, *Fawlty Towers*. Whatever the case, many in the village like James, a semi-retired migrant refer to how in comparison to the village, the town 'might as well be another world'.

Judy arrived in the town in the 1980s. Now in her seventies, she is one of the leading lights of the community in Tocina. She moved to Spain after she had met and married her husband in later life. Far from an example of a process of 'intellectual draining', she is a former teacher who taught at a progressive school using Montessori principles and later became a lecturer in psychology in Oxford. She lives in a small, but cosy apartment high up in a block of flats in the centre of town. On a visit, she makes us a pot of tea whilst I sit on her chairs piled high with cushions, from which you can take in the view to the sea over the tops of the apartments in the town. The flat is full and welcoming; there are watercolours of the local beaches, and the walls have photos of her cats and odd postcards from places visited by friends across the world. The dark wooden units are stacked high with books, including a large encyclopaedia of Spain and numerous Spanish and English history books. I spot a video of *Pride and Prejudice* and we share a laugh about how the actor, Colin Firth, is adored from the ages of seven to seventy. On one visit, she sat at her table piled high with papers, including information she had collected on her trips out, tickets for excursions she had been on and books that she was currently researching. Judy is a keen member of several clubs run for and by foreign residents: the American Club, the International Club, the Royal British Legion and *the Serenaders*, a choir group. When I first came to do fieldwork, Judy used to run the Labour Club, a small group who met for the odd lunch and to watch relevant films. Now Judy devotes her time to running the local history group, which organizes a series of lectures on topics such as Phoenician and Roman Spain, the Battle of Trafalgar and the Spanish Civil War. After starting it up, Judy tells me, 'the club is going from strength to strength' and the popularity of it has surprised even her.

Every month, the history group has a lecture, accompanied by lists of extra reading and a visit out to one of the sites spoken about later in the month. The organizers go on exploratory tours to find out what is there, prepare the trips and establish what facilities are available for the mainly older members of the group. When the lectures stop, a few of the organizers meet up socially. I ask where they choose to go and Judy says that it is up to them:

> ...any of my favourite places. It's very good really — I get to follow my interests and everyone else seems to love it. Yes, I'm surprised — when we went to Cabras, we had to hire two coaches as the trip was so popular. On the way up, I was telling stories about the civil war and the refugees on that street as it was the *día de Andalucía* (Andalucía day). But when we stopped for a coffee halfway up, the people in the other coach heard and wanted me to go in there and tell them about it too.

Judy refers to how, because the history club travels as a group, the organizers can barter down the price of trips. The last excursion was a tour around a sherry house, where she explained, 'you can do the tour for €2 and get wine tasting for €2, but we managed to get the whole lot for €3'. This is important to Judy, who as a widow, must be thrifty in order to enjoy all the opportunities of life in Spain. Judy thrives on the hard work required by her involvement in the clubs, and is even now busy with a weekly slot on the radio station as 'Doctor Jude' (referring to her doctorate in Psychology). She is helping to establish the radio station to 'help cater for all the arts and cultural side of things'.

Judy occasionally calls in to the *hogar del pensionistas*, the day centre for older people. It is a vibrant meeting place in the centre of town opposite the cultural centre, mainly used by older Spanish people but sometimes frequented by some Northern European pensioners. The foyer is maintained by Pepe, a charismatic receptionist, who welcomes you into the bright and airy building. The windows are wide open to allow those inside to see the throngs of people passing by in the busy street, from the enormous meeting area and bar. Suspended above the bar there is an iron grate, decorated with fairy lights and flags (including the Spanish flag, the EU, a Union Jack, a Welsh dragon, a Scottish thistle). On the back wall there are flags from Barcelona FC and Liverpool and a paper sign written in capital letters in English – 'WELCOME. OPEN TO EVERYBODY'. On the outside door there is also a *menu del día* written on paper, available at the bargain price of €4.50. This buys you a simple regional meal consisting of a soup of chickpeas and noodles, a main course of breaded veal and chips, followed by a dessert of flan. In the morning the room is full of Spanish older men playing dominoes, but at lunchtime, they return home for dinner and the room empties out. Occasionally I go with Judy for a meal who, like me, appreciates the good value, and she chats amiably in reasonably good Spanish with the cook and bartender, an Argentinian couple who have been there for five years. On other occasions, there are a few other retired foreigners in the centre, such as the group of friends who go there for a bite before their Scottish country dancing meeting over the road.

Just up the road from Tocina live Ray and Lilian in a small flat in an apartment block overlooking the sea. They only arrived four years ago in Spain. This is their second marriage for both Ray and Lilian and they sold both of their houses in Britain to move there permanently. However, they moved from their holiday home in a remote village to the coast after eighteen months because of their feelings of isolation and loneliness and explained, 'we couldn't speak Spanish. But we like the culture and friendship of the Spanish. They have a calm, lovely way'. Both had wanted to leave England as they did not like the weather, but they return to England three times a year and still make frequent phone calls back. Yet they explain that where they live,

> there's not so much of the English. It's more international...in July and August, this is where the Spanish come. Most of our friends are international, we quite like to be away from the Brits. There's Swedes, Germans, French, Polish. We came here for a way of life.

Ray and Lilian both feel much healthier and certainly don't miss what Ray described as the 'antiquated health system' in Britain. In particular, the weather eases Ray's arthritis, 'England is *yuck*', Lilian explained, 'here our health is better and time doesn't drag, we're not bored at all. I am involved in the cultural side of things, I go practicing twice a week for choir, whilst Ray goes to golf. It's difficult fitting it all in!' They moved specifically to the apartment so that they had something they could manage in old age. This decision was informed by their experiences helping out in a voluntary ecumenical centre *Lux Mundi*. As trained nurses they had often been called out to 'rescue' people who had got themselves into difficulty. They have since distanced themselves from the centre because it took too much commitment, but Ray explained that the experience, 'made us think. We wanted to be safe and not have to travel far. There'll come a time...'

Ray and Lilian are both spiritual healers and expressed surprise that they were able to meet other spiritual healers when they came to Spain. Lilian explained,

> we thought we would leave it all behind. I've never had a filofax, but we keep one out here. We say you have less time when you're over sixty-five...I think there's only eighteen hours in a day, five days a week instead of seven. It's because socialising takes longer. Lunch is at 12, but finishes at 6 and yet, you've only been for 'lunch'. That's the lovely thing here, and there are all the other nationalities you can enjoy life with. We wouldn't want to live in town though. If you live in Spain, you want to live with the Spanish....You have to think Spanish, live the ambience. We take siesta sometimes.

The couple both expressed how they feel very much at home in Spain. 'I'm often ready to go home before the end of visits to UK', Lilian described. 'Here, we're learning and growing all the time. We learn about different customs and it's definitely broadened our outlook on the world and life'.

Ray and Lilian are involved in many of the community events, including trips out and regular social meetings or luncheon events. In Tocina there is certainly no shortage of places to eat and drink; the winding streets are full of restaurants: Spanish fish-bars, English, Chinese, Mexican, Indian restaurants and of course, a Spanish flamenco show-bar. The town environment is also characterised by various gift shops, clothes shops, car-rental facilities, ice-cream counters and a couple of charity shops. Slightly away from the main bustling tourist area, there is a second hand English bookshop, which is the central place in which the foreign population rents out English language videos and can buy and sell books. They can also find out on the corkboard at the entrance the name of an English plumber, builder, childminder, Spanish teacher or details of housing to rent. It is also a place to pick up the free weekly newspapers and magazines produced by and for foreign residents, which feature articles written on topics as diverse as football hooliganism, the story of Rosa Parks and an account of memories from an eighty-seven year old (in *The Marketplace*, August 2000*)*. Contributions are regularly written by well known foreign residents in the town and village; Judy often contributes features on history. The advertisements in *the Marketplace* magazine also inform readers of local details; in a recent edition the opening of a new Cornish pasty shop was reported and there was a page dedicated to 'the Roast on the Coast' which advertised restaurants where a good Sunday lunch could be purchased.

Not far away from the second-hand bookshop is *W H Smiffs*, which sells an impressive range of novels, good life abroad books, Spanish cookbooks, books on language tuition, maps and cards. If you require a packet of Murray Mints or dollymixtures, *Allsorts,* an old-fashioned sweet shop can meet your needs. Walking in one direction, you will pass the numerous English bars, including *Pirates, the Market Tavern,* and another with a large sun-shade that describes the food on offer as *a taste of England in Spain*. Venturing inside one of the bars, in a very quiet period there are just a few other people, maybe tourists, eating English breakfasts, whilst others eat typical British meals such as steak and kidney pie with chips, cabbage, peas, carrots and gravy. There is a smell of chips and malt vinegar. The furniture is covered in green velour upholstery and glasses hang above the dark wooden bar, including old-fashioned thick handled pint jugs, and there are Victorian-style pictures on the wall. A *'Hammers'* flag (indicating West Ham football club) is on the wall just above a chalkboard which lists the food on offer — steak and kidney pie, lasagne, savaloy and chips, chilli con carne, and a range of puddings which include apple crumble, chocolate cake and lemon meringue pie. The only Spanish there is a *'perros no'* sign ('no dogs') which is just next to a 'no passing wind' joke sign. The TV is on all the time, tuned in at the time to Sky News. Over the road in another, it is very similar. It is run by a friendly young woman who used to be a tour operator here, who explained the nature of their regular custom:

> I don't know how many of our regulars are retired. Some of them don't seem to do anything but always have money on them. I don't know how they do it, but you don't ask. Lots are retired early, I guess. We couldn't survive without the regulars, it keeps us going over the winter, but lots of them go back now. We've just last night said goodbye to Sandra and Paul, Bob and Jean, Pat the Hat, Ann and Barry.

Many of the retired migrants in the study rely exclusively on the infrastructure offered by the expatriate clubs (see Chapter 7) for their social lives. An example of one of these clubs in Tocina is the American Club, which meets just up from *Calle Higueres* (known colloquially by some migrants as 'Post Office Street'). The description of the club is misleading, as although it is run by Belle, an American, not all of the members are from North America; a sizeable proportion are from Britain or Germany. Belle can always be spotted at the Chinese restaurant on Saturday lunchtime. She puts a decorative American flag at the top of the table, denoting the occasion as the meeting of the local chapter of the club. She also lays out a number of magazines, with the latest news of the club administration, travels of members, members' birthdays and monthly calendar of forthcoming events, including the large Thanksgiving supper held near Fuengirola, a tourist hotspot to the West of Málaga. Sometimes only a few people will turn up, although there are often around fifteen to twenty people. Some eat a three course special lunch with red wine, others order just a pot of jasmine tea.

The group has been using this venue for a while now, but during the course of my fieldwork, the group had to move the venue four times because the bars or restaurants were judged unsuitable or the expectations of the proprietors and the club-members did not match. However, Belle currently experiences a good relationship with the Chinese manageress, who often brings her back little gifts when she returns from visits abroad. Of late however, some members have dropped out of the club gradually as they do not like to eat at lunchtimes. I asked Belle about this, to which she shrugged her shoulders and explained pragmatically, 'you can't please everyone!' Other members include Bill, an American attending the club. He is somewhat of an inspiration to other members as he was in a wheelchair for a long time following a serious operation, but now walks with crutches. Bierta is a soft spoken German woman who comes to the meetings every Saturday for just a couple of hours, as she is keen to return to her husband, Jack, who stays in their house a few miles up along the coast road. Jack still goes daily into town in the morning for a glass of beer or two however, much like Elizabeth he regretted that he no longer saw people he knows anymore. 'Some days I can sit there and not a soul I know goes by', he said.

Just a few streets up from *Calle Málaga* is the International Club of Tocina, which, unlike the American club owns its own premises, which were purchased in the late 1980s. It would be easy to miss the clubhouse, as it is a small, unprepossessing building. It is tucked away in a quiet residential street, where older Spanish women can be seen sweeping clean their open doorways or crotcheting whilst waiting to sell their beans or avocados displayed in boxes to passers by. The club is open on Tuesday, Thursday, and Saturday afternoons and some evenings. The meeting room is fairly small and full of tables and chairs next to a bar, which is run by volunteers. Hanging on the walls are pictures (such as such as a church in Segovia) which are painted by members attending the club's art classes. The club was originally formed in 1974 and is now registered as a charity so can offer subsidised drinks to members, who must register and pay fees. The club membership is claimed to span twenty nationalities, although the majority are British. Members come in to chat or to swap videos in the carefully organised video-library which is run by Daphne, a British woman who has recently moved to Spain. She took the job on with her husband William, a retired Sergeant Major, to help keep her busy and fend off her feelings of homesickness. Since taking over, the couple have colour-coded the entire video system to make it more efficient. In addition to the video library, there is darts, scrabble, an art club, a writers' club, a bridge group and regular trips by coach to Gibraltar and other places of interest in Spain. On a club day, the place is packed, with people having a beer, wine, brandy or coffee. On one occasion, the barman called out over the noise, 'be quiet you lot, the digger can't hear himself work' making a joking reference to the relentless sound of the roadworks going on outside.

Back in the town walking towards the west of the town, tucked into some apartment blocks by the side of the very British freezer shop *Iceland*, is the meeting place of the Royal British Legion. This is a well-established association in Britain, catering for ex-servicemen and their wives. Although the club in Spain is a recognised official branch of the British-based charity, it does not have premises of its own, meeting instead on Wednesday lunch-times for a social gathering at the *Golf Hole*, a small, cosy English bar filled with comfortable padded booths in velour yellow and green furnishings. It is open to the public but its regular clientele are also the club members and golfers from the golf society. On the wall, there is a painted caricature of different golfers distinguished by their red noses and inebriated condition. The bar is run by a lively British couple, who dish out *tapas* of anything from *estofado* (Spanish stew) to cottage pie or liver and onions. By virtue of regular use, it feels to members (and myself as time goes by) a home from home (as Dixey notes on the use of bingo halls 1988).

A usual Wednesday afternoon sees the bar fill up with the regulars, chatting over a glass of wine, beer or brandy about anything from news on other members and their families, health issues, memories of war time, forthcoming events, fundraising possibilities and tales of visits to Britain or to other destinations abroad. On one occasion, Robert and Sam discussed the problems they were having with the Spanish chef at their usual luncheon venue. The conversation was interrupted by the arrival of a couple Tony and Jan, to which Robert commented, 'Oh look, the snowbirds have come in...but they're deserting us next week. Yes, they grace us with their presence when they choose and then they're off'. Tony explained later to me, 'We prefer to describe ourselves as swallows...the priest in our local church says from the pulpit when we go there, "the swallows have arrived" and then here, the priest says the same when we come back'. Like other clubs, the British Legion has a fluctuating membership because of the comings and goings of seasonal migrants like Tony and Jan.

The association puts on popular social events, ranging from its weekly meetings in *the Golf Hole* to its monthly luncheons. The main event of the year however is the annual Remembrance Service (see Chapter 7) which is followed by a special three course luncheon (typically including roast beef as a main course). The club attracts all sorts of people; on one occasion William (the former Sergeant Major) was in the *Golf Hole* dressed in designer suit with cravat and wearing skiing sunglasses. He was talking about his recent trip with his wife to the Panama Canal. Harry 'the Hat', a soft spoken man from the East-End of London was sitting next to him, dressed in a green baggy cardigan with a vest underneath. Les was also there, a former lorry driver, swathed in tattoos, wearing jeans, white T shirt and trainers, looking tanned and fit, despite recovering from six heart attacks in four months. Judy was also there, herself wearing leggings, jogging top and trainers and she joked with Les, 'Now look at him. Larger than life and twice as ugly!'

Like other clubs, the British Legion has a strong welfare responsibility towards its members. In fact, there is a wide network of voluntary services run by, and sometimes for, the Northern European migrants in Spain (Huber and O'Reilly 2004). For instance, a small number of English speaking volunteers (including Judy) run a translations service at the *ambulatorio* (outpatients' clinic). The clubs also rely on voluntary personnel, comprising a Chair, Treasurer, Secretary and committee members, whilst jobs are carried out by others to support club activities. Thus in the International Club, volunteers not only manage the video library, but work in the bar and organize trips out. There are also fundraising events (such as fashion shows) and people serve in charity shops for other organisations including CAS (Costa Animal Society) and CUDECA, a charity established to fund a hospice and palliative care for cancer sufferers (see also O'Reilly 2000a). Other more informal, ad hoc opportunities for helping out arise, which see migrants involved in activities such as delivering flyers for events, putting up posters, writing articles for the expatriate press, offering lifts or doing others' shopping if they are ill. The consequences of migrants' work are admirable;

not only are there lavish, well run social arrangements but the charity work engaged in by the community helps others in difficult circumstances (see Chapter 5) and raises money. For example, in the poppy-collecting campaign for Remembrance Day undertaken by Royal British Legion members in 1998, the local branch collected 1,040,204 pesetas (around €6,250). Every member or volunteer who helped in the campaign received a personally typed letter of thanks from the secretary of the campaign, who gave details of the total raised in each collector's box.

To conclude this introduction to the context, it is worth also introducing some of the many people who live in the number of urbanisations built on the outskirts of the town. One of these is *Los Jardines*, an urbanisation full of houses built in a pseudo-Andalucían style with winding trails of terracotta tiles weaving between well maintained grassy verges rich with heavily scented *dama de noche* and *bougainvillea*. It is mixed-use; some properties are owned privately as holiday homes by Spaniards or foreigners and some are let through travel agencies, whilst others are permanent homes for retired migrants, like John, in his seventies and Annabel, in her late fifties. They moved to their house there having lived in the Caribbean for ten years, where John had worked as a technical plastic engineer. They had rented out their home in Britain, but in their absence it had been wrecked by unscrupulous tenants. Annabel explained how she felt she had nothing to go back to England for: 'If you make me go back, I'd curl up and die', she commented. When looking for somewhere to retire, they already knew they liked the climate of Spain and had a friend living there who was enthusiastic about it. When Annabel first came to Spain, she literally had only one week to find somewhere to live and they spent the first six months in Spain renting whilst work was being done on the property. They explained how they were put off buying a *cortijo* (farmhouse) in the countryside as 'at our age we want security' and felt content that any battles they had to fight were fought by the officials of the *comunidad* (community offices) who run the urbanisation.

'It's absolutely super!' Annabel told me. 'We found it no trouble making friends. Dolores in the *comunidad* was superb as the go-between the solicitors and the French lady we were buying the house from'. Their biggest concern was around health, so they took out an insurance policy for three years. However, Annabel also told me of her experience using state healthcare. Although she had been advised by others to go back to England, she maintained, 'we've been treated extremely successfully. The aftercare is ropey, because the Spanish rely on their relatives…but the medical side was first class!' Annabel went on to explain how, 'it's not like being on holiday…well, I suppose it is compared to England. John plays golf a lot, but we don't join in the drinking set, although it's here if you want it'. Annabel trained in massage and reflexology in the Caribbean. She offers these as services from time to time at home, an activity than earns her 'pin-money' and she also goes to keep fit at the *salon,* which is a meeting room in the urbanisation centre. Near the salon there is also a bar, swimming pool and a grocery shop. Annabel also goes to a gym and tries to learn Spanish but she complained that she does not get the opportunity to speak Spanish outside of lessons. John, in contrast, believes he is too old to learn Spanish, but claimed that through knowing twelve words, he can get by. 'So many of them [Spanish people] speak English', he explained, 'this means you don't bother....five or six years ago, there were no interpreters, for example. Now, it makes you lazy'.

The couple maintained that they had no intention of ever leaving Spain. They admitted that there were things that irked them about living there, including the eight weeks of the year they called 'the silly season', when they were disturbed by holidaymakers in the urbanisation at 2, 3 and 4 in the morning. To overcome the disturbance however, they had a cooling system put in so that they do not have to open the windows. They also expressed how they miss certain products from Britain. John explained how they are,

> forever asking people to bring them things, or we go to Gib [Gibraltar]. Although now there's any type of food you want. It's very international here and convenient to have the things you get used to. It's been a battle fought and won.

Annabel continued, 'we've never had any problems with the Spanish. We get on with the gardeners around here really well. We're not the sort of people to row though...we respect different ways. We tolerate — we're in Europe now!' 'The only problem is the smoking everywhere', John added, 'And the Spanish bring their kids everywhere', complained Annabel:

> ...changing nappies on the table, they have no sense of personal space. I have a friend who married a Spaniard and had a problem with this open house business. She lives in a village where there are only thirteen people, it was unbelievable. Even here, the builder had garlic in his pocket to ward off vampires. But we have friends of all nationalities, Swiss friends...there is the International club although we don't like clubby things. When you get here, you clutch at straws, then you find your own level...It's not my scene [the club-life], I don't fit in. In the urbanisation though there's not two the same nationality and that's how we like it.

They explained how, 'there're all sorts of interesting people' there, and explained the further benefits — a better lifestyle for a limited pension budget. 'We work to play', says John, 'there's just no use worrying about the future'.

SUMMARY

The chapter gives an insight into the range and variety of experiences of some foreign residents growing older in Spain, showing their multiple orientations and attachments to the place in which they live. Having positioned some individuals in their social context, the remainder of the book will address the key analytic themes of how their aspirations for ageing well in retirement are experienced through a careful balancing act of the inherent contradictions of those desires. The following chapter interrogates the first theme of time, showing how desires for free and spontaneous time use are ultimately matched with concerns for using time productively.

4 The Time of Our Lives
Temporality and the Life Course

One rainy Saturday in late November, at the International Club, I sat with Molly and her friend, Hazel, at their usual table towards the back of the club. It was very busy inside and the windows were steamed up. She pointed to the paintings on the walls by members — variously of fruit or landscapes, 'you know there's some that are really professional now. They sell as they're quite good'. I agreed with her. She continued, 'Of course I'd never be able to do anything like that. I get too tired'. Our conversation turned to the subject of Charlotte and Gerald, who were regular faces at the club. Charlotte had recently suffered a bad fall and had been in and out of hospital for a while. Hazel commented, 'well you know about Charlotte and Gerald don't you? She's very bad.... She doesn't even get to sit out on the terrace now'. Molly added, 'But I don't think that enough was done when there were things that could be done. I mean I used to see him walking miles in front of her telling her to hurry up. It's a shame, she should be looked after'.

A whistle was blown, signalling the end of the library session and Molly swallowed down her coffee quickly. She gathered her magazines such as *Woman's Own* and *the People* that she collected that morning from the magazine swap offered by the club. She was keen to leave, as the club house was getting too busy. 'You know us', she smiled, 'we have our own little routine — we're off for our chicken sandwich at the café around the corner'. I looked around and said hello to Bob on the next table, who invited me to sit with him and his friends. He was pondering on the practicalities of moving house as he was selling his house nearby Freila to be with his wife in New Zealand. She had already moved there to be near their children, as she required regular dialysis. Now Bob was trying to make sense of what to do from some advice in one of the free magazines...'there's all these regulations, you have to have copies of everything, they can't just take your word for it. And the law says you need such and such, so you go down to the Town Hall and say, I need this and they say, what's that?' he sighed. The biggest problem he faced was in arranging the transport of his two dogs, but he refused to leave until he could take them with him. The other couple sitting with Bob were also planning to move to France soon, and explained, 'we used to live up in the hills, but found that too isolating. Then we moved down to an urbanisation and hated it. But we've been here seven years, it's just time for a change, time to move on'. I asked them when they're going. 'Pfffff! We haven't even looked at any houses yet, and besides, we're off to Morocco next week on an International Club trip'. 'That's right', said Tom, cradling a brandy, 'we're hoping to sell our wives whilst we're there'.

I caught sight of Linda, a Scottish woman, at the bar. She was always the life and soul of the party, although today she seemed quite distant and disinterested in my social pleasantries. After a few minutes, she told me abruptly, 'we can't stay here any more, my husband's ill, we're leaving'. I expressed my sympathies and asked when she was going. She replied, clearly upset, 'that's the 500 million dollar question...I just don't know, it's all up in the air'.

The last chapter showed great diversity in orientations to lifestyle and place amongst retired migrants in Spain. Nevertheless, this vignette, of a typical social meeting in one of the foreign residents' clubs shows that one fundamental challenge shapes their lives in Spain: they are all negotiating growing older. The lifestyles they live are influenced — and occasionally violently disrupted — by the irreversible fact of their ageing (Adam 1995). Ageing, a process too slow to apprehend directly (Hockey and James 2003), occurs simply as time passes, which means that perceptions of ageing are bound up with wider questions of temporality. In these migrants' lives, questions of how people pass their days, their plans for wider vistas of life times and, for some, how long they can even stay in Spain, are influenced by their ageing and as such, merit closer attention. This chapter focuses on time and how it is perceived, experienced and reflected upon, in both people's daily lives and their imagined trajectories of life.

A central issue to emerge from this examination is that many retired migrants in Spain construct certain stories about time to help to sustain positive ageing self-identities. They describe Spain as a place in which it is felt that time is more flexible, spontaneous and unhurried. Moving to Spain is associated with disengagement from time-conceptions governing former lives, still so evident in the lives of others 'back there' in the homeland. Structured time-use and the imperative to beat the clock are presented as conditions of the past, whilst the putative speed of that past is contrasted with the slowness of the retirees' present. And, perhaps most importantly, this time of the life course is 'theirs'; experienced as 'me-time', rather than life lived at other's bidding. However, the chapter shows that friction arises in sustaining these temporal fictions, because of contradictory cultural messages around free and structured time. In typical busy working lives, we often yearn to 'work differently' (Nowotny 1994: 136) to have 'more' time and less time pressure, an experience imagined in retirement. However, on the other hand, too much free time is culturally evaluated as 'weighty' and 'heavy', informing imperatives rather to 'kill' time and avoid 'stagnation' (see Lakoff and Johnson, 1980). For retired migrants, this contradiction becomes even more pertinent, when considering how as Adam (1990: 128) argues, 'life is lived in relation to our finitude'. Thus I show that whilst rejecting structured time-use is one means of enjoying free time, on the other hand, migrants attempt to 'fill' (rather than waste) time, through routine and planned activities. Contradictory orientations of structuring time use which resonate with ingrained orientations of industrial time as a valuable resource, thereby impel people towards productive time-use long after paid productivity ceases. As a result, some temporal conventions that are expressed as being shed in moving to Spain are simply reintroduced to uphold positive self-identities in people's 'life-times'.

Analysis of this tension can be aided by considering some relevant work in sociology and anthropology, which sheds light on how notions of time are culturally produced. Much empirical research neglects the detail of time (Rosaldo 1993) perhaps because it is such a 'deeply taken-for-granted aspect of social life' (Adam 1990: 9). However, there is a long theoretical tradition of work on the subject. Durkheim explored the social nature of time, emphasising it as a core category through which humans variously experience the world, whilst Evans-Pritchard (1940) demonstrated how there is variety in the culturally constituted time-universes of different societies. Lévi Strauss also distinguished between 'hot' societies, which internalise their historicity and are governed by a non-reversible conception of time, and 'cold' societies in which people live according to static and cyclical notions of time, although Gell (1992) argued against such cultural variability in conceptions of time.[1] Leach (1966) helpfully explored two ways in which time is apprehended, first through repetition and recurrence of certain natural phenomena such as the rising and setting of the sun. However, the inevitability of death instils a second awareness of time as non-repetitive, linear and irreversible, a 'psychologically very unpleasant' fact (ibid.: 125).

More recently, social scientists have suggested that not only should we explore abstract notions of time, but look at the 'timings' of life, or the qualities and experiences of time lived in social, historical and material practices (James and Mills 2005). This directs attention to how time is experienced and understood through metaphorical and symbolic cultural constructs. In Western capitalist societies, time is often conceived as a mechanistic and quantitatively valued resource (Adam 1995). According to Lakoff and Johnson, this is a 'structural metaphor basic to Western industrial society' (1980: 66) in which time is ideologised as something to be saved, wasted, filled, sold and budgeted (Adam 1990: 104–126, Thrift 1996). These beliefs are instilled from early childhood, for example, everyday practices of rewards and punishments are used to impart time-disciplining on the body, so that children come to understand time as 'a commodity which is subject to an exchange relationship based on both discipline and/or liberation' (Christensen, James and Jenks 2001: 203). And it continues through the life course, as in working lives, periods of labour are exchanged for the free time of holidays and ultimately retirement. For those in paid employment, 'free' time is a compensation that must be earned through work (Clarke and Critcher 1985), a valued resource to be purchased before it can be consumed:

> The free time of the holidays remains the private property of the holiday-maker; an object, a possession he has earned with the sweat of his brow over the year; it is something owned by him, possessed by him as he possesses his other objects... (Baudrillard 1998: 154)

Such notions of time as value are, according to Adam, not universal, but a culturally learned and historically developed conceptualisation 'peculiar to a Western way of life' (1995: 64). In 'Time, work-discipline and industrial capitalism', E.P. Thompson (1967) demonstrates, for example, how this conception has developed. His analysis depicts how workers' perceptions of time between the Middle-Ages and mid seventeenth century fundamentally changed, through a shift away from task-orientation in pre-industry towards timed labour. This created a distinction for workers between 'their employer's time and their 'own' time' (ibid.: 61). Time-use became subject to moral evaluations through which it became a sin to waste time in idleness, a notion enshrined in the Protestant ethic and still evident in the contemporary dictum that, 'time is money' (Christensen, James and Jenks 2001: 203). This temporal consciousness and restructuring of work-life laid the foundations for the shift to industrial capitalism, although by the nineteenth century 'labour won some time for itself from capital in order to call such time 'free': free from work and for producing things for the profit of others' (Inglis 2000: 3), as discussed previously. Foucault (1977) also demonstrates how time-management became a technique of disciplining the body. The monastic model used by Benedictine monks (Adam 1990, 1995) inculcated time-discipline through strictly regulated timetables, which were punctuated by the ringing of bells (Thrift 1996). These techniques spilled over to wider society to instil concern for time-keeping which has become taken for granted practice; in twentieth century Western education, for example, time segregation and punctuation is evident in the use of timetables, bells and calendars of the education year (Adam 1995).

Not only are apprehensions of time shaped by culture, but experiences of time may vary by age. Leach states, 'The feeling that most of us have that the first ten years of childhood 'lasted much longer' than the hectic decade 40–50 is no illusion' (1966: 132). Adam argues that this is because the metabolic rate is lower for older people so that 'the experience of the speed with which time passes is consistently different between the young and the old' (1990: 79). The perception of a quicker passage of time for older people is perhaps also heightened by the recent history of Western post-industrial society, in which technological advances have led to an accelerated culture of speed (Nowotny 1994). This perception of time itself speeding-up, compounded by the ontological knowledge of the universality of the death experience, she suggests creates a deep 'escape' orientation. In relating this argument to the topic here, I explore retirement migration as narrated by migrants as a similar attempt to escape to places that enable them to live in a less frenetic time-world. With these considerations in mind, I consider how time in Spain is understood, articulated and experienced by retired migrants.

EXPERIENCES OF TIME I: 'FREE' TIME

'I don't need to wear a watch here anymore' was a statement made by a respondent in the Costa del Sol in King, Warnes and Williams' study of retirement migration (2000: 119). This was indeed a dominant narrative of migrants repeatedly articulated during my ethnographic research, which suggests that they enjoyed a different sense of time than lived in the past. For some, physical movement to Spain is represented as a juncture distinguishing an entry into this other way of life. As Willy, a village migrant stated, 'the thing is, when you come here, the past is past. It doesn't matter. Nobody gives a shit. That's it. When you step off the plane, it's a new you'. Whether the migration is permanent or involves a more fluid and gradual process of sojourning,[2] creating a 'new' life in Spain nevertheless is often presented as a major event, a 'career break' or discontinuity in the life story (described by Humphrey 1993: 172). For some this pivotal turning point alters the fundamental meaning structure by which they orientate themselves to the world particularly when the move coincides with a definitive life event. For example, Emma moved following divorce, Molly moved following her mother's death and William decided to move when he was diagnosed with high blood pressure and realised that time was, in his words, 'frittering away'. For others, like Richard, an expatriate executive, there are more continuities between his former and current life, but he still nevertheless refers to how when he writes letters, he has 'to be in the right mood, as in my *previous* life' (my emphasis). This resonates with Biggs, Bernard, Kingston and Nettleton's study of people moving to retirement communities in Britain, who show how the move is cast as an epiphany from which a new life begins (and see also Keith-Ross' 1977 *Old People, New Lives*).

Willy's articulation of 'the past is past' suggests there are possibilities of freeing oneself from past identities and reinventing the self in the present (see discussion in O'Reilly 2000: 81–82 and Chapter 6). Such themes become particularly pertinent when coinciding with retirement, which offers the chance to redefine the self outside of work identities. Movement becomes cast as a temporal and spatial reference point through which nega-

tive aspects of lifestyle and character can be relegated to a former identity. Sharon, a retired social worker, told me, for example, since living in
Spain, 'I am more content, less exhausted, I am not the person I was', whilst
Davinia, a retired head teacher talks about how 'you don't bring the presence and the pressure of your career and self-esteem. That's a heritage of the
past. You have to build a new one'. Similarly, Jim a former builder told me,
'I took early retirement. I worked in Central London as a building man for
the dental council. Living there was stressful. Here, I've time to do things:
I can take an hour to shave. I was governed by the clock in England'. These
accounts are typical in emphasising a past life governed by time-pressures,
which is now discarded in favour of a more relaxed orientation to time.

The different sense of time is also demonstrated through a relaxed attitude
to planning, as a few people told me, 'I came here [a number] of years ago,
and never planned to stay'. This extends also to thought about the future;
most people told me that they planned to stay in Spain 'forever', although
over time it transpired that some people were simply testing out Spain for a
while, and other people curiously upped and left to return suddenly to Britain with very little notice to their friends. Yet their original assertions correspond with a general theme expressed by Chris, who explained, 'there's
no point worrying about the future, we'll see what happens' (and see John,
Chapter 3). This did not mean the future was unimportant, rather that,
as for a few men in particular, the 'see-how-it-goes' approach to life was
developed in response to an imagined schedule of estimated or unknown
remaining length of one's 'life time'. For instance, Don, a man in his sixties,
told me over coffee in his palatial villa overlooking the sea,

> We don't worry about the future. We have to live life as it is, as I
> know in my family genetically nobody lives past sixty-nine years old....
> I know the time's coming for me to die. I'm very rational about it. Its all
> genetically programmed you see, I've got eight more years and I plan
> for that moment. I'll die before my wife, although she doesn't like to
> talk about it.

Don's assertion brings sharply into focus that, despite attempts to manage
his future, the extent and duration of the present of his third age is in reality, unknown. This means that for retired migrants, assertions of lack of
planning, spontaneity and 'seeing how things go' are often actually lived
in the framework of a generalised 'retirement plan' (see Ackers and Dwyer,
2002). The plan, contingent on an unknown temporal boundary may
involve for some people, 'the idea of subsequent return 'home' at the point
at which they needed support or when either partner died' (ibid.: 159).

However, this awareness of 'a time left to live' (Jerrome 1992: 50) also
powerfully informs the imperative to 'live for today'. It is used to justify
life-choices, ranging from the act to migration itself to other consequent

events. For example, when Lilian and Ray (Chapter 3) moved from an inland village to the coast, they lost a significant amount of money. They justified this by observing that, 'shrouds don't have pockets!' And as Don explained further his theorising of his life-span, 'some accuse me of being pessimistic, but that's how I know things to be, and it makes me realise I am here to live, in the *now*'. The fact that this time off has been earned through years of working also informs the notion that this is 'me time'. Having spent years subject to the demands of the work or family routine, Roger, a retired brigadier, explained at the British Legion that his life in Spain was 'pay-back time:' a reward for previous hard work. As Roger expressed, 'you get here, reflect on your life and realise that you've spent all your life doing other things apart from living it. When you get out here, you have to live the reality of life'.

Making the most of the 'here and now' is articulated as facilitated by living in Spain, where people express that there is an intrinsically slower tempo of life and opportunities for more 'quality' time. Migrants following in the footsteps of social scientists such as Lévi Strauss, distinguish different time-qualities of 'traditional' and 'modern' societies, narrating their move from Britain to Spain as a migration from a place governed by a rapid, linear, chronologised time to one with a slower temporal order. This idea gains support through place-based myths propagated in tourist brochures and publications that describe life in Spain as unchanged over centuries, evident in the repetitive nature of the ritual year in Spain. Mintz observes that life in 'tradition-minded Spain' observes 'a yearly round of feasts, fairs and holy days' (Mintz 1997: xiii), and, whilst processes of development might threaten to disrupt notions of an unchanging canvas, much of this part of Spain's touristic appeal continues to rest in images of unchanging traditionalism (Oliver 2002, Barke and Towner 2003).

An important contributing factor to this image of Spain's orientation to time is the ubiquitous stereotype of the '*mañana*' temporal dimension, which refers to a spirit of completing tasks without care for the pressures of time. It refers to how plumbers, builders or electricians might promise that work will be done tomorrow (*mañana*) but in reality they mean an unspecified time in the future. This laid-back image of Spanish (and particularly Andalucían) life has some veracity; Spanish friends commented on their relaxed regard for time as a positive characteristic. Interestingly, it was also described as a feature which set them apart from incomers who, for instance, were observed to continue to eat at fixed times throughout the day. A Spanish woman referred to how, 'my friends like to ask me about our customs, about the festivities or times for eating and things like that... they try to adapt to Spain. But, you know, they always keep their customs of their meal times and such'.[3] And yet, as she intimates, the principles of a more flexible approach to time and adoption of *mañana* are sometimes positively appropriated by migrants (see O'Reilly 2000: 114); Marco, an

Italian estate agent who sold properties to expatriates, spoke of this condition when he said,

> Where in England could you get an atmosphere like this? You LIVE! You have to learn how to live it. I see people in my office buying property, and they sit there, nervously twiddling, not knowing they do it. They're still in the rat-race. When I come back from London, honestly, it takes me three days to get back to normal.

The relaxed, flexible and laidback approach to time-use in the town and village is contrasted to a Northern Europe or a Northern Spanish regard for time, where, as Bill explained one day in the American Club, everything works '*en punto*' ('on the dot'). Reg, overhearing Bill talking added, 'Britain is a go-getter society', he said, 'everything is timetabled and planned. It's all set, with no freedom. That's why I left there. I got fed up with it'. Barbara, who lived in the village also confirmed, 'I hate the time element that you have in England...here you can bask in the freedom'. In fact, as Marco suggests, to fight against the relaxed approach to time in Spain is seen as futile and frustrating, whilst to adopt it engenders a sense of belonging (and is used by migrants to contrast themselves with tourists engaging in hurried activities, Gufstafson 2002). Sally, for instance, referred to her alteration of character in moving; originally a buyer for a large pharmaceutical company, she was now retired in a house in the centre of the village:

> I've become more tolerant and easy-going, I think because you *have* to. You just have to accept the fact that the Spanish like to talk and use the shops as a meeting place. People push in or pop around and then they are chatting for ten minutes. That's nice though...in England, they've forgotten how to talk.

Sally's observation implies that the regard for time used by local Spanish people is reminiscent of a way of life that used to exist in England. Certainly a sense of temporal traditionalism and timelessness is read in the rural heritage (see Fabian 1983, Oliver 2002 and Lund 2005). Not only does this support ideals that in moving to Spain migrants see themselves as moving 'back in time', but the non-urgent Spanish approach to time is projected with moral qualities. The unhurriedness is read as evidence of community, and reflections are tinged with nostalgia for a more moral bygone past of rural England (see Chapter 5).

This is, however, a very fragile vision, as romantic ideals of a timeless place are under threat through regional development. A real estate agency recently put up a sign in front of the village that pierces these ideals through its grand statement, '*bienvenidos a Freila, el futuro está aquí*' ('Welcome to Freila, the future is here'). The timelessness is seen by migrants as giving way to a fast-paced progress-oriented vision of change. For example, after being away from the village, on my return, I walked through the village and saw Anya, from Germany cleaning her car. She reminisced about her time in the village, explaining how when she arrived for a short-stay many years ago with only a few suitcases, she had little known she would end up staying for life. But she complained, 'I don't know if it's to do with getting older or its just being here, but life seems so busy these days, everything is changing so quickly'. In the face of these changes, many retirees I knew engaged in practices that defied the effects of change and upheld ideals of past 'community'. Many still left their doors open and Joy, for instance, indignantly refused to lock her car doors when we drove back to the village inland where she used to live. These practices, symbolic of community values of the past are particularly important in respect to feelings of personal security in ageing. Sally told me,

> It's a lovely feeling to know you can leave your door open, and the kids run in and out. Here, the kids are respectful of the elderly and aren't afraid of looking soft. It reminds me of what we've lost in England... You could never lie dead in your house here, because villagers always ask if they've not seen you for a while.

The climate also bears considerable influence on the apprehension of time passing. The seasonal climate changes are dramatically evidenced in the landscape as the mountains bear the different colour and vegetation of the seasons. During the year, the high season (see Chapter 6) is experienced to 'drag on' because of the heat. At this time, clubs often stop programmed activities, migrants return to Britain for visits and as Judy explained, 'the place fills up with strangers' (contrasting with Brody's (1973) observations of tourists' summer visits helping to affirm local identities in a village in the West of Ireland). The winters in Southern Spain can also be quite unpleasant and incredibly cold. When I went to visit Judy, for instance, in March in her apartment, she asked me what the weather was like outside: 'it might look sunny, but once you get out...it's been the coldest winter on record in Spain for quite some time', she explained. During cold spells, Elizabeth lit all her fires and had additional direct heating from gas stoves, but this did little to combat the coldness emanating from the cool stone walls. Yet despite these dramatic differences in climate, the longer duration of the sunny period in between adds to a qualitative perception of stretched time. Sarah, for example, told me in mid-October, 'in Britain at this time, everything's closed, people are wearing grey raincoats. Here, you can sit outside from April to November, and have the freedom to watch the stars in the evening'.

The feeling of having 'more' time is also created through the different daily and weekly rhythms in Spain. Perceptions of slower, unstructured time are aided by the breakdown of former sharp demarcations of 'work-time' and leisure time amongst retired migrants. People joked that they forgot which day of the week it was, as there is no particular qualitative difference in the ways the periods of weekdays and weekends are spent. In this part of Spain, there is a long break in the middle of the day (between around 2 p.m. and 4.30 p.m.) when shops close and some workers return home for dinner. Rachel, a semi-retired women in her fifties, told me as a result how she felt, 'there are two days in one in Spain. You get up, do your things, have a glass of wine at lunch time, have a siesta then get up, and it's like you've got another day as the shops are all open until 9 or later. It stretches the day'. At a lunch meeting that had started at 12 p.m. and still had the odd straggler at 8 p.m., I was also told by Joy that 'time here is elastic'. We had arranged to meet later that week for the village fiesta, and although she told me it was to start at 10 p.m., she added, 'you know the Spanish, you've lived here for a while…it doesn't mean a thing'. And indeed I found myself going along to impromptu and unplanned events, and whilst this element is common to most ethnographic research, here spontaneity is mentioned by migrants as particularly characteristic of the context. When I bumped into Rachel, a woman in the village, she broke her prior dinner arrangements to spend time with me saying, 'that's what I love about Spain; the spontaneity. I'm supposed to be going for a dinner with the girls, but I'm sure they'll understand'.

EXPERIENCES OF TIME II: PRODUCTIVE TIME

Although I have shown that moving to Spain is equated with adopting a less structured and pressured temporal order, it is also the case that prior associations of 'timed social life' (Adam 1990) are not so easily disregarded. I have shown that the finite life span informs an imperative to live for today, but it can paradoxically become more difficult to uphold such a carefree attitude to time when one considers it will ultimately come to an end. The tension is expressed by Mary, who I referred to in Chapter 3. Living alone, she described herself as, 'a batty old woman in the studio' as she fought an increasingly difficult battle to maintain her large house in the country. Occasionally, she questioned this existence. Going over these thoughts during a series of visits, she explained that her motivation was to feel a sense of productivity from her life before she died:

> I feel that, you know as you get old, that perhaps you haven't done anything…that you'll look back on your life and it was a washout. I suppose I'm trying to stop it being a washout. It's like I want to look back and say that I've achieved something. That's it, I had a choice at some point, I either went to the beach, arranged to meet for coffees, played board-games, or I threw myself into something like this. At least now, before I die, I'll have a couple of properties to sell.

Mary's explanation reveals a concern for productive time, formed in response to the acknowledgement of 'time as the boundary to life' (Adam 1990: 30). Yet here however, the spectre of time 'running out' reinstates the cultural valuation of time as a finite 'resource' or a quantity discussed previously, which can be squandered, wasted or used inappropriately (Lakoff and Johnson 1980). Amongst retired migrants, deep rooted cultural myths and moralities about time use are very much in evidence, whereby too much unproductive time is presented as dangerous, and leading to 'stagnation'. Chaney observes that, 'the standard assumption has been that an excess of free or unstructured time will create a variety of 'problems' culminating in the possibility of self-disintegration' (1995: 212). Jahoda (1982) shows how time structure is vital for psychological well-being and its absence, for example, in conditions of unemployment, 'is seen as presenting a major psychological burden' (Haworth 1997: 25). And Deem confirms that for some older women, having 'time on their hands', 'far from being a scarce resource, comes to be dreaded' (1987: 115).

In Spain, I was often warned by other foreign residents of the dangers of unoccupied time or spending too much time on my own. Angela, a younger woman who had given up work early, cautioned, 'all the time here, it makes you think a lot and you can become introverted and worry too much what other people are saying about you' (see Chapter 6). Jim, a retired teacher told me how the bar-owner in the village had warned him of the dangers of 'getting sucked-in'. He had been told that if he went 'with the flow' too much, the inevitable late nights in bars and late morning starts would be unsatisfying. By pointing out that he had seen people 'wasting' their lives, the bar-owner reaffirmed the moral valuation of time as a resource. Ironically therefore, despite migrants' refrains about 'not wearing a watch', sentiments claiming efficiency in time use are asserted in equal measure. As Clarke and Critcher (1985) point out, even in 'free' time, existing modes associated with the realm of work are woven into workers' leisure (also see Nowotny 1994). In this way, leisure time is still cast as something that should still be used 'properly' and constructively, so a spectre of time-disciplining and a work ethic still influences retiree's lives in Spain. It also forms the basis of a defence against perceptions of migrants indulging in permanent tourism (see Chapter 7). As Judy showed during our first meeting, she was concerned to defend herself against the notion that 'we all sit around drinking gin and tonics all day'. She also pointed out on another occasion how annoyed she was at people who come from a nearby town to the history club lectures and 'get there halfway through'. She said, 'It's no good not being there from the beginning, they haven't got the thread and try to catch up, but it disturbs the speakers'. On another occasion, a dispute had been caused in the meeting room at an urbanisation after a Spanish lesson overran into the next group's time-slot by five minutes. And such attitudes may be surprising to visitors who have the impression that the retirees live with little regard to the clock. Amanda explained,

People expect you to be the same as them. You know I had a couple of visitors and by the end they were in a mood with me, saying, 'what's the matter with you?' But I just didn't want to stay up all hours all of the time. For them, its two weeks, but you know, for us, well we could end up doing that all the time.

In Spain, temporal structures are created anew because predictable daily or weekly routines and habits offer a form of security following migration, an event which alters prior circumstances of 'practical normality' (Misztal 1996: 108). In particular, the adoption of voluntary roles in the clubs can compensate for the absence of statuses in retirement (Jerrome 1992, noted in Hepworth 1998). As King, Warnes and Williams (2000: 148) point out of living in Spain,

> Individuals may find themselves living in what J.G. Ballard (1996) calls an 'affectless zone', without conventionally defining activities and structures (work, family, neighbourhood etc.) This allows them to invent new roles for themselves. One role which is adopted by older people, some time after their arrival is that of a volunteer.

Voluntary activities may include running charity events, working at the charity shops, producing newsletters, printing tickets and menus, arranging events, running fundraising appeals and organising campaigns. Yet, as others have shown, for older people in retirement communities, talk of full schedules and busy lives becomes a regular refrain in their lives (Fitzgerald 1986, McHugh 2000). Cruikshank notes how Sun City resident's 'race with time' is met with social approval (2003: 159) whilst Ekerdt (1986) speaks of a 'busy ethic' akin to the work ethic in retirement (see Chapter 5).

As a result of engaging in many new activities, it is common to hear a conflicting narrative amongst retired migrants, that rather than time slowing down, it 'flies'. The claim is used to deflect the possibilities of stagnation, boredom and apathy, which are accusations sometimes levelled at others. For instance, Suzanne complained, 'It's the way people live here, day-in day-out, sitting around with nothing to do with their time apart from sit around and talk about the fact that they do nothing'. Charlie, a man in his eighties, also spoke sceptically about the 'people who come and pretend they are not growing old...who try and live in the past, although time is speeding up...who have no real interests...and get very, very bored'. Other judgements about time-use were typically addressed at the often younger foreign *alternativos* (hippies) who as Joy explained, were seen to do nothing of value with their time and 'expect a free ride'. Alternatively, migrants like her, felt they had *earned* the break. This no doubt placed me in a difficult position; I felt myself that I had to justify being in Spain because I had not earned the right. One day, for instance, I was caught sitting on a bench in the town reading a Spanish magazine during a break between interviews in the exhausting heat of the day. Tony, a retired British friend, was passing by and called out, 'so this is what they call research is it?' As a result, I often worked long hours to compensate for this perception and felt curiously satisfied when a club member, busily sorting through club business first sighed, 'we don't have a minute, we just don't have time to spare', but then exclaimed in response to the queries of another, 'Who's she? [pointing to me] She's is here to study us...No, she's a hard worker, she doesn't play all the time'.

To combat slippage into 'wasteful' time, retired migrants also reintroduce their own personal time-discipline through new self-imposed rituals. Catherine, a woman who had taken early retirement, was infamous for her extended visits to bars, but still talked of her need to reintroduce a timetable into her life that was familiar to her from her former life. She said, 'I still like to live the same as before, you get used to your routine don't you? I make Thursday the day to go into the town, otherwise you say you'll slip down there [on other days] and then aimlessly wander about'. Meanwhile the cycle of seasonal migrants' movements, who return to the UK for summer, help impart a calendrical rhythmic organisation into migrants' leisure experiences. The clubs run according to a timetable that mirrors the Northern European education systems' term-times, in which activities are planned between late September/October and May/June (high season) with a break for Christmas and Summer. A woman at the International Club described in December, 'we've broken up for Christmas now', using identical expressions used to describe the educational year in Britain. Furthermore, yearly rituals such as the Remembrance Day and Thanksgiving Dinners are marked by a meal that is held in the same venue, following the same format annually. Once a month, at the American Club, birthdays are also celebrated with champagne and cake, a practice which O'Reilly (2000a) suggests creates a feeling of continuity in the transient community. As the opening example showed, Molly followed her visit on Saturday to the International Club with a chicken sandwich afterwards at the same café with her friend. After my six months absence, she said, 'oh nothing changes, we're still here, we're still going for our chicken sandwich afterwards'. The routines break up, structure and organize time and as Jerrome (1989) points out, rituals found in associations for older people help to ground aspects of self-identity which may have been threatened by change.

Nevertheless, like Molly, I also found comfort in the regularity of club activities to give structure to hours, days and weeks that were otherwise stretching limitlessly ahead. I found myself adopting a weekly round that included International Club on Saturday morning, American club on Saturday lunchtime, Tuesday morning: Spanish lessons, and Labour club or International Club on Tuesday lunchtime. Wednesday lunchtime I would go to the British Legion, Thursday I would again go to Spanish lessons, on Fridays would be the monthly British Legion luncheon and monthly lectures of the fine art club were on Sunday evenings. Others also referred to their own busy schedules which were constructed according to their own preferences. Such routines create a reference point for the individual whilst the habitual nature of the meetings helps to establish trust relationships in this transient arena (see Chapter 6). Yet it is interesting to note that although migrants lived in their own routines, they often distanced themselves from this impression, as they evaluated routine negatively as a form of stagnation or monotony seen in others behaviours, particularly amongst older people in the homeland (see page 83).

Indeed, Hazan's (1980) study of elderly Jews in London shows how repetition of activities in their socially insular world became a means of effectively freezing their social condition. It creates a kind of timelessness, which helps to halt problems of ageing and deterioration. Similar findings are observed by Huby in an East London day-centre, who points out that although the participants see themselves very differently, to the outside world, 'the impression [is] of a group of people suspended in an eternal present of bingo, reminiscence groups and day-trips' (1992: 41 and see Golander's 1995 work on nursing wards). In Spain, the time-rich environment is broken down into repeated standardised chunks of productive time, which stretch and disrupt linear time conceptions, as well as instil comfort because this is the way things have always been done. Again and again, when I returned, it was suggested that nothing changed, but at the same time *everything* did, especially in the composition and well-being of people attending the clubs. And, whilst the impact of regular change is downplayed through ritual, its positive benefits are nevertheless paradoxically asserted as introducing novelty in the social scene. Thus, whilst on the surface, as Molly maintained, nothing changes, the American club president Belle, explained, 'It's always changing, there's always fresh faces...as one lot dies, another lot comes, it certainly stops it being boring!'

The two orientations I have identified thus far towards both free and newly structured time, however create practical dilemmas for migrants in their choices about time-use. Taking on new work roles is a means of being productive and filling time, but this approach nevertheless chafes with the orientation identified previously towards spontaneous 'me-time', in which one spends one's time at one's own bidding. In this light, taking on new responsibilities again may simply contradict these principles; Sharon, for instance, the retired social worker believed that she had become 'more selfish' following her move and explained, 'No. Now I feel that I can't waste my energy on organisational activities here. I feel like I've done my bit before and ended up a total wreck'. She also emphasised the value of retirement time through being choosy with her acquaintances and engaging only in worthy new friendships as she stated, 'at my age, I won't put up with nonsense from other people'. Furthermore, Lilian and Ray (see Chapter 3) were involved in helping out at an ecumenical centre for some time, as Lilian was formerly a nurse, but she explained,

It became too much of a commitment. When you are retired, you want your time to be free. You can say, 'I've done my bit, now's the time for myself. You know, to go swimming in my own personal swimming pool, the sea, and enjoy myself!

As a result, there may be difficulty of fragmentation which many older people's clubs face (see Jerrome 1992 on UK-based clubs). When I met Judy attending the clinic as a voluntary translator, she acknowledged how much time she had to sacrifice just in order 'to keep things going'. Although Judy finds great esteem in her work, she acknowledges that the time investment is not always reciprocated by others, and told me, 'mostly, people come because they are retired and they don't want to get things going, and then when we do, of course people are always dying off'. This corresponds with the difficulties faced by the Anglican parish committee, who faced difficulties in stability when new priests came for short terms one after the other because, as the churchwarden explained, 'we don't have the cash to make long term investments in the priests...they're constantly changing'.

Moreover, others may find that they lapse in their commitments as they are influenced by the holiday ambience and relaxed approach to time. For instance, the secretary of one club was unable to present financial reports in time for the annual meeting because he went on a three month holiday at short notice. Again this left older and longer established people to bear the brunt. I visited Judy, for instance, on a Thursday when she was given the task to complete the editing of the newsletter of the American club before it went off to print the day after. She had very short notice for this task, because the person assigned to do the job had also decided on the spur of the moment — without warning — that he/she was going away on holiday. Judy said, 'at the moment I'm trying to shed jobs, not take them on....but nobody's interested in taking things over'. And Joy, suffering badly with arthritis at the time, found herself running around town putting up posters for a forthcoming event at the Cultural Centre. When I went to visit her, she said she felt exhausted and complained, 'my friend told me to delegate. Good idea, but what happens when there's no one who wants to be delegated to?' The time-consuming 'work' can be physically and mentally draining, particularly amongst people who are older and health considerations may make the job more time-intensive and affect how easily the job can be done.

Moreover, in this type of 'work', time is given voluntarily, and 'payment' is through rather more abstract terms such as others' gratitude. Favours based on temporal rather than material investments create unspecified return obligations, and the fact that people's time is spent arranging other's enjoyment (in club trips and activities) renders it particularly grating on occasions when little or no gratitude is shown for the work involved. For instance, Sandra felt other club members showed a lack of commitment and when I pointed out that they probably appreciated her time, she said, 'Thanks! Thanks! You don't expect thanks for doing this task. Nobody gives you thanks!' And yet on another occasion, Judy was upset when she informed Sandra that she couldn't attend an important meeting of the British Legion. She recounted to me how Sandra had dismissed her breezily with an "Oh don't worry', as if it didn't matter in the slightest... 'Well, if I'm so easily missed, 'I wonder why I bother at all', she expressed. The allocation of 'me-time' is judged by the same principles of use-value as in Britain, and when little renumeration is felt, the time investment is likely to be reconsidered.

BETWEEN TIME NOT THERE/THEIRS: FREE TIME IN LEISURED RETIREMENT

The chapter shows that in the light of past influences of time-bound working lives and in the face of new expectations associated with this stage of the life course, time assumes a particular salience. Migrants express desires to inhabit more relaxed temporal modes than their previous lives allowed. Moving to Spain is articulated as a move towards a more self-determined approach to time: a move away from lives in which time is controlled by others. This idea is spatially mapped out in comparisons of Britain and Spain, with migrants praising what they perceive as a 'Spanish' flexible approach to time-use, which is appropriated for their experiences of leisure, and this is contrasted with the time-poor 'rat-race' of Britain (or other place of origin). However, although knowledge of the finite and limited time of the lifespan to some degree underpins this drive for 'free' time, it also fosters an opposing orientation, which encourages more productive and routinised time use. Not only has this time off been 'earned' through work, and thereby still judged as having intrinsic 'value', but free time, although much desired, can be a poisoned chalice, becoming weighty and provoking boredom and apathy, which are especially important to avoid in a good retirement experience. Thus to avoid the possibilities of wasting time, a temporal disciplining that governed many people's former life still influences their time-negotiation. The structured 'inward notation of time' (Thompson 1967: 57) impinges into leisured existences, too deeply embedded to be completely disregarded.

As a result, in retirees' lives, there is a tension ensuing between free and structured time. And this dilemma occurs precisely because of the particularities of the Western life course, as migrants are squeezed into an extraordinary condition between time as 'not theirs' (devoted to their working lives and families) and time as not there (inevitable mortality). The 'me time' of retirement becomes valued as incredibly precious and precarious, with much to be squeezed in, a fact all the more ironic given that it is also paradoxically a time of 'earned' relaxation, in which it is, for once, socially acceptable to slow down. Yet, rather than purely experiencing time slowing down through moving to Spain (although as I have shown, this is indeed one side of the coin), there is equally a paradoxical pressure to pack more in, and this creates a feeling that time is speeding up. As Viv complained, 'I'm so busy, that's the thing living here, time goes so fast. I'm not just talking a day or week, but months'. And Lilian asserts that she has 'less time' in Spain and now owns a filofax, a symbol of timetabling that she had never possessed before she came out to Spain. Perhaps this productive activity is pursued with such great gusto to overcome an association of ageing with 'slowing down' (see Chapter 5). Certainly all of this, in summary, suggests there is a paradox at the heart of retirees' experience of time: the ideal of a positively ageing existence is one in which time is apprehended as passing both more quickly *and* more slowly, of having more time but yet less time. It is curiously a desire to have time in abundance (as Janet stated, 'more time to do things') but yet simultaneously 'no' time (as Elizabeth stated, 'time? It just goes').

The next chapter explores how similar contradictory tensions are felt in negotiating bodily ageing, as people experience both a freedom from societal expectations, yet also create new obligations for managing ageing and dependency.

5 Does Age Matter?
Positive Ageing and Place

I don't know why someone doesn't write a book about how alive every-one is here. They're all bounding around with so much energy. It's so different...anyone who would prefer to go to Florida after seeing this lot must be crazy...they're all brain dead there. It's because it's all organised for them there, all this organised living...pah! There's bingo at two, charades at four, we'd go brain dead wouldn't we, play-ing bowls all day? (Belle, an American woman explaining the benefits of retiring in Spain to a prospective resident)

Let's face it, if I was in England I wouldn't be going on cruises like I am now. (Viv, urbanisation-dweller in Tocina)

I argued in the previous chapter that there are contradictory tensions in negotiating time in migrants' retirement in Spain. In this chapter I explore how ageing is negotiated with reference to space and place. I show that migration invites the possibility for creativity in sculpting a positively age-ing identity in the new location, because, as the quotations above allude, it allows an imaginative spatial relocation of certain social constructions of ageing. Spain is depicted as an environment in which ageing can be experienced in radically different ways to the homeland, offering enjoy-able experiences of ageing, including a disregard for social conventions, an irrelevance of age, new leisure experiences and a cultural respect for older people. This is contrasted with ways of ageing experienced by others, whether that is evidenced in those adopting the 'wrong' attitude, particu-larly in the homeland, or in positively valued 'other' (Spanish) experiences of retirement. However, as in the previous chapter, it is necessary to exam-ine to what extent these ideals of ageing can be maintained, particularly when the materiality of the ageing body intervenes and impinges on the ability to interpret ageing subjectively. In other words, how is the material-ity of the ageing body negotiated in conjunction with choices for positively ageing lifestyles of leisure and sociability?

Again, I show a paradox at the heart of migrants' experiences. On one hand, a positive experience of ageing is claimed through the adoption of a subjective approach to ageing, where 'age does not matter'. They celebrate the possibilities of engaging with new activities and maintaining personal autonomy. However, as in the consideration of temporality, there are internal contradictions to be wrestled with. The common experiences of ageing ironically form the positive basis of a shared identification, giving ageing an ultimate significance in the society. Furthermore, the conditions of good ageing — whilst no doubt liberating — can also, when experienced in the social context, lead to a reinscription of societal expectations in a period apparently free of them. Not only is there pressure to be active and look good in contexts where new 'younger-old' people arrive all the time, but the regular activity, voluntary commitments, socialising and consumption of alcohol and rich food risk hastening the onset of more negative experiences of illness through people 'overdoing it'. Moreover, there are significant risks in growing older in the Spanish context where state provision of care is limited, and one's peer group is older and limited in its ability to provide care. As a result, social expectations appear urging preparedness for the moment at which people's lifestyles may ultimately need to change. Ultimately, a balance must be struck by people that allows for both making the most of life in the present, whilst respecting their bodily limits now and in the future.

AGEING I — A NEW LEASE ON LIFE
THROUGH ACTIVE AGEING

> You're as old as you feel. I feel about one. (Roger, explaining his age of ninety-two)

Thompson, Itzin and Abendstern's (1991) book, *I Don't Feel Old: the Experience of Later Life*, refers to common view held by older people today, and reflects a point of view subscribed to unanimously by those I was researching in Spain. The assertion suggests that prescriptive chronological and physiological markers of age can be resisted; ageing is instead interpreted as a subjective experience that is under one's power to manage and disguise through masquerade (Woodward 1991). Such subjective understandings correspond with the theory of the 'mask of ageing' in which the visible ageing body is experienced as a mask that disguises a youthful or ageless essential identity of the person beneath (Featherstone and Hepworth, 1991).

Certainly, a dominant narrative amongst migrants in Spain was their claims to feel more youthful through moving away. According to a paper written by a resident in Spain, migrants 'revel in the new sense of youth' (Price 1992, unpaginated) as people feel liberated from work and former responsibilities. Indeed some people drew metaphorical parallels between their current period of life and earlier stages of the life course (see Hockey and James 1993) as they told me they had not felt such freedom since they were teenagers. Some also employed a role reversal of sorts with their adult children in Britain, who were depicted as possessing characteristics normally associated with parental control in contrast to their own claims of more irresponsible behaviours. For instance, on one occasion, Bob's daughter was visiting him and his wife. At a social meeting during this time, Derek, Bob's friend suggested how unlucky Bob was to have the 'misfortune' of two women to 'watch what he was up to', referring to Bob's wife Amanda, and his visiting daughter. 'What are you talking about?' Bob countered, 'you've got *two* daughters in England'. At this, Derek responded, 'Ah ha, but they are like some dark force in the far beyond, over there.... they can't see what I am up to, thank God!' This attitude resonates with the observations by Stephens' (1976) in her study *Loners, Losers and Lovers: Elderly Tenants in a Slum Hotel*, where she found that older people may prefer to stay in less desirable surroundings in order to enjoy 'illicit' pleasures (at least in the eyes of their children) such as alcohol and sex. Moreover, the average older age of the social group meant that chronological age was reinterpreted anyway, according to the average age of people there. Younger migrants in their fifties, sixties and sometimes seventies were regularly described as 'youngsters', or as I heard, 'young pups'. When Judy told Molly that she was seventy, Molly, considerably older, replied, 'oh well, you're just a spring chicken then!' In another conversation, a woman reported how at seventy-four years old, 'I'm only a youngster' in comparison to the 'amazing' ninety year olds at the same club.

This social interpretation of older age is encouraged by certain environmental and cultural aspects of place. The mild climate encourages a relaxation of life course expectations around dress, with little consensus on what should be worn (O'Reilly 2000a). Migrants usually wear casual summer clothing such as T-shirts, light dresses or, commonly for men, shorts. Moreover, the availability of cheap fresh produce in the locality is also cited as enabling a healthy old age; as Charlotte and Gerald maintained, 'eating the Mediterranean way...that keeps us young'. This perhaps relates to cultural stereotypes in British commercials, which portray the Mediterranean lifestyle and diet as associated with longevity and healthy old age. A recent olive oil spread advertisement, for example, depicts how lively behaviours in old-age are induced by consumption of the family produced olive oil. Eighty year old men are shown enjoying football matches cheered on by their devoted wives or indulging in strip-shows in front of an adoring elderly female audience.

These social interpretations of older age are nevertheless underpinned by genuine material reasons why people may feel more youthful. Most importantly, the milder climate is cited as reducing aches and pains from arthritis and rheumatism (O'Reilly 2000a, King, Warnes and Williams 2000). Migrants experience a different quality of life through the diet and outdoors lifestyle, which enables more physical activity. Retirees can pursue year round outdoor exercise which may have been restricted previously

(Warnes 1991). For instance, Tony got up every morning and swam in his pool daily, Lilian swam every day in the sea and Les regularly swam in the sea from one end of town to the other. In Les' case, this physical activity was merely a continuation of a former lifestyle, rather than necessarily adopted upon retirement. On the other hand, the tradition of taking a siesta is also regularly adopted, which allows for a mid-afternoon rest.

However, as Shilling suggests, the general increase in engaging in leisure pursuits in the latter part of the twentieth century has been closely associated with rationalizing processes that make sport 'closer to, rather than further away from work' (2005: 101). His observation is particularly true in old age, where physical activity is undoubtedly a source of moral esteem. Williams' (1990) study of older Aberdonians shows that activity is seen as a generator of good health, a means of renewing one's reserves and keeping illness at bay. In particular, activity requires mental determination, and the effort invested means it can be socially evaluated as a form of 'work' (ibid.: 34). Indeed, for retirees here, the dominant self-narrative of busyness, activity and mobility (in 'doing things') is contrasted with disavowal for those who do not entertain themselves and get bored (see Chapter 4). It is evidence of the 'busy ethic' (Ekerdt 1989) or continuation of a work ethic (Williams 1990) in which retirement is justified through addressing leisure or activities with the same determination previously invested in family or work life.

There is, as such, a discourse of esteem for those in the community, such as Judy, who are 'on the go'. Gustafson (2001) documents how Swedish retired migrants emphasise mobility (in the sense of travel between two countries) because it is associated with other positive traits of freedom, independence, adventure and initiative, but the observation is equally applicable for understanding day-to-day evaluations of active lifestyles. In this sense, being 'on the move' is employed in narratives as a leitmotif of good ageing in opposition to images of sedentary lifestyles. Barbara, a former expatriate who lived in eight different countries, described, for instance, how 'she couldn't sit still' and that to avoid feeling bored, she would often 'flit off on her own'. Les referred to how in Spain, 'you don't get the opportunity to rot as you do in England'. And Doreen, who, at eighty-one years old was soon moving back to Britain, explained how she planned to inject her life there with the same vim of 'go[ing] away, around and about, all different places' that she had experienced in Spain rather than 'sit[ting] and mope[ing]':

Doreen: I'm joining a group [in England] and they go to big houses and we get the chance to go to these houses and some of them you couldn't go to. And then I'm going to join the bowling club. I like playing cards.

Caroline: Right

Doreen: So, more or less you've just got to go on. I think that it keeps you alive out here [in Spain], it keeps you younger, when I go back home [Britain] now…Yep, well when I go back home, I look at the people of my age and I say, 'what are you doing?' [with a sad voice she imitates older people there] *'there's not much you can do in a limited time, all we do is sit around and watch television'* [reverts back to her voice] 'Can't you go and join something?' [reluctant voice] *'well, yes, I suppose we could'*… and 'cos here I've got my car and I go around all about, all sorts of places, I go away, around and about, all the different places.

Caroline: Yes, I think I've found…

Doreen: I think that's what you've GOT to do, you can't sit and mope, everybody gets bad days, it doesn't matter how old you are, everybody gets bad days don't they?'

Doreen's explanation emphasises a particular attitude of activity and mobility that she imagines is less observed by her peers in Britain, and by doing so, she downplays her own 'oldness' by locating it in others in Britain. In another example, Judy, Ann and Molly were complaining about the noise from the *discotecas* during the *feria* at a social morning at the International Club, when they mocked themselves for their attitudes. Ironically inhabiting stereotypes of older people, they laughingly mimicked the phrase, 'It wasn't like that in my day', in wizened voices, and Ann exclaimed, 'Gosh, we sound like real old crones!' This concurs with Hurd's (1999) observations of women at a seniors' centre in Canada, whose collective statements of 'we're not old!' distanced them from association with ageist stereotypes. Others have also argued that such strategies of distancing from identification with 'oldness' occurs not as a form of resistance to ageing, but rather to the oppressive stereotypes associated with being old (Andrews 1999, Gibson 2000). Rather in Spain, those people who can maintain active and mobile lifestyles into late old age and resist 'oldness' are lauded; Molly described Rose, a woman she knew of around ninety years of age who attended many of the International club's events and trips, as 'amazing'. On one of the clubs' organised trips to Granada, the woman let Molly in on her secret. She kept her sunglasses on to hide from others the fact that she was actually sleeping on the bus. Molly thought that this was an amusing and clever way of disguising the tiredness Rose felt as a result of the highly esteemed activity.

However, Andrews argues, this 'redefinition of certain — desirable — types of old age as "young" (1999: 301) is nevertheless a subtle mechanism by which ageism functions. In other words, despite the function to resist stereotypes of ageing, these distancing processes nevertheless cast 'old age' as something that can be — and implicitly should be — transcended. It implies that if an individual, such as Rose, can choose not to feel or act her age, it supposes that others, by contrast, choose to inhabit 'oldness'. In Spain, at times, showing 'oldness' is judged as provocative of negative social commentary; for instance, when I met Nathan and Birgit they contrasted their lifestyle of regular international travel with that of their less active neighbours, Charlotte and Gerald. Birgit said, 'they're old. Well, when I say old, I don't necessarily mean in age, but well, they're *old*. Other people we know are much older in years, but are younger'. In Birgit's assignment of particular moral qualities to styles of ageing, 'oldness' again is negatively evaluated and avoided through displacement onto others. This resonates with themes from Chapter 4, in which the future and by implication, problems of ageing and death are not to be worried about now.

The subjective approach to ageing is even more in evidence when people experience physical ailments, which at least in the public fora of the clubs, are discussed using a 'mind over matter' approach to ageing. Les, an enthusiastic man with an intense lust for life explained how he had recovered from a series of heart attacks. 'Mind over matter' he explained, 'putting your mind behind something. The doctor commented on how super-fit I am and that [way of life] I will continue, although of course it's getting harder now'. As a former Sergeant in the Army, Les was used to engaging in intense physical training. His heart attacks were interpreted as an indication of, as Jerrome describes, 'a 'slowing down' rather than a 'giving up' (1989: 161). This 'mind over matter' approach employs mechanistic models of health (Williams 1990) through images of the body as a machine, which is conceived of as a separate material entity that is programmable and malleable through the mind. Les described an incident when he was near to death in which he was saved by the doctors, 'jump-starting me. It was like they kept plugging me in, jump-starting me back to life!' Les' friends, Robert and Jan, who had moved back to England as a result of Robert's mobility problems, used similar mechanistic imagery to explain his health problems. Jan explained, 'Bob could hardly move, but they've pieced him up. He's got nuts and bolts all up his back'. Another man (also referred to in this study as Bob) described his operation for removing cancerous polyps using the expression, 'they simply nipped them off'.

For men in particular, the ageing body was not hidden, but regularly displayed to reveal bravery and courage in overcoming health difficulties. Some pulled their trouser legs up or lifted their shirts to show others their scars. For example, I visited Tony one day and had not seen him since a serious operation. He took his shirt off and described graphically the whole process, narrating the medical procedure through his scars, which he explained one by one from those on his throat to those on his abdomen. Bodily marks were sometimes displayed as 'battle-scars' and recounted as evidence of the courage of individuals. They were also used to justify temporary immobility or reduced activity, given the moral emphasis on activity as 'work'. Jack, for instance, wore a brace after falling outside his house. When I visited him, he was lying down on the sofa, a fact that he explained immediately by raising his shirt and patting his brace. At eighty-two years old, he admitted that he realised only recently that he was 'old', as he explained he found it difficult to understand scientific literature that he used to devour ten years ago by tapping his skull and stating: 'my brain's not as active as before'.

The separation of the body-mind and mechanistic imagery of the objectified body is mobilised to support the aforementioned image of the retirees as being 'young-at-heart', despite physical ageing (Featherstone and Hepworth 1991). It marks a shift in their self-conceptualisations of the body, from its taken-for-granted status in youth towards the awareness that one *has* or possesses a body (Nettleton and Watson 1998) which might need to be coaxed to function properly. Williams (1990) describes this tendency (particularly in working class families) to draw attention to functional or mechanical aspects of health, whilst Featherstone and Hepworth (1995: 44) argue,

> The dominant image of the body as a machine which can be serviced and repaired, and the array of products and techniques advertised, cultivate the hope that the period of active life can be extended and controlled into a future where ultimately even death can be mastered.

According to Turner (1996), the ability to transform the body through medical interventions leads to a mythology of endless renewal and rejection of ageing and death.

However, it is interesting to note that the references in everyday narratives of health and illness are more often employed at the point at which the futility of such images is extant: at moments of bodily failure, weakening or challenge. Thus, whilst the explanations attempt on one hand to refute the diminishing capacities of the body, they seem also to be employed to restore subjectivity over what are dehumanising and frightening experiences. In this light, Les' discussions of his heart attacks were at once a celebration of his 'survival', a mastery of medicine and indeed confirmation of the importance of his mental attitude for managing his body. But it was also an occasion in which he acknowledged and made public some evidence of his body physically 'wearing out'. In fact, those heart attacks became a turning point after which he modified his lifestyle. Rather than consuming his usual beer at the British Legion, he drank only soft drinks. He also talked enthusiastically how he had now time to pursue his new interest, a much less strenuous activity of painting model aeroplanes, following his abandonment of his previous punishing fitness regime. Similarly, Jack gave up going to the local karate club three years ago because, 'it wasn't fair on the boys', because they did not know how to conduct the hard semi-contact sport with him. And despite his recent lack of activity, he maintained that he would however soon return to the gym, in a reduced capacity to do upper body exercises. This shows that the new limitations are incorporated into a continued narrative of active ageing.

Mechanistic images of bodily functioning are also found in reference to mental activity, which is considered an equally important element of good ageing. It was often suggested by migrants that those retirees who move just for the climate would suffer inertia and the loss of their critical faculties after a few months, confirming the productivity ethos observed in Chapter 4. Adhering to the clichéd but important constituent of successful ageing of 'use it or lose it' (Rowe and Kahn 1998) more cerebral activities such as Spanish classes, bridge club or history club which might require reading and study are justified as a kind of exercise for the brain. Many people attending Spanish classes went with less conviction that they would learn the language than a belief in the importance of the activity as good mental exercise. Linda explained, 'I'm not very good at Spanish, but it keeps me alert, it keeps my grey cells ticking over'. Similarly, social participation is encouraged as integral to a healthy mental disposition, and felt to fend off problems of homesickness and depression. Joining in with club activities is seen as an opportunity to try out new experiences, learn new skills and 'stretch' oneself. Judy recounted the experiences of someone who recently gave a speech at the history club:

> He's not the world's best speaker — those at the front said they noticed his trembling hands, but we all helped him out with pointing out things on the diagrams. I had to tell him when he had five minutes left and he said when he felt my hand on his shoulder he was the most relieved he's ever been. This was because he'd never spoken off the cuff without having it written down in front of him. All these new experiences when you come!

Social participation also offers new opportunities for companionship and romance, particular given that interactions in the clubs often involve light-hearted 'flirting' and teasing. New relationships are looked upon fondly and cherished as a hallmark of migrants' less ageist society. This is commented upon often in comparison to Britain where romance can be seen as something wrong or a focus for amusement at this stage of life (Hockey and James 1993). Considering that some new relationships may follow the death of a spouse, they may also take alternative forms. For instance, Judy was widowed in Spain, but was subsequently engaged in a relationship with Ted, based on a mutual arrangement whereby she lived in Tocina and he lived the other side of Málaga. They alternated weekend visits, allowing Judy time and independence to pursue her interests and hobbies. Another couple, Roger and Pat met and married in Spain following the death of their former spouses although they had agreed that when they died, they would be buried with their former spouses. Annie and Peter also met in another area in Spain, but in this case, they had met when they were with other partners. Following divorces, they moved to Tocina to escape what they described as 'unbearable gossip'. This latter example hints at how relationships and flirting, whilst encouraged, have to be managed to avoid social censure (see also Chapter 6).

The forging of close relationships with others, both romantically and otherwise, is particularly aided by relaxed norms of regular alcohol consumption. As McDonald (1994) and Harvey (1994) show, drinking alcohol can be demonstrative of a performance of non-conformity or associated with the breakdown and challenging of social conventions. In Spain, the comparatively cheaper cost of living compared to Britain means that migrants can more often afford to go out for meals and drinks. Annie and Peter were not wealthy by any means, but asserted that they 'couldn't live like this [in Britain]...we'd probably at best get a double bedsitter, and no possibility of going out to have meals or drink wine'. Indeed, at a luncheon meeting, I was explaining to Peter, who lived in the town, the aim of my research. 'What you will find', he said to me in reply, 'is that the reason why most people come here is *this*', as he pointed and tapped at the top of a bottle of wine. Whilst this is hardly a serious reason for migration, Peter's point is nevertheless valid in the sense that social mores on alcohol consumption are relaxed in both the club events and more informal social gatherings. Migrants are free to take drinks at any time of the day, as club meetings are often at lunchtime and the idea of routine is still psychologically based in the 'other world' of England (as Chapter 4 shows). Forster, Hitchcock and Lyimo suggest that perhaps this is characteristic of expatriate life more generally, as they state, 'Drinking, sometimes quite heavily, was a feature of European expatriate life' (2000: 65) although they observe that in military arenas and former colonies, alcohol consumption required regulation.

The freedom of alcohol consumption meant that drinking was, for some people, excessive and problematic, as I will return to later. It also has social consequences; in one club, a man regaled the tale of how an inebriated older woman had flashed her G-string to everyone at their party that weekend, although it was generally agreed that this was 'going too far' (see Chapter 6). For the majority, however, enjoying a drink is much more expressive of a community and egalitarian ideology (Macdonald 1994) which means that avoiding a drink is sometimes considered strange or as even verging on rudeness; Lynn, for instance, felt that she was an outcast precisely because she did *not* drink alcohol. I often enjoyed joining in with a drink, but on one occasion, I attended the funeral wake of a friend when feeling unwell, and my attempts to find a soft drink were interpreted by those handing out drinks as insulting to my friend's memory. Indeed, the woman I was with commented that it was the wine itself that kept her healthy (Oliver 2004). By doing so, she drew on the wider metaphorical link made between alcohol consumption and longevity in popular culture, drawn for instance in joking references relating older people to fine wines maturing with age. A well known poem — that I have seen in pubs in Britain — was sent in by a migrant to *the Marketplace*, a magazine for expatriates. It demonstrates this metaphorical fusion of alcohol consumption with longevity and shows how drinking is symbolically linked to experiences of a 'good' old age:

The horse and mare live thirty years,
And do not know of wines and beers.
The goats and sheep at twenty die
And never taste scotch or rye.
The cow drinks water by the ton,
At fifteen life is almost done.
The dog at fourteen packs in,
Without the aid of rum or gin.
The modest sober bone-dry hen
Lays eggs for years and dies at ten.
But sinful, ginful, rum soaked men
Survive till three score years and ten.
And some of us — the mighty few
Stay pickled till we're ninety-two.
                    (The Marketplace: October: 1998)

Independence, the family and life course

> When I get to that stage, *I'll put myself* in a home. (Lynn, village dweller, talking about the future [my emphasis])

Migrants' subjective approach to ageing however has important implications for familial relationships. Arber and Ginn (1991) point out an emphasis on avoiding dependency, whether on children or on others, is a fundamental concern for older people. This is enabled through migration. The maintenance of independence is stressed through the process; King, Warnes and Williams suggest that in moving away, 'Retirement migrants to Southern Europe have clearly broken their moorings; or maybe their moorings were never that strong anyway' (2000: 97). Longino's work on retirement communities in the United States also reports that most people did not make the decision to move in consultation with children and concludes that 'the degree of expressed independence in making the final decision to move is substantial' (Longino 1982: 254).[1]

Certainly the maintenance of autonomy was expressed as a particularly prevalent issue for many migrants in Spain with children in Britain, as they presented the move as evidence of their independence. Doreen, for example, referred to how her children enviously encouraged her travels, and laughed when she told me they have difficulties getting hold of her because they do not know where she is on the globe at any particular point in time (Oliver 2007). Yet other children are more protective of their parents and attempt to act as guardians, a position often borne of fear that something will go wrong. For some retirees, these attitudes are unwelcome, and are likely to be met with strong assertions of independence. For example, Molly bought her flat in Tocina following an inspection-holiday without consulting her children. She explained that her family had been angry with her, assuming that she had, in her words, been 'twizzled'. This opinion arose, she suggested, because her children, 'couldn't quite believe that I was capable of doing things on my own'. For Lynne, similar concerns marred a trip back to Britain to visit her family. During the stay, Lynne's children had organised a day out to the seaside for her benefit. However, she explained to me how she had been purposefully demonstrative during the trip, because she felt her independence was being compromised. She complained,

> I live on the Costa-del-Sol. Why did they think I wanted to go to *Weston-super-Mare?* I admit that whole day I was cantankerous, I knew what I was doing, but felt I couldn't stop my reactions. I just felt so aggravated that I was being told to do all these things.

Molly even admits that one of the advantages of moving was to get away from the responsibilities for her children. She said, 'It sounds silly, but you don't get involved in their problems. You tend to have the nice times, and as the saying goes, 'what the eye doesn't see, the heart doesn't feel'. This concurs with Amit and Rapport's (2002) observations that some long-distance movements framed in terms of 'adventure' and 'escape' entail disjuncture with previous relationships, rather than continuity. It reminds us that analytical focus on transnational *connections* potentially obscures the ways that former relations are altered following migration (Chapter 1) as well as the ways in which migration may be related to events in the family life course. Indeed, Hareven points out that 'it helps us to view an individual life transition (such as leaving home or marriage) as part of a cluster of concurrent transitions and a sequence of transitions that affect each other' (Hareven 1982: 2). And, certainly for some of the migrants in Spain, moving away is part of a process of realigning parental responsibilities. For example, Pete's parents moved to Spain when he began university. Pete saw his parents intermittently not only because he had his own busy job, but his partner Elsa was a teacher, which meant they could only travel in the school holidays, when the costs of flights increase substantially. Whilst Pete was pragmatic about this, for some adult children left behind, their parents' move away can also be experienced with sadness. I talked with another woman whose mother lived in Spain and she described how hurt she felt when her mother moved. As the youngest daughter, she felt her mother had abdicated on an expected responsibility to help out with her children. This was particularly upsetting for her as the youngest child, because she felt that her mother had been around to help her siblings when their children were young.

However, the increased independence experienced through migration does not mean that migrants' family ties will necessarily be diminished. Many older retirees in Spain regularly had visits from children and grandchildren, who referred to how the Costa was a more desirable destination to visit than previous residences. Such families experience 'intimacy at a distance' (Jerrome 1990: 194) and valued the 'quality time' they experience in visits (see also Huber and O'Reilly 2004). For instance, Doreen maintained strong ties with her children and grandchildren, who called her 'Nanny Spain'. Ackers and Dwyer (2002) also suggest that whilst migrants often move back to receive care, family connections are also mobilised when migrants may have to visit or move back to *give* care (see also Warnes 2004). Migrants' stays in Spain are cut short because their adult children need their help, for example, following divorce or illness, showing how migrants are enmeshed in a 'web of interdependencies or reciprocities that form the cycle of care in their lives' (Ackers and Dwyer 2002: 149). This may equally involve children moving to be near their parents in Spain. John and Jane had moved to Freila in the late 1980s, but over time, both their daughter's family and Jane's older mother came to live in Spain. Their daughter moved back after an unhappy year of 'testing it out' but Jane's mother died in Spain. Similarly, Pete's sister and her husband decided to move from London to Spain with their young child, after Pete's mother saw an appropriate job advertisement in Spain. Their daughter, who is fluent in Spanish, was keen to move away from their small flat in London, and decided to accept the job near her parents in Spain rather than a comparable post in Brighton, although both generations have since moved back to Britain.

It is interesting to note therefore, that although claims of independence from families are common, kin-based responsibilities are liable to become activated again at different stages, particularly as people get older (although see page 109 for contrasting cases). Jean was happy to live in Spain until she had a stroke, at which point she began planning to move back to be near her sons (see page 110). When I spoke to Doreen about her plans to leave Spain at the age of eighty-one, she explained that it was partly a result of her children's wishes that she would move nearby to them in the South of England. On the other hand, she described that it was very much her own decision, as she said of her children, 'they're great. It's: "Mother, you make up your own mind", because they said if we say anything and anything goes wrong you'll only blame us'.

However, it should also be noted that claims of independence hide complex motivations, particularly because they are often linked to a discourse of concern for children's welfare that aims to avoid 'burdening' them. When explaining her move to Spain, Dolcy told me firmly, 'I always said I'd never trouble them...I'd hate to feel a burden, they've got their own lives to get on with, their own things to do, they don't want to feel like they have to care for you'. For a number of women in particular, it was common to hear such opinions expressed because of their own experiences of having been the primary caregivers for older parents. Molly's assertions of independence is understandable when contextualised with reference to her former commitments, when, as an only child, her retirement at sixty coincided with the responsibility for caring for her dependent mother. Following her mother's death, she moved to Spain, a decision explained simultaneously because both her 'children had their own lives and it wasn't fair to burden them', as well as because she felt that when her caring responsibilities ended, it was time to do something for herself (see Chapter 4). However, there is little evidence as to whether children concur with the representation that they see their older parents as burdens; such notions need to be critically examined through exploring childrens' perspectives in a wider consideration of shifting transnational family responsibilities, which whilst outside the scope of this project, offers an interesting avenue for further research.

The discourse of avoiding being a burden however has wide social currency amongst retirees in the expatriate community. For instance, it was appealed to by Monica's friend Belle when Monica's husband died suddenly, as Belle advised her not to make any immediate decisions about whether she should move back to Britain. She explained: 'Besides, you can't always be a burden to your children now, can you? I mean you can move back with them, but they might not want you there all the time'. Belle's encouragement for Monica to stay in Spain rested on the premise that there are plenty of friends around that can become important replacements for kin ties (as Jerrome 1990 also found in the UK). Belle even used the idiom of kinship (Bell and Coleman 1999) to explain her attachment to the American club, explaining, 'I always say the American club is my family'. And Joy described her close friend Kate as 'the sister she never had' (although see Chapter 6 for a further discussion of social relationships). The commonality of age-shaped experiences can certainly form the basis for intense friendships, and these can encourage the reinvention of self following retirement or widowhood, particularly for women, as they do things they had never done or had only ever done in a partnership (see Cruikshank 2003). For instance, Joy felt supported by the all-female embroidery club, 'it's catharsis. You get onto to the most intimate subjects, and you'd never get that if the men were around'. And Molly discussed how Judy, following her husband's death was always 'bounding from one place to another', commenting, 'it's lovely to see her like that though. She wasn't like it before her husband died. And I'm pleased for her, so many widows around here sit and get more depressed, but she didn't do that'. Yet it is interesting to observe that the strong social ties are also as much a draw as kin ties for some men too. Shortly after Bob had moved to New Zealand to be near his wife (see Chapter 3), she died. He found that his children 'had their own lives' and he missed the social support of his friends in Tocina, so he moved back again, this time to a more convenient flat in the town.

The ageing 'other': Contrasting experiences of retirement in Spain

I have explored how many Northern European retired migrants express desires for independence, which are met through migration. However, it is curious to explore their reflections on others ageing in Spain, as they often praise more traditional models of intergenerational sociability evident in Spanish family life. This section explores the different cultural approaches to ageing perceived in the locality and explores the genuine differences between some Spanish and migrant populations' experiences of and attitudes to retirement. This different approach, I suggests, offers a contrasting background by which retired migrants position and interpret their own activities. This 'otherness' is compounded by actual social distance which is found between most older foreigners and older Spaniards. As Alicia, Elizabeth's housekeeper, explained,

> The foreign retired people think and live in another way. And the Spaniards have a more sedentary life. Here in Spain, it's more like, "I sit down, see what's happening and then I go home and eat" ... and then they go, for example, to the day centre. They [foreigners] also live in a different way, living until they can hardly walk. They eat out with friends, they go out, they come in... and the Spanish don't. At least in Freila they don't. They have the odd day out when they eat out with their children but it's not as often as the foreigners.[2]

The differences between foreign and Spanish retirees' lifestyles are influenced by their contrasting life and work histories. Older foreign residents enjoy social activities of eating and drinking out, but in this part of Spain, emphasis on retirement as a period of consumption and leisure is relatively recent. Jesús, my neighbour, told me that many of the older people in the village may still be reluctant to indulge in luxuries or even pay for simple pleasures such as whisky at fiestas, because of memories of previous hardships in their lives. He explained, 'they have that fear, "ay, just in case..."' (*'tienen ese miedo, "ay, vaya que..."'*) established through suffering years of poverty and only comparatively recently benefiting from economic growth. It is also the case that, certainly in the village, the majority of retired Spanish people still had family land or a continued association with the family businesses, which means that retirement is not the standard practice that it is in much of Northern Europe. Manolo, for instance, was in his mid-seventies and ran a small bar that he opened as regularly as he wanted, although recently, he had taken his daughter-in-law on to help at the bar. He looked after his own land and animals, and helped out Mary, his employer, an Englishwoman who lived opposite (see Chapter 3). Similarly, María's father Paco was in his eighties, but like Manolo, he continued to cultivate his trees and crops in the *campo* (country) on a daily basis. Sometimes he walked the mile or so distance to his land, or sometimes María drove him there, especially after he began walking with crutches. He returned in the afternoon to dinner with his wife in the village, where he helped run a kiosk in front of their house, selling confectionery. This sometimes involved him working until the early hours of the morning. María, Paco's daughter, reflected:

Foreigners retire at sixty-five and don't do anything else. And here nobody retires. Here, a man who works on the land will work until he's eighty. He doesn't retire. Foreigners retire....they go to the beach to walk, they have their houses and they always have somebody in to help them. It's not like here. Here it's only now that the elderly are starting to go out on trips! And that's only some, not all of them. Not here [in the village]. Here nobody retires. Because everybody has a piece of land, they have some tiny thing, some tiny business... and everyone works until the last day.[3]

The older women similarly continue with domestic responsibilities, looking after the house, family businesses and helping in care for the extended family. For example, Consuela, Manolo's wife, helped to organize and clean the bar. Until a few years ago, she walked on a daily basis over the hillcrest to the village, a mile or two away. However, it is interesting to note how her activity changed; a while ago, I returned and called in to visit after having not seen her for a year. In that short time, Consuela's appearance had altered radically. Her hair, which the previous year had been short and dyed auburn, was now completely white and secured tightly in a bun. She explained that she no longer went to the hairdressers or coloured her hair because it grew too quickly. She spent most of her time at the house, sitting outside on the terrace where there was a sink, cooking area and tables laden with produce, such as beans, old cheese and meat for the dogs. She told me that she had been to the village earlier, but had started to tremble and had to sit outside one of the bars drinking water with sugar added. She explained that she preferred to stay at the house, because it was '*más abierta*' (more open) and there she tended her animals and land; she had three horses, numerous hens, fruit trees and a herb garden. Her daughter-in-law now brings her shopping to the house.

Consuela's reliance on her daughter-in-law reflects the different welfare system of Southern European 'mother-daughter' economies (see Ackers and Dwyer 2002: chapters 3 and 5) which place more emphasis on family care. Although socio-economic change and urbanisation have disrupted traditional family life over the past few decades, the family continues to be an important source of support to overcome the relatively underdeveloped social welfare systems which lag behind other major EU countries (Dunphy 1995, Giarchi 1996). This was confirmed by María,

It's like an obligation or a duty that we look after them [older relatives], that they don't lack anything. So when they're really ill in bed we help them. It's like an obligation....We don't think so much of using old people's shelters or homes, no. We think more that they should be in their home, in peace, with the children there to help them.[4]

As Inma Hurtado Garcia (2006) points out in her ongoing research, given these expectations, Spanish healthcare staff members read the absence of foreign residents' family members as disinterest and perceive this distance as cold or unfeeling. By contrast, in Spain, families are generally expected to deal with chronic care, whilst state provisions for older people mainly fund social activities, such as the *pensionistas* (day-centres) in the town and village. The club in the town provides activities such as computer classes, Tai Chi and regular trips. There are also schemes governed by the *Instituto de Mayores y Servicios Sociales* (IMSERSO) for retired people who have paid social security in Spain that entitle them to take highly subsidised group holidays in low season in hotels in other regions of Spain. These initiatives, along with regional social and economic transformation have begun to dismantle traditional age-expectations in Spain. For instance, women's mourning practices involved wearing age-appropriate attire, such as dressing in black and not cutting one's hair, practices which help to mark age-status (Blaikie 1999). These are no longer expected, although Alicia explained that her grandmother, who died in her eighties a few years previously, had nevertheless dressed in black from the age of twenty-eight until her death. She said,

> We, as we say, "prepare to die". We lay down and we give up on every-thing, including our appearance. Yet this has changed over the years.... now if you see eighty year old women, they're in bright colours and they go out more than before.[5]

The shift towards notions of active ageing apparent in Spanish society is however particularly ambiguous in the region. Older people are seen as holding an important link with the 'traditional' past, and are employed as such in tourist-directed social constructions of the region. For example, the figure of 'the older woman in black', whilst becoming less an image in reality, is used in postcards or photographic representations of the region to advertise 'traditional' Spain. In the village last year, a coin-operated machine was also established with automated mannequins of two older women, one of whom was in traditional black dress (see Figure 5.1). The figures, 'María' and 'Dolores' held the secrets of how life in the village used to be, their age linking them to a time viewed as 'traditional'.

It is interesting to note that retired migrants often stress these more romanticist elements in their reflections on Spaniards. Jim described, for example, 'the Spanish, they're the salt of the earth, people live here the same way they always have'. Jock, a man in his seventies, also captured the contrast he sees between his lifestyle when he described how he dashes around from place to place and often goes into Freila where he knows 'all the old fellas'. O'Reilly (2000a) also explains how British residents regu-larly referred to the visibility and intergenerational respect offered to older people (see Figure 5.2, a common sight of older people regularly sitting

Figure 5.1 'Maria' and 'Dolores': a tourist kiosk. Photograph by author.

outside passing the time of day). Joy nostalgically suggested that this intergenerational care was something that had been lost in Britain, explaining:

> the Spanish go everywhere in hordes. The families take care of each
> other. You know some women have to remain single to look after their
> mothers, and then when their mothers die, they're in black for the rest
> of their lives. You think things are changing but they're not. It's how it
> used to be in working class families in England if you were Catholic.

These reflections are curious however, as whilst images of a Spanish
more 'traditional' way of growing 'old' is admired from a distance, it is
unlikely that migrants themselves feel they offer a lifestyle that should
be imitated. Retirees' own couching of their move to Spain in terms of
enhanced independence suggests that the alternative witnessed in Spain is
not realistically a desirable option applicable to them. The reflections can
instead be interpreted as useful in migrants' narratives of their recasting of
retirement. Featherstone and Hepworth observe that changing conceptions
of retirement occur through dismantling a traditional image of retirement
of days gone by, with an encouragement towards 'adopting a modern outlook' (Featherstone and Hepworth 1990: 271). In this light, older migrants'

Figure 5.2 Spanish older people on the street. Photograph by author.

celebration of traditional images of ageing in Spain helps support their choice to move to the location — as it is associated with a healthy diet, a slower, community oriented way of life and more respect for older people. Yet, the reflections also help to create a backdrop of 'otherness' and difference which also proves useful to contrast their own identities. In other words, they can be used to both confirm their choice of moving, yet position themselves and their own activities in contrast: as more 'modern' to their 'traditional' and as 'younger' to the Spanish 'older'. This contrast was captured by Alicia, as she laughed about the possibility of her employer pursuing the same lifestyle as the older Spanish people around, 'Elizabeth...would die if she needed to go to the Day Center for elderly people!'6

AGEING II — 'YOU'VE GOT TO KNOW HOW TO HANDLE IT': THE MANAGEMENT OF OLD AGE

It's a matter of attitude. You have to prepare for your retirement from when you are a child. If you just work all your life and don't develop any hobbies outside, then you are going to get here, and within a few months you'll get bored and depressed. (Prospective migrant, greeted with murmurs of approval at a club luncheon)

The first part of the chapter reveals positive feelings in how ageing is experienced by migrants in Spain, and shows how ageing is downplayed and considered irrelevant through a subjective approach, assertions of independence and adoption of a 'modern' approach to ageing. However, this section reveals the paradoxical importance of age, examining how age nevertheless maintains social salience and requires acknowledgement, reflection and new regulation, particularly in a context in which deterioration is read in the competencies of both oneself and one's peers. People must pay careful attention to the management of their active, leisured lifestyles, particularly when new expectations are created around how one should age well, to both avoid the possibility of 'overdoing it' and to extend the period of activity. These reveal limits to the 'freedom' imagined in life in Spain.

The salience of age: Cohorts and common ageing identities

When Judy explained that she has lived in Spain for ten years, she also sighed an acknowledgement, 'that means we're ten years older than we were'. Despite the emphasis on feelings of agelessness explored previously, Judy's acknowledgement points to the inevitability of material, bodily ageing as a fundamental condition underpinning migrants' experiences in Spain. As Judy shows, time spent in Spain is measured *vis à vis* generational compatriots, in which the length of time in the site is a marker of sorts of increased age, which is especially compounded by the loss of peers in one's cohort. Belle referred to the progression of retirees at an American club meeting, at which Bierta reflected, 'well, I suppose me and Jack are getting past it now — we're part of the old lot, but then if we thought about moving where would we go?' Her observations demonstrate the position of many older residents I met, who felt nostalgia because many friends within their own cohort have died or have had to move as a result of failing health. For instance, Elizabeth referred to how her close friend moved to a residential home in Sussex and Derek, her close friend, died unexpectedly. Elizabeth's other friend Jean was due to return to Britain soon and two other friends from the village had recently moved to the coast, leaving Elizabeth socially isolated and unwilling to start making friends anew (see Chapter 3).

It is not so much the actual age-differences between different migrants that are significant, because in many cases, a person's age is not even known to her friends. Rather it is that new waves of migrations form different groups of 'young old' people and when other younger migrants move in, they tend to reflect on differences between the cohorts. For instance Annabel, a woman in her late fifties (see Chapter 3) pointed out, 'there's a different group here [in the urbanisation] than ten years ago. Those before were more community-oriented, and we're more outward looking'. Not only do the new migrants gradually change the composition of the migrant community, but their activities also become a subject for reflection of longer established (and often genuinely older) migrants, who consider their age and capabilities in comparison. Thus Molly reflected on her decision to avoid too many activities, because she was too tired, considering the club life the province of 'the young old, that's who it's good for, those in their fifties and sixties, you know who like all the "association-mania"'. At eighty-four years old, she repeatedly referred to herself as an 'old fogey', and 'an antique', wilfully inhabiting the stereotypes of old age that others so vigorously denied. Sharing tea and biscuits at her house after a morning at the International Club, she said,

> I don't do anything extra apart from the International Club. I get too tired. I think that's sometimes a problem here, too many people being active. They try to forget they're getting old, but you know, when you get older, you need to be slowing down, to realise that you can't do everything you might like to. Instead, they speed up, rushing through everything they wanted to do when they were younger. No, I'd be too tired.

The subjective downplaying of age observed previously is also undermined because paradoxically old age is positively mobilised and emphasised as the basis for a 'we-feeling' of community belonging (discussed in Chapters 6 and 7). Judy acknowledged: 'we're all old here' (see also Keith Ross 1977) pointing to how a common culture can be built on a shared history and generational difference in attitudes (see also Williams 1990 and Chapter 7). Blaikie argues that the barricading in or 'encrustation' (ibid.:177 referring to Kastenbaum 1993) evident in some age-segregated communities formed following retirement migration in the US, Britain or in North-South migration in Europe is motivated by older people's desires to preserve identities under threat, and their feelings of estrangement from wider societies where their values are not upheld. In Spain, these sentiments are evident; for example, an article in the local free magazine was entitled 'youngsters get it wrong' (see also Chapter 7). Judy's partner, Ted, in his seventies, also explained how old age was important in shaping a different perception, which he described as:

> Something that happens, and it's not until you get there that you realise you have a completely different way of looking at things than younger people. Of course no one wants it to happen, but when it comes, you realise it immediately. It's when a young girl passes and you know they wouldn't as much as look at you. It's a different mentality entirely being old. When such a mentality comes upon you, you've got to know how to handle it.

Acknowledgement of the shared experience of old age can also be used for positive ends, particularly in challenging mainstream attitudes. For example, Bill, a former journalist, wrote an article based on his own frustrating experiences of dealing with inadequate wheelchair access and, over time, succeeded in lobbying for more disabled car parking spaces in the town. And the Chairman of the British Legion in the area was campaigning to develop a funded system of repatriation for members who find themselves with no financial means to cover it themselves. Moreover, people benefit through confiding in others the practicalities of dealing with bodily ageing, when experiences of ailments and health issues are shared with others in the knowledge that they are ageing too. Tips and remedies are passed on, as discussions focus on issues such as dealing with high blood pressure, tiredness, water infections and experiences of operations, and these are often quite graphically described. For instance, when Joy was suffering bad arthritis and a period of impetigo, she cast this physical deterioration as a process of decay. She told me, 'I just feel like I'm dying slowly, rotting away', resonating with the alternative vision of activity as something which stops people 'stagnating' or 'vegetating' (see Chapters 4 and 5 and Mason 1988). However, whilst this explicit acknowledgement of the body helps some people, others found discussion of the materiality of the ageing body countered their positive experiences of retirement. Thompson et al's (1991) research showed that some older people may be socially uncomfortable solely amongst people of their own age and this was certainly the case for Amanda, a woman in her late fifties and in good health, who became more and more disgruntled with the public airings of ageing-related problems at one club. She said to me,

> I do get bored. All the conversation revolves around operations and drugs etc. It gets me down sometimes...I feel left out, which is silly, I've got nothing to complain about, surely that should be good?

The body and consumption

The exposure of ageing I have identified, however, is highly ambiguous and does not extend to the diminishing of concern with weight and appearance. This is particularly marked for older women, for whom connotations of youthfulness are especially disadvantageous (Bury 1995). Whilst migrants feel less prescription around clothing, the social events nevertheless also present many opportunities to 'dress up' and the context of leisured sociability means physical presentation is still very important. As Katz explains (2005: 33), there is now available a range of, 'bodycare techniques for masking the appearance of age'. In this part of Spain, 'anti-ageing' therapies are ubiquitously advertised in the free press. These range from acupuncture, chelation therapy (an artery cleaning process), magnetic field treatment to cryotherapy (a process that uses liquid nitrogen as a means of 'freezing the way to better looking skin', and removes, 'unsightly skin blemishes' that might include age-spots and warts). Less dramatic processes of bodily modification, such as weight loss, can also be aided for a fee. Thus Josie, an American woman, spent a considerable amount of money on herbal meal replacements from a local company in an effort to lose weight. One afternoon, she made a large lunch of pasta for me and her beloved cat, but sat at the table herself miserably struggling to swallow down the foul tasting liquid.

Such pressures on bodily appearance and healthy lifestyles are particularly difficult to negotiate in the leisured environment, where the communal sharing of rich food and drink is an integral part of sociability. A typical luncheon run by the clubs involves a three-course meal and at least half a bottle of wine per person. Yet the ethos of enjoyment clashes with the requirement to maintain the body and this puts pressure on the individual for restraint. Viv, on her latest diet, complained at an American club social gathering, 'It's not easy when you're here to enjoy yourself. Can you imagine at all these social occasions, getting out your flask of cabbage soup, and meeting for drinks, but having no drinks!' At an American Club meeting at the Chinese restaurant in town, Bierta ordered a meal one day, commenting, 'I might as well say goodbye to the diet today I think'. When she poured some wine she continued, 'when I go to bed at night after this sort of thing, I feel bad and say I won't drink anything but water tomorrow. But tomorrow never comes', again demonstrating the long-term dilemmas between health and enjoyment involved in her retirement lifestyle. As Viv's assertion shows, giving up small pleasures contradicts the ethos of enjoyment, which is so fundamental to retirees' lifestyles. Belle solved this problem by eating only small amounts of her Chinese meal, commenting, 'I think its fine to eat this sort of thing all in moderation of course, because it's all nutritional'. Pointing at the wine she justified, 'even that's nutritional, it's full of vitamin C'. Yet these contradictory pressures for enjoyment –but not excess — bear heavily on those who do not necessarily fit the ideal. This I shown in the following vignette of women talking at the British Legion:

Patsy: Well you know the Spanish, they let themselves go don't they? They take so much care of themselves and then they have children and...

June: Yes, like their thighs are enormous!

Patsy: Well, I'm always the same, always have been. But its laziness isn't it, getting fat?

Both women look embarrassed when they realise that their other companion, Amanda is larger. Patsy looks at Amanda:

Patsy: Well don't you think it's a problem being larger? You can't be happy like that.

Amanda refuses to reply.

As I have suggested before, the discourses of freedom espoused in Spain are experienced more as a loosening of norms, a kind of 'flirting' with freedom, rather than abandonment of previous expectations. This is particularly seen around alcohol use, whose positive evaluation is particularly fickle. At the same funeral in which I was reprimanded for turning down a glass of wine, disparaging comments were quietly directed at one lady whose 'varicose veins and red nose' were explained by her 'drinking too much'. And during my fieldwork over two years, Charlotte and Gerald's behaviour became the topic of social censure. Initially the couple were seen as widely popular raconteurs, celebrated for their fondness of wine and their consequent spirited behaviours. Their names provoked affirmations that 'they drink like fish!' which is an ambiguous statement that both approves yet passes commentary on their actions.[7] However, over a period of time, the positive evaluations of Charlotte and Gerald's activities waned, as they started to suffer the combined effects of alcohol consumption and old age. Charlotte suffered incontinence in a volunteer's car and was seen to lose her wig at a social occasion. She began to withdraw from circulation and no longer attended the clubs. At this point, discussions around Charlotte focused on her ill health, suspected Alzheimer's disease and mental health. At the same time, people also muttered how she was in the 'advanced stages of alcoholism'. A respected member of the expatriate community commented quietly to me one day, 'No-one wants to get involved and help them. They've now got a reputation as two alcoholics, two old winos really', following a number of noisy disturbances at their flat. One afternoon, their neighbour Birgit pulled me to one side and told me that that Charlotte was in a terrible state. She described how Charlotte kept falling and on one occasion she fell through a glass table. She said,

> Fortunately, she didn't cut herself, but it's too much for Gerald, he's almost blind and in his eighties now. He has to call out ambulances in the middle of the night, and he can't speak Spanish. The problem is that they are poor too, so they can't afford to pay for things like taxis to the hospital [20 kms away] in the middle of the night. Lots of times, we have to go in and help...one time, in the middle of the night we went in to help her get up, and get her into bed after changing all her pads and everything. I think Gerald's accepted that they have to go back. He does accept he needs help, and does ask us for help, but the main point is, he just doesn't want to admit that its time to go.

Although Charlotte needed round-the-clock nursing, the couple were estranged from their children and the responsibility fell mainly onto Gerald to care for her, despite his own mobility problems and failing eyesight. When I saw him, he was furious that they had been 'turfed out' of the hospital in the early hours of the morning (as the Spanish health service relies on family-based aftercare). Birgit pointed out,

They won't accept her into hospital...not if you're at home. They assume that you have someone to look after you....its like when Nathan [Birgit's husband] was in hospital...he was given an orange, but he had his arm up in the air, so of course he couldn't peel it, and couldn't ask. It's things like that.

The local branch of the Royal British Legion paid for nursing assistance for a few hours a day whilst the Chairman tried to arrange repatriation. This, he explained, would not be easy because by that time Charlotte was too frail to get onto an aeroplane. Charlotte died a few days later, although as the Chairman pointed out, she could have lived much longer. Gerald died six weeks after Charlotte.

Time to go: Caring conflicts and being prepared

Charlotte and Gerald's story is on the whole, thankfully rare. However, it demonstrates some of the issues identified by Mullan (1993) in her research for Help the Aged on British retirees in Spain. She highlights some of the difficulties facing the growing numbers of people who moved to Spain in the 1960s and 1970s when fit and well, who are now growing older. Some have limited financial resources to fund their care, particularly when dependent on state pensions that are vulnerable to inflation. The cost of living in Spain is no longer as cheap as it has been and many continue to live in socially isolated or poorly constructed properties unsuitable for older people. Whilst one must be mindful that the media often over-emphasise or sensationalise problems (O'Reilly 2000a), a recent report quoted the president of Age Concern in Spain stating that this problem is worsening (Stevens, *the Observer* 2006). And, even if rare, the difficulties unwittingly faced by some people can nevertheless be serious (see Hardill, Spradbery, Arnold-Boakes and Marrugat 2005). During my fieldwork, I heard a story circulating about an older woman who was found dead in the winter, some weeks after she had died alone at her house in the seasonally under-populated urbanisation.

The horror of such events may be exaggerated or distorted by word of mouth (see Chapter 6), but such stories nevertheless instate a need for people to be pragmatic about the risks of their lifestyles in Spain, particularly as they grow older. Thus, the irony of living amongst similarly aged peers is that whilst it encourages a reconceptualization of retirement, nevertheless the evident frailty, experiences of illness and deaths of others in their midst regularly remind people of their own ageing. For example, one afternoon, when Belle and I sat talking at the end of a meeting of the American Club, she reflected on how knowing how other people had fallen provoked a fear that it would happen to her. This encouraged her to sustain her mobility through particular strategies, as she explained,

You know I always hold on to the rails because it's so easy to fall if it's dark and you can't see, you get to the bottom stair and miss it and that's all it takes. In my apartment, I hold on to the rails and I count the steps. But people see you and keep saying, Belle, are you OK? And that bothers me, I don't want people to say are you OK? I understand why they do it and I suppose I did it with my parents.

Whilst clearly the avoidance of dependency remains a fundamental concern, Belle referred to her shifts in lifestyle and gradual cutting down of commitments. She explained her retirement from a key job in the society: 'You know it's just too much and I'd done it for a while. And nobody's grateful anyway, they complain too much. I guess I'm getting older now, I realise'. Her struggle is a reminder of how, as Laslett (1989: 153) explains:

> everyone in the Third Age, especially when he or she is threatened by the Fourth, ought to be aware of when and how to withdraw. To be properly sensitive to the judgement of friends, neighbours, acquaintances, and people at large, expressed, implied, or for reasons of delicacy merely hinted at, is a demanding duty.

For some, the responsibility for withdrawal occurs through a gradual cutting down, or giving up of activities (see Jerrome 1992: Chapter 8) which precedes planning for the 'time to go', whether that means a move back to Britain, a move into specially adapted facilities or withdrawal from the social scene. These negotiations are arrived at with the contribution and help of others in the society, although the point may be delayed for as long as possible and readjustment made through a number of small steps. Often the changes wrought by old age are adjusted to with further physical moves within the site or even back to Britain (see King, Warnes and Williams 2000 and Chapter 7). These cases provoke mixed feelings for remaining migrants; whilst Judy felt genuine sadness at the departure of Doreen, her close friend, she acknowledged it was a 'sensible thing to do'. Yet there is also sympathetic understanding — up to a point — for those who try to avoid it. When Roger and Pat were deteriorating quickly, there was a discussion at the Remembrance Day luncheon as to why they didn't go back 'to a nice residential place in England'. Sheila pointed out, 'it's psychological, isn't it? To move back would be like giving up wouldn't it? Like admitting, well that's it, that's your life gone. Nobody wants to get like that'.

This is not to say that all older migrants adapt their lives as dramatically as moving back to Britain (or country of origin)[8] and some fail to make adjustments altogether. Particularly for migrants who have lived in their houses for many years, such as Elizabeth and Mary, there is reluctance to move, even if, as in Mary's case, this involves a daily battle to stay on top of things. She said of her imminent trip to hospital,

I am just going for a check up but I'd rather not know. I'd rather run around for six months and then drop dead. If it's the big 'C', then I don't want to know. And I don't want to be pumped full of drugs or be on a drip or anything – I'd rather keep going here until I pop my clogs. I keep thinking of selling here [the house] anyway as its too much work and it's too big to keep on top of. But I like it here.

However, even in these cases, there was still an emphasis on 'being prepared'. When Mary said these things, she had been frantically sorting out her will before going into hospital. She also had some insurance that her need for care could be met through a subtle shift in her Spanish employees' responsibilities. Whilst Manolo and Sebastián, who Mary had known for years, looked after her land, house and affairs, increasingly the moral responsibility of her care also fell upon them. I vividly remember the fear Manolo expressed when we both went to investigate why Mary had not answered her [open] door, despite us having a previous arrangement to meet. In the case of Elizabeth, Alicia's role had also gradually shifted from housekeeper to include some care responsibilities for Elizabeth, although full-time care was prohibited by Alicia's own family responsibilities. When Elizabeth needed more help following an operation, she paid other people to come in and care for her although she did not like the intrusion. On the other hand, she considered Alicia as like a daughter, as she said, 'what would I do without Alicia? There's no way I could manage at all'. Alicia also felt genuine concern for her employer as she told me, 'the union between her and I is much more than she can ever know' (*'la unión entre ella y yo es mucho más que ella pueda saber'*).

In cases where people do not have either close Spanish employees or children to help, or indeed when kin ties are weak and are unlikely to be mobilised following ill-health, the responsibility falls on people to finance the majority of their social care themselves. Whilst registered retired migrants are entitled to full state health cover under form E121, under which they are issued with a health card, many people hold private health insurance. This may be within Spain, or may be in Britain; indeed, Tony, a seasonal migrant had a number of operations in a private medical centre in the UK and used his second home in Spain for periods of convalescence. Those relying purely on state provided medical services in Spain find that family members are expected to assist with personal care and there are very limited local care services (see King et al 2000:182–184). A report in *the Observer* (Stevens, 2006) also suggested that some Spanish doctors are now refusing to treat expatriates who do not speak Spanish. This is due to the risks of them misunderstanding diagnoses, as well as borne of indignation at the limited resources they receive because many foreign pensioners are 'invisible' because they do not officially register. Moreover, those requiring chronic care are confronted by a limited number of state-funded care home places, whilst private care home placements are unfunded by either the Spanish or UK governments (Age Concern España 26 November 2003). This leads to a situation, as Josie said, 'if you have money you can always get care. But if you don't have money, what do you do?' In cases where longer-term social care is needed and people do not have the finances to cover it, the responsibility therefore tends to fall onto spouses, neighbours, friends and people in the voluntary organisations.[9] And whilst society functions through interdependency (Arber and Ginn 1991) and some care responsibilities are undertaken willingly, sometimes these roles are taken on simply because there is nobody else to help.

This presents dilemmas particularly for some retired women migrants, who must negotiate the balance between societal expectations and the fulfilment of their own aspirations (Ingrish 1995). In some circumstances, however, there may even arise conflicts as to who should adopt the role of 'carer' and who the 'cared-for'. For example, Josie, who herself was ill and planning to move to a residential home in the United States, was preoccupied by the plight of her neighbour, Rose who was unable to cope on her own. She explained,

> Betty [another neighbour] rang home to her sons but they told her, 'She won't want our help, she's so independent'. After that, she fell down and burnt her arm and she's not capable of looking after herself...but the sons use the 'independence' as a good excuse. She wants to sell her house and move back, and an offer was put in. But the sons were called, and they want $10,000 more. People stay on and on and on, not thinking they will need help. So Rose now has help ten minutes a day, but that's with a helper not really a nurse. She is always falling over, it's horrible, but they [her sons] don't want to be bothered.

Josie felt obliged to help, even though in other circumstances, given her own health difficulties, she would be the 'cared-for'. Similarly when Joy suffered a nasty bout of food poisoning, her older and infirm German neighbour still relied on her to do tasks and odd jobs. When her own infirmities meant Joy was unable to help, she felt extremely guilty at what she felt was her negligence when shortly afterwards, the woman was found dead following a fall. Although negotiating care relationships seemed particularly problematic for women, some men articulated similar concerns. For instance, Bob, who lived in his isolated large house alone whilst waiting to move to New Zealand (see Chapter 4), was unsteady on his feet. Before he retired to bed at night, he put a piece of cardboard up in his window, on which was a written explanation (in Spanish and English) that if it was not removed in the day-time, this would indicate that something had gone wrong. He expressed how he hoped, 'somebody would come in and find him', and explained that he thought he could rely on, 'people who would advise on my funeral and tell Edith [his wife]. At least I hope they would tell Edith if anything happened to me. It's very insecure here though...you see I could die out here and no-one knows'. He referred hopefully to, 'Spanish friends who think I'm like a granddad. I know that they would sort it out, stick me in the wall up there[10] and look after the dog'. But when I asked him why he did not seek more help, he said that in addition to pride, it was also that, 'everyone's old here. It's not fair to put on them, when you don't know which one of you is going to die first'.

The scenario of migrants with limited resources (and few or unwilling relatives) getting into difficulty, is however, generally seen as something to be avoided at all costs. The urgency to prepare for dependency is even more acute given that, as the example of Rose demonstrates, distance may hinder assistance of older relatives by their families, with a reduction of time spent on care 'at a distance' (Joseph and Hallman 1998). As Young, Seale and Bury (1998) have demonstrated, friends may represent an important resource, but are not a substitute for family-support in experiences of serious illness. This is particularly a problem for migrants who are not well-integrated 'joiners' (Jerrome 1992) or who are geographically isolated in the *campo*. For example, Jean was a loner who had successfully renovated her house in the village, learned Spanish to communicate well and pursued her own interests in music and literature rather than joining the social scene. Yet she had a stroke that left her with little capacity to remember what she had learned; she could no longer communicate in Spanish and was distressed whilst awaiting migration back to Britain to live with her sons. The risks presented in such stories are capitalised upon by the private care and insurance market who stress the moral responsibilities for individuals to take care of themselves. An article/advertisement for investment for long term care in the expatriate press for instance states,

> We are grateful to our partners, family, neighbours and friends for popping in and helping out when we are not feeling well. It's nice to have somebody to make a cup of tea, prepare a meal and tidy around the house while we rest and get better. The carer is happy to help out. It's only a few hours, for a few days of their lives. There is nothing like a bit of TLC — Tender Loving Care to make us feel good. A problem comes when TLC turns to LTC — Long Term Care — when you need help not just for a few days but for the rest of your life. Will the carers be able to adjust their lives to give the attention you need? Would they be prepared to? Of course, as an expatriate your potential carers may live hundreds of miles away. And how would you feel? A burden? Guilty that you were disrupting other people's lives? (Savidge, Nov 1999)

It is important to note the important role that is played for people with little kin support or financial means to pay for care, by associations with a domiciliary service (such as the British Legion) and other charities (such as Age Concern). However, there are sometimes slippages in terms of who bears the ultimate responsibility. When Margaret was released from hospital following her stroke, volunteers accompanying her from an expatriate association had arrived at a Nursing Home, where it was understood she had a place. However, they were told that the staff had no knowledge of Margaret's admission. At this stage, it would have been impossible to seek readmission into hospital, so Margaret returned to her flat and the British Legion had to arrange a home-carer for her. However, it is extremely difficult for clubs facing an ageing membership to provide care when they have only minor support from social services. A discussion paper, written by the area chairperson stated, 'We cannot sustain long-term care for those requiring constant attention who are without funds' (Brooks 1997: 1 and see Mullan 1993). For some caught in the poverty trap, repatriation, funded by charitable organisations, is the only answer. I was told by a British Legion spokesperson in the area of my study that although repatriation had occurred on rare occasions in very negative circumstances, the lack of formal procedures for repatriation was a source of considerable concern. He explained how some people will stretch their independence until the very limit, and said, 'people don't like to admit that they need help'. In the AGM speech, he gently reminded members about the imperceptibility of ageing, stating how 'the future' in fact arrives rather gradually: 'Yes, we're all getting on…One day we are seventy, one day seventy-five, then all of a sudden you realise, you can't lift a bag'. His statement was an implicit reminder to members of the expectation that, whilst retiring to Spain offers the chance for positive experiences of retirement, it is nevertheless the individual's responsibility and moral duty to plan for the future, especially in the face of limited institutionalised provisions.

SUMMARY

The chapter shows a number of pressures existing in negotiating ageing in migration to Spain. On one hand, there is a loosening of age-based prescriptions and evidence of a subjective approach to youthful ageing. The perspective often coincides with a temporal, social and spatial deferral of feared aspects of ageing onto other people (as I also expand upon in other chapters). Negative aspects of ageing are socially distanced, located as the domain of the very old, seen as the fate of those who do not possess the right attitude or located elsewhere, 'back there' in the homeland. In this way, the place of Spain is employed purposefully to re-imagine the ageing process as one managed 'well' in the here and now, and considerable evidence shows how people's lifestyles in a sunny and sociable environment are widely enjoyed. On the other hand, whilst ageing is constructed as a malleable process, there are limits as to how far the material realities and challenges can be downplayed, a fact particularly made evident in the progression of age-cohorts. The social scene also places an imperative on people to manage the ageing body, which exerts limits on how far migrants can and should go in the pursuit of their enjoyable lifestyles, particularly when some associated aspects, such as alcohol and rich diets, are understood as being detrimental to health and visible appearance. Thus, whilst constraints on behaviours are loosened, these only go so far, and migrants face contradictions between pressures for health, and their engagement in other enjoyable pursuits. Moreover, the length, extension and limit of active lifestyles must be carefully judged according to considerations about the availability of care from kin as well as the availability of financial resources in contexts where social care is expected to be provided by the family. In risky negotiations, migrants' must weigh up their reluctance to lose independence against how they will manage as they grow older, and ultimately where that will be. Migrants thus live according to tacit expectations for managing their bodies, adjusting to change and being prepared, although, as I have shown, there are nevertheless varying degrees as to how far these new societal expectations are respected.

6 Community and the Individual in Migrants' Spain

As the last chapter demonstrated, retired migrants emphasise their inclusion in a warm and welcoming community of other foreign residents. This community is sustained through informal cooperative networks, governed by an ethos of 'helping each other out' (O'Reilly 2000a: 124) particularly through voluntary work by retired migrants (see King, Williams and Warnes 2000: 148–152, Huber and O'Reilly 2004, Verlot and Oliver 2005, and see Chapter 5). Upon moving to Spain, new residents find it easy to make new acquaintances (O'Reilly 2000b) in a social life governed by a spirit of camaraderie and loosened social etiquette. Differences seem to matter less, as O'Reilly points out, 'there is an explicit agreement that it should not matter what you were in the past' (2000a: 129). This echoes Fitzgerald's analysis of retirement communities in North America, where, 'no-one gives a hang here what you did or where you come from…It's what you are now that matters' (1986: 219). Perhaps, as I suggested in Chapter 2, such features suggest an emergence of 'communitas' amongst migrants, the common feeling of union arising in liminal conditions which stresses 'personal relationships rather than social obligations' (Turner 1969: 112).

However, as in the previous chapters, this chapter discusses the number of contradictions experienced in the reality of the 'community' ideal. Turner points out that 'communitas does not merge identities' (1974: 274) yet, as the chapter shows, the levelling ethos, the reduced importance of previous status and the possibilities for masquerade presents risks for migrants on a number of levels. First, the egalitarian communitas downplays the former achievements and certainties on which individual identities have been built. Whilst this has advantages, it also diminishes the importance of the moorings on which people's identities have been constructed. And second, it requires people to trust others at 'face value': believing that they are who they say, that their words are genuine and their friendship can be relied upon. This is a challenge in a transient context where it is hard to find out 'who you really were' (O'Reilly 2000a: 112, see also Huber and O'Reilly 2004). In light of these potentially disconcerting factors, in this chapter, I show how other social practices arise, including gossip and reputation-management processes. These processes may appear incongruent and even antithetical to the community cohesion so widely espoused. However, as the chapter shows, they are fundamental to enable expressions of individuality, expose infringements of the egalitarian ethos by others, force information about self and others to be made public and aid the process of validation of others' trustworthiness. These practices are paradoxical; both risking the fragmentation of the community yet wholly necessary to maintain the egalitarian 'community' of strong-minded individuals.

I: MIGRATION: 'THE GREAT LEVELLER?'

One day, I joined in with an early morning outdoor water-aerobics class in a hotel complex on the outskirts of Tocina. The arbitrary grouping of people of different nationalities all hopped about, grabbing hold of each other in a watery conga dance and passing the ball between their legs, with little care for age, status or nationality of the person in front. The various shouts in English, Spanish, Dutch or French merely added to the atmosphere, as did the objections to the odd accidentally misplaced hand amongst the mixed group. 'Come and join us', shouted the instructor to various other people walking by on the side. I was, regrettably, unable to get to the early class on a regular basis without my own transport, yet a few months later, the instructor visited the village where I lived. When she saw me, she greeted me warmly and enthusiastically by name, despite having met me on just that one occasion. To this day, the group sticks in my mind because it was particularly indicative of the relaxed social codes in the migrant context. The event held a 'structure-dissolving quality' (Turner 1974: 263) in which social boundaries were relaxed and status hierarchies seemed less important.

Certainly a spirit of familiarity and informality governing social relationships is evident in much of community life. The peer support available to retired migrants in Spain is particularly valuable in this stage of the life course, especially in the face of other losses incurred at retirement (Jerrome 1990, 1992, Arber and Ginn 1991). Research on Swiss migrants in Spain shows they have four or five times more close friends than those over sixty-five in Switzerland (Huber and O'Reilly 2004), whilst the social relationships may also be more intense as people have more time to spend on friends (see Chapter 4). In particular, the welcoming domain of the clubs provides the ideal breeding ground for new friendships, as Les and Amanda explained their relationships with Bob and Jan at the British Legion, 'we've formed a very close friendship, it's because we're two very happily married couples, we refer to these two as *Cod 'n' Chips'*. 'Chips' (otherwise known as Jan) replied in a joking style customary in these contexts, 'What? I've still got the bruise from where you kicked me when we first met!' The employment of informal nicknames was common across all the clubs; some I heard included *Miss Music*, *Jack the Hat* and another couple of women, *the Aunties*, signifying a rather tongue-in-cheek or light-hearted discursive style evident in the social scene.

It is also notable that in Spain, the clubs have mixed memberships both in terms of background and nationality, particularly given that both Okely (1990) and Arber and Ginn (1991) indicate that class and gender differences often influence the patronage of older people's social clubs. This evident openness in Spain however leads to social contact between, as one woman described, 'people you'd never come into contact with in Britain'. Although I show later on this may provide grounds for dissonance, it nevertheless promotes a sense of freedom from conventions dictating social intercourse in Britain and is cited as evidence of the tolerant nature of the newly made society. One day, I attended an embroidery group meeting, an informal group of around seven women of different nationalities and backgrounds. We met at one of the members' homes and sat around the table chatting for many hours. The women swapped news, yet over the day, the conversation often reverted back to the topic of difference. The women discussed how migration was 'the great leveller' and praised people who lived in their community as tolerant and easy-going. When anything with the slightest whiff of essentialism was raised, other participants set it right, repudiating the tendencies of, as Kristiana described, 'generalising and making generalisations about others'. Differences in background and financial capital were also minimised. This is also revealed by Annie and Peter in their interview (which turned into an occasion for inviting their friends Claire and Brian over for drinks):

Peter: As they say the quality of life is so much better over here, the warmth, and I suppose the climate makes you feel happier because it's so sunny and nice.

Claire: I think the other thing is that people take you for what you are rather than who you are, it doesn't matter if your dinner plates don't match or you're drinking out of plastic cups.

Annie: No, it doesn't matter a damn.

Brian: No. Your dinner service is not important here.

The discussion refers to a lack of importance of material trappings in Spain, confirming O'Reilly's (2000a) observations of a re-evaluation of former status following migration. Tom, a former psychology lecturer was baffled by the lack of interest in his past life, as he explained, 'it's strange, but I thought I'd be asked what I did before much more when I came'. This ethos however supports the previously explored narrative of migration as an opting out of the capitalist rat-race into an idealised community-life (see Chapter 4) in which again, images of rural Spain are employed to support such stories. Willy, for example, although not retired, had nevertheless 'downgraded' and given up his job as a businessman in London, instead doing building work as and when he could. He often sat in Bar Antonio in Freila, and, when I passed, he regularly called out for me to join him. At that point he generously put my drink on his tab and expressed his satisfaction at living in the village. His pleasure at living in 'my utopia' as he described it, emerged from the fact that he felt part of a community in which, 'Here, nobody cares [about status]…It's a small village, they look out for you. I mean in England you'd [referring to me] go into a bar and get hit upon, but here, they'll protect you'. Annie and Peter also described their Spanish plumber as 'a sweetie' before concluding:

Peter: If they know you live here, if they see you around, in a small town like this, in the winter particularly if they see you around then it's…

Annie: What is so *very* nice is to walk through the town…it's still a village heart here and not like a city and I get '*Hola*', '*Buenos días*' and whatever from about 6 or 8 people who don't know me, but just know me by sight…

Peter: That's right

Annie: …I'm part of the village life which…I'm not just a number here, I *live* here and they know that and that is very, very nice I think.

Assertions of self in egalitarian community

However, whilst the effects of 'the great leveller' of moving are no doubt experienced as liberating, it nevertheless strips individuals of taken-for-granted sources of identification. This may be disconcerting for some, for whom the anonymity provokes rather a more forceful reassertion of the self. Indeed it was notable that when I asked some Spanish friends of their views on retirement migration, it was less the community spirit than the regular tensions they saw occurring between the *extranjeros* (foreigners) which provoked commentary. María speculated that the tensions she witnessed were borne of foreign residents' concerns to uphold an air of exclusivity. One man commented that it was foreigners who introduced fences (*vallas*) into the region to mark out their private property whereas previously boundaries were marked through less exclusivist markers of boundaries, such as trees (see Rozenberg 1995). María mused further:

They [foreigners] annoy each other. They get on each other's nerves because they want to come to Spain to be unique, to have an 'England' or a 'Germany' here for them, to be here with *their* laws and *their* rules…. [She imitates foreigners] '*What's mine is mine and nobody steps in*', and '*I don't know you at all*' and '*everything's mine*', and '*it annoys me that there's another foreigner next door*'. They'd like to have everything for themselves….Even though they live next door to each other, they fall out. It's always because of something, because of a boundary, noise, a siesta, whatever it is... There's the example of Jenny and Isabel: fallen out. Ruth and Frida: fallen out.[1]

Many foreign residents themselves admitted that difficulties arise in social relations because they felt, particularly at their older age, it was not easy to suppress key aspects of former personal and professional identities. King et al suggest, 'an individual on the threshold of retirement has experienced six decades of learning, socialisation, effort and experience. Much of a person's make up is their biography' (2000: 5). And when people pride themselves on their independent and assertive nature, friction may emerge in communal activities. Mary, for example, explained why she was reluctant to go the clubs, as she said, 'I suppose I could go to the clubs, I could just walk in, but I think I'd upset people in the end. I'm not very good like that, I always come out with what I think'. Joy, at the embroidery club, also excused some perceived bad manners of a friend and said, 'they probably didn't mean it. It's like me, I can't get away from the fact that I was a school teacher. I sometimes come across as aggressive'. Bierta also observed that, 'people here have different educations, manners, money, ways of life. It's no wonder that cliques form'. These comments seem to suggest that whilst on the surface, differences in background, economic and cultural capital are less important, they are nevertheless factors that cannot be erased. Thus whilst Willie argued that status did not matter, he also regularly complained that there were plenty of who he called, 'the Daphnes and Rogers', the 'people who come and flash it around that they have a five bedroom place' (and see other comments around taste in Chapter 7 which shows how consumption and style is an avenue for the reassertion of past taste and provides a new basis for social differentiation).

Others who hoped to move to Spain to feel freedoms from societal expectations in Britain also expressed disappointment at the continued existence of some social prejudices in the community. Although in the town there was a thriving gay scene for men, one older lesbian woman I spoke to, for example, was terrified of others' social opinion about her sexual orientation and the repercussions it would have on her friendships. She lectured in Manchester on gay consciousness years ago, but said,

> With all that I did...'be proud' and all that, here I am and I'm too frightened to tell anyone at all that I am a lesbian. If they knew down at the Fine Arts club, few people would speak to me.

The woman explained that when she wore makeup to a Christmas party, 'everyone was completely shocked'. '"How pretty you look," they said. "You mean I look the same as the rest of you,"' she replied. And during my fieldwork, she went on a visit back to England and returned less satisfied with life in Spain. '*Freedom*, they call it in Spain' she said. 'It's not free in Spain, at least in England I was free'. When she finally moved away from

Spain, in a subsequent correspondence, she told me how her initial reaction was relief when she finally moved back to her native city, beginning her news, 'finally I've escaped the gold shoes and matching handbag brigade!'

It is not uncommon in other social contexts of ageing (Keith 1977, Counts and Counts 1996, Okely 1990) to find conflicts emerging within group situations. For example, Myerhoff's (1986) account of Jewish older people in Venice Beach, California, explored definitional ceremonies as performative displays of strength to others and themselves. In these social dramas, 'the style was agonistic, much adrenaline had flowed and a good fight indeed offered clear cut evidence of a continued vitality' (ibid.: 268). Although the dramas rarely changed anything and rather led to the reiteration of common membership, they were nonetheless important for allowing people to be 'heard from, seen, authenticated' (ibid.) in a context where people were without the props of earlier identities, lacked an established history and felt invisible to mainstream society. In Spain, people's loss of sources of identification through the combination of retirement and migration may be rectified in similar ways through assertive expressions of opinion, as an Anglican priest in Tocina explained:

> Often the people who come here feel estranged as they used to have grand positions. They come and are seen as nothing, just another person. Perhaps this is why some people seize on conflict and blow it up out of all proportion.

Taking on new positions of authority in the clubs is one important means of overcoming anonymity in the new community. However, the desirability of jobs may however mean that authority structures are disproportionate to membership; O'Reilly refers to the example of a dancing group whose committee of twenty-five people catered to less than a hundred members (2000: 129). The informal nature of club organization also means that authority must be maintained through individual charisma rather than official means. Organizers have to be firm to deal with the divergent wills of other people, and this is not always easy because people react against expressions of power, as Judy observed, 'all these people were formerly organizers. They don't like being told what to do'. I was involved in a discussion between Judy and Sharon about a recent club event which exemplified this issue:

Caroline: How was the trip?
Judy: Yes, it was good....Of course it was a shame that I couldn't sit with Janet and Ted (Janet's partner) because they'd [club-organizers] allocated seats [on the coach].
Caroline: They told you where to sit?
Judy: Well, it saves problems.
Sharon: Well, that's *really* silly, I think. Couldn't they just do it on a first come first served basis?

Sharon felt that her age influenced her objections and her wider reticence to participate in certain clubs. Retirement was a time in her life, she explained, when she would finally 'make her own rules' rather than adhere to 'pettiness'. She maintained she found some of the club leaders 'a small group trying to dictate' and described those in power as 'little Hitlers',[2] echoing observations reported in Counts and Counts' (1998: 193) research on the RVing community in the US. Speaking of similar conflicts found there, they suggest, 'people whose key values are freedom and independence struggle to maintain their autonomy, while trying to impose their will on others. The result is tension and confrontation' (1998: 194).

One example of the difficulties facing organizers in Spain occurred because of problems in the seating plan at the American club dinner-dance. I was due to be seated with a party including Bradley and his wife Kate, who were American seasonal migrants, as well as David and his partner, Sharon, who were both English permanent residents. We were sharing the table with another group of people, which included a couple of American people, and Tom and Ernest, two singers who were due to sing after dinner. As we planned to sit down, we noticed that the name places had been moved around by the other party, which had left our group relegated to the back of the table and Sharon pushed out of her place. The events followed:

David: This is just not on! Not on at all!
         [Tom and Ernest sat down and folded their arms, the American woman also took what was Sharon's seat.]
American Woman: Belle [the chairperson of the club] said it was OK.
Bradley: But you might also have asked our permission first!
         [Belle came over, busily checking that everyone had found their seat.]
Belle: Is everybody happy, everything all right?
David, Sharon, Bradley and Kate: NO! Absolutely not.
David: You've let them take our seats!
         [They complained to Belle, who tried to smooth things over with appeals towards having a good time. In the end, we reluctantly took our seats at the other end of the table and managed to squeeze everybody on. Over the starter, the American man tried to establish how deep the rift was.]
American Man: Is this going to be a war then?
David: Yes, if you like. This is war. You're the sort of person who steals your seat then pushes you off the bus.
         [The American woman continued arguing with Sharon but their conversation ended abruptly.]
American Woman: AND HAPPY THANKSGIVING TO YOU!
         [She turned her back pointedly on us. The conversation with her own party at one end of the table continued.]

American Woman: I've been in Spain since 1962. I used to read the letters of the locals and write letters back because they couldn't read.... Times have changed so much. Things were so different then. You wouldn't have found this sort of thing going on at a Thanksgiving dinner then.

[Between courses, a woman got up to lead the dancing and it was announced later on that she had just got engaged to her partner. The people on my table did not join in the dancing.]

Kate: I must be getting old, I just feel past it. I've always been past it, I think.

[Finally, after dinner, the brothers got up to sing the Star Spangled Banner. Belle wanted everyone to sing the Spanish national anthem, although few joined in.]

David [laughing]: Well that was a shambles, wasn't it?

[The dancing resumed and people mingled from table to table. After a while, Viv joined us.]

Viv: When does everyone go?

David: When Belle decides.

Kate: This is getting too much! Whatever Belle says, goes.

[Later on, waiting for the coach, I stood talking with another woman, Monica.]

Monica: I understand it...so many people have just got on my nerves today. I thought for a while it was me, you know that I'm just not tolerant enough, but sometimes here, however much you look for the good in someone, you just can't get on with some.

In the face of strongly expressed differences of opinion, public figures like Belle may find their roles fraught with difficulty. They must try to smooth over social relations, but avoid overt demonstrations of power which could be perceived as 'pulling rank' to suit partisan interests. Moreover, they face being a target of personalised criticism about the ways that things are run, which is particularly upsetting when it comes at times when they may be struggling to keep up with their jobs. For example, I asked one former club member why she did not go any longer to a club, and she explained that as the chairperson had been ill, she had got frustrated by some of the confusion she faced in booking places at luncheons and complained, 'by the time you get to the luncheon, it's chaos'.

Maintaining harmony is, however, imperative for club-leaders, as dissatisfaction is demonstrated by people voting with their feet when they leave clubs and exploit the multiple other possibilities. People are discerning about which clubs they attend, because membership requires significant financial commitment (as Mason 1998, notes in her study of women's leisure activities). People must pay for joining fees, drinks, luncheons, activities and trips out (whose average cost ranges from €6.5 for a lecture to around €25–30 for a day trip). O'Reilly (2000a) suggests there is a great sense of competition between clubs, and perhaps this is because without sufficient membership, some clubs may be forced to close. Indeed I heard how dissatisfaction with the way that one club was run provoked members to create a breakaway faction of the club in a nearby town. In another example, one couple were evicted (undemocratically they asserted) from their jobs as travel organizers of a club. They claimed the election which saw them voted out was rigged and complained, 'they [the committee] quote the constitution but break it themselves'. In response they set up their own travel club and organised an identical Christmas trip to Benidorm. Both clubs attracted a sizeable number of participants, and the rival groups travelled five hundred kilometers to stay at the same hotel at the same time at Christmas, but had little to do with each other. This echoes Sallnow's (1981) analysis of the breakdown of communitas in Andean pilgrimage, where he revealed how a rival pilgrimage was staged as a direct challenge to the official one, and where factionalism and conflict coexisted with brotherhood and egalitarianism.

In summary, sustaining the community ethos in Spain is not easy when the individuals comprising the group are keen to preserve their individual autonomy.[3] An interesting parallel is provided in Cohen's study of Whalsay, Shetland, where the closeknit and isolated society is run according to egalitarian principles which inhibit individual distinctiveness. However Cohen shows how codes, joking behaviours and other means of allocating distinctive characteristics of individuals help construct difference whilst simultaneously upholding the cultural integrity of the society. However, this is possible in Whalsay because it is a more stable and enduring island community. In Spain, it is somewhat harder as the sociability is influenced by particular conditions of transience which have further consequences for trust and social relations. I interrogate these further in the following section.

II: 'THERE'S A LOT MORE TO THEM THAN MEETS THE EYE': TRUST AND REPUTATION

> There are some faces that tell me everything at once. Yours don't convey anything. Jean-Paul Sartre (1947: 19) *Huis Clos* (*No Exit*)

On one occasion, I sat at a social event with two migrants, Margaret and Wilfrid, who I had come to know well in my time in Spain. The conversation was easy and relaxed, in large part, I assumed because the two also knew each other. Yet when Wilfrid got up to the toilet, Margaret asked me discreetly what his name was. She explained quietly, 'I just don't know... because people come and go all the time here, you remember faces but not names'. The occasion demonstrates how when social relations are made in transient conditions, sometimes, little more than superficial knowledge of others is known, and 'acquaintances' are more likely to be made than friends (O'Reilly 2000b). As Catherine complained about social relationships, 'it's all done in pubs and cafes. They [other people] don't know a thing about you!'

As I have explained, the regularly changing makeup of the society can be felt as liberating and it certainly encourages the communitas explored previously. However, it just as much encourages an opposing trend of curiosity and speculation about potentially interesting former identities 'hidden' underneath the surface. Even in the close-knit British Legion, Bob commented, 'the thing is with people here, there's a lot more to them than meets the eye. You can't take anyone at face value. For instance, take Roger over there, he was in a group that dropped in Polish waters, the other man negotiated a submarine'. On another occasion, I had a two hour lunch with Don and his wife, believing Don's explanation that he had been a 'battery salesman'. Following an invite to coffee, I was confronted with their luxurious home, at which point Don mischievously revealed how the sorts of batteries he sold were for spy satellites, an evidently lucrative business. Whilst Don's masquerade in downplaying his past status was a harmless joke, Alice observed seriously, 'A lot of people around here pretend to be something they're not. Course they do — who would know if they've got 1000 pesetas or 100,000?' And as Josie said, 'you can say whatever you want about before...that you're a nuclear physicist. How can you check it?' This is a pressing issue given the social constructions of the Costa as a region popular for criminals on the run (O'Reilly 2000a: 72–75) and certainly some retired migrants I met had fallen victim to various scams. An eighty year old woman I knew had finally given up pursuing a legal attempt to recoup thousands of pounds from an unscrupulous builder and some property agents, who had simply disappeared with her money. This suggests that issues around trusting others are particularly pertinent in Spain.

Sociologists have explored how social relationships are reliant on the investment of trust to create friendships, which by nature are voluntary, non-exploitative and based on reciprocity (Allan 1989). Academic interest in the salience of trust in modern society is growing (Misztal 1996, Phillimore and Bell 2005) and whilst it has shown that trust is difficult to define (Seligman 1997) it can be explained essentially as a belief in the honesty and values of those around. However as Giddens (1990) has shown, trust in modern societies can no longer be taken for granted but requires work and self-management (Misztal 1996). Constructing trusting relations between individuals is a risky business, as it involves an attitude of accepting dependence on another person at the risk of betrayal or rejection (Luhmann 1979). Moreover, trusting relations also require time, as Nowotny comments, 'Trust presupposes expectations of a longer-lasting relationship, it is based on expected durability. Short-term interactions negate time, and where time is neglected, responsibility also dwindles' (1994: 14). In Spain, the lack of secure knowledge of others, transience and limited time over which friendships have been made, therefore heightens the risks implicit in trusting relationships in Spain. Jackie, a younger woman had come to the conclusion that,

> You can't confide in people here. I wouldn't let personal things away, because you don't know how others take it. For you, it could be really serious, but another person could read it lightly. You all take things in different ways don't you?

Jackie's refusal to enter into trusting relationships is certainly one option to overcome the risks, although it is somewhat extreme. However, I suggest that in response to these concerns, a number of behaviours emerge within the society. These practices include speculation about others through gossip, attempts to 'get to the bottom of people' and a concern with reputation. Such behaviours might appear at odds with harmonious community relationships aspired to by migrants, but as I show, are indeed rather vital: to both stamp out the risks inherent in trusting others at face value and to attempt to establish some shared values in the transient community.

Gossip and reputation: Knowing the others

'If you don't have a reputation, you'll get one anyway', Lynn Motson, the owner of Andalucian village house in a small inland village not far from Freila, told me. I had asked her to explain the tiled description on the outside of her house that read: *'casita de that Lynn Motson'* ('the little house of that Lynn Motson') when we met for coffee there. She was surprised that she had not heard of my visit before through the village 'grapevine', as she said, 'usually the *tambores* (drums) would've told me that you're here'. Lynn was not alone in mentioning the heightened significance of small talk in migrants' interaction. When I went to talk on the expatriate radio, the radio-show host even told me, 'we call this place Rumoursville' (and see other examples in Oliver 2007). In the first week of fieldwork I was discussing my project with Pete, a younger builder in his forties, who also emphasised these features:

Pete: The people in Tocina are bad....I mean, its such a gossipy goldfish bowl down there.
Caroline: Oh, great, what am I letting myself in for?
Pete: No, It's OK, but they're a funny lot. Every now and then I go down, and immediately I am filled in with the gossip about everyone. But, that's what you get if you choose to live in a goldfish bowl.

Although gossip is found in many other contexts, I was interested to discover why it was so prevalent in Spain. I suggest however that it is one of a number of related practices — such as concern with reputation and information retrieval — which directly or indirectly address the risks involved in engaging in trusting relationships in Spain. They are key mechanisms by which people attempt to elicit details about others, tease out their 'true' nature and thereby confirm their trustworthiness.

In Spain, a good reputation is the central source of social capital, especially given the apparent reduced importance of former occupational status, background or wealth (as explored in Part I of the chapter). Good reputations are earned through being predictable and trustworthy characters, as people get a good name through community-building activities such as helping others out and sharing one's skills (as a lecturer or musician etc.). This explains the esteem that Judy is held in; her reputation derives from her public roles as organizer and lecturer, and her local knowledge. However, by engaging in such activities, Judy becomes a known character, demonstrating Misztal's point (1996: 127) that, reputation is an 'important social capital which facilitates people's willingness to cooperate by helping to overcome a scarcity of information'.

However, reputations are usually constructed through building a stock of knowledge about a person based on past behaviours (ibid.). Where this is limited or lacking, the most important means of gaining knowledge of others is through word of mouth (ibid.) wherein gossip provides information for compiling 'mental "dossiers"' about others around (Brison 1992: 13). Certainly in Spain, eliciting information and probing about others was part of a normal process of sociability. This was demonstrated to me on a number of occasions when people offered me tips and tactics for obtaining what they saw as 'real' research data rather than presentations of 'a front'. I was advised, from their experience that I should 'get them drunk and then the truth will come out!' whatever that 'truth' might be. Some people's reputation was even based on their ability to extract information. Christine said, 'I ask questions and get people to spill all', whilst John said, 'It's amazing to see Christine at work...she makes people feel so comfortable and then they tell her everything'. And a conversation I had with Tony at the American club revealed similar concerns as he said,

> I suppose I'm good at the art of conversation. That's why you're doing well...you're easy to be with, you listen and people feel comfortable around you. They feel safe and so you've lulled them into saying things they probably wouldn't reveal otherwise. It's the same with me. I know I'm a good conversationalist...it's hard after being in sales so long to be quiet, but you know the secret is to say very little, but just ask questions, pepper in the odd few things that are interesting to them. Then you've had a conversation where they've been talking all the time and they go away and say, oh yes, Tony is fantastic company!

The apparent similarity between my research and others' activities provoked some anxiety on my part, particularly as it was not my intention as a researcher, as Tony had interpreted, to 'lull' anybody into anything. The difficulties presented by my activity and role were also revealed when I went to a social gathering with John and Christine. They had invited a retired neighbour that Christine considered I would be interested in talking to. Early on in the evening, however, Christine said, 'I'm interested in what you do and how you do it. I'm going to watch the questions you ask and see how you get people to reveal things about themselves'. The evening was a little uncomfortable; I was cautious of Christine's interest, because she implied that I was 'really' investigating something other than I said whilst she was also suspicious that I was constantly trying to lull *her* into a false sense of security in order to get information from her. Quite out of context, late in the evening, in mid-conversation she exclaimed, 'You're doing research aren't you?' revealing how my job as an ethnographer hit upon the central sensitivities around trust and privacy of the community. Undoubtedly these factors influenced my methodology because 'hanging out' would have simply confirmed my activities as suspicious, but they also helped retrospectively explain some initial reactions to my presence, as mentioned in Chapter 1.

The negative effects of speculation and information probing can, however, in eliciting information, create the contrary effect of further provoking more concern amongst people for privacy. Many people echoed Catherine's expression that she 'keeps herself to herself'. I also felt these concerns, when I became aware of speculations about a friend I had to stay. Joy had known I had a visitor almost immediately, but she laughed mysteriously when I asked how she knew, joking, 'I have my spies out and about!' Indeed, it seemed that keeping oneself to oneself simply placed the individual at a higher risk of gossip, because it suggests that individuals have something to hide; Bok (1981) explains that where information is scarce and when people wish to find out more about others than they are able, gossip is more likely. As such, the migrant community, whilst friendly, was also sometimes experienced, as Joy described, as 'incestuous' and claustrophobic. This echoes Percival's study of people in sheltered housing (see also Kinoshita and Kiefer 1992 on a Japanese retirement community) where gossip was 'integral to social interaction in these settings' (2000: 306) for reinforcing norms in a close-knit environment.

In this area of Spain, certainly environmental factors promote the prevalence of gossip. For those living in the village, the proximity of people's houses does not allow for much privacy, as the older dwellings are often intertwined and divided irregularly according to family inheritance arrangements, with overlooking balconies and rooftop terraces (see Figure. 6.1). Brandes (1980) and Gilmore argue, in any case, that gossip is an endemic feature of Andalucían societies[4] which helps to create group solidarity through the 'invisible fist of a public opinion' (1987a: 52) whilst maintaining an image of harmony amongst those at odds with each other (Gluckman 1963, Szwed 1966). And this is compounded by an uncomfortable

Figure 6.1 The proximity of houses in the village. Photograph by author.

sense of surveillance caused by the presence of tourists in the village. Willy told me that he had woken up in his village house to see tourists peering through his windows, whilst Elizabeth's secluded courtyard was featured on postcards and had become a magnet for tourists (see Chapter 7 and Oliver 2006). Despite these factors, foreign residents living in and around the village nevertheless perceived the coastal areas as most claustrophobic, an image supported by the visual distinction of the mass coastal strip seen in opposition to the dotted and isolated houses of the campo. The coastal dwellers were, as Elizabeth described, a group living 'on top of each other', representing an unreal 'giant performance and theatre', in contrast to a perceived normalcy of life inland.[5] Barbara, a woman building a house in the *campo* with her retired husband also confirmed, 'on the coast, everyone gets in each other's pockets. It isn't normal. I have a normal life. I work doing the jobs in the way I want to'. In this way, gossip is kept in check through being cited as evidence of other's boredom and lack of activity (see Chapter 4 and 5) as a means of 'beat[ing] empty time to death' (Bergmann 1993: 75).

Gossip and reputation: Defining social values

As much as gossip is minimised as the behaviour of the bored, it never-theless proves particularly important in Spain, where in the face of tran-sience, it helps distinguish people as 'members' of a community (Brison

1992) and also states and preserves some societal values. Ironically, it plays a powerful role in preserving the community egalitarian ethos explored previously. This is because untraceable social opinion becomes an important means for addressing any unwarranted assertions of exclusivity or claims towards a superior status (Bailey 1971) when individuals 'stick their head above the parapet'. For instance, one anonymous letter printed in a newspaper attacked a previous commentator for his opinion, who was told that he, 'oozes around with the sense of direction of a rotten carcass'. Another, addressed to 'an odious moron' was written under the pseudonym, 'H.F.Rottweiler'. I was also told of a magazine slot in Almeria, where *Jeanne 'n' Tonic* has her own social observation feature.[6] And 'that' Lynn explained how, when she received unexplained visitors at her house who arrived in expensive cars, she was subject to rumours speculating that she was a prostitute when, in fact, her visitors were Jehovah's witnesses (see Oliver 2007). Such practices can be understood as a reaction to perceived attempts of people 'getting too big for their boots', where damage to their reputation through the rumour mill is the means of bringing them back down to size.[7] Thus Lynne's individualistic tendencies and reticence to disclose information provoked rumours, which, in turn, invited a refutation of the allegations. Any attempts she made to offer evidence to the contrary would signal her willingness to participate in the social group.

Hellum's work (1998, 2000) on gossiping amongst foreign wives in Greece also shows how the practice functions to discipline and position the women in particular gender roles. She argues, 'in a society where "everybody knows everybody" the network becomes a tool for social control' (1998: 27). This notion is supported by Tebbutt's research which shows how working class women's gossip establishes a 'self-policing system' (1995: 76). In the migrant community in Spain, word of mouth commentary not only preserves the egalitarianism, but similarly makes public any perceived excesses within the framework of loosened social constraints. Discussions both celebrate risqué activities but yet mark the point at which the freedoms are perceived as being taken too far. The discussions of Charlotte and Gerald's drinking habits provide one example (Chapter 5) but another theme of discussion was relationships and flirting, as, for instance, one group of women revelled in the story of how one man hid the pants of a girlfriend under the pillow whilst seducing another woman, who had no idea of his indiscretions. Yet, again, public commentaries also mark the limits of such practices; Keith-Ross' study shows that notorious flirts were a source of concern in a retirement community (1977); in Spain, careful negotiation of flirting behaviour is required. For instance, one man was asked to leave a club when his flirting offended some of the women. And, whilst Tony described himself jokingly as 'an old reprobate', he found himself in trouble when others anonymously reported to his wife (who was in Britain at the time) that he had been seen driving other women to club activities, despite this being an entirely innocent activity. As such, lone women also felt particularly vulnerable to gossip in a context where many club members are married. Brigitte complained, 'women don't like you because they think that you are one of the single women who are out here looking for a husband. Of course, if you are talking to their husband, you are going to sleep with them!' Finally, gossip deals with perceived one-upmanship around ageing; being excessively active, for instance, was likely to incur commentary if it was seen as 'showing off'. Monica, who was recently bereaved by the loss of her husband, stated to the agreement of others in the vicinity how she was, 'sick to the back teeth' of hearing about the adventurous travels across the globe of another couple, particularly in light of her own personal sadness.

As this last example shows, such practices are not only useful for constructing community values, but are simultaneously helpful for individuals to express their personal views. On one hand, the discussions allow for self-affirmation through comparison. Bok describes, 'Part of the universal attraction of gossip is the occasion it affords for comparing oneself with others, usually silently, while seeming to be speaking strictly about someone else' (Bok 1984: 92). Sharing information is also a means of building intimacy with others in new social contexts, and as the former example of Christine shows, knowing information about others is an important resource in Spain, as people stand to gain prestige and status through the tactical 'micro-politics' of reputation (Paine 1967, Bailey 1971, Haviland 1977 and Bok 1984). Finally, these practices offer a means of dealing with the frictions that naturally appear over time in the social society where potentially one should be friendly with everyone. They allow people to find their own intimacies and set their boundaries in friendships. As Don and his wife described, they were overwhelmed by the 'ready made group of friends' available in Spain, but explained how it took them a year to 'sift out the bad'.

However, the frequency and sociability of social contact means that when people decide to break social bonds, the rupture needs to be ostensibly demonstrated. Thus Elizabeth referred to how when she walked down the narrow street in the village she blatantly ignored people she disliked. And Jenny told me how baffled her daughter was when she visited, because she saw her mother ignoring people and walking straight past them. Jenny's daughter pointed out that this form of behaviour was completely at odds with the outlook she had adopted before in Britain. And this underlying threat of broken bonds renders intimate relationships vulnerable; Joy's sister-like intense friendship with Kate (see Chapter 5) broke down when Kate met a new partner and she was perplexed when two close friends simply ignored her at a gathering. She had once considered them great friends, but without explanation, the couple simply started to ignore her. These factors helped convince Joy that she should leave Spain.

THE PARADOX OF COMMUNITY

> What happens when a community that idealises communal harmony is faced with internal conflicts and contradictions? (Falk Moore 1978: 32)

This chapter has explored how benefits of community life are met by other mechanisms which help deal with some of the related difficulties associated with the paradoxical drives towards community and individualism. On one hand, the ease of life, the emphasis on social contact and the perceived commonalities of those choosing this way of life (including their age) help establish a strong community. However, whilst the benefits of such a lifestyle are obvious, there are hidden paradoxes within the communitas, because of concerns about personal autonomy. The necessary recreations of authority, whilst offering new roles and sources of identity, disturb egalitarianism and provoke resistance from others, and the transience and possibilities for reinvention render friendships subject to scrutiny for their trustworthiness.

As a result of such tensions, the sociability in the expatriate community is accompanied by conflicts and other forms of social control. These both help to enable the expression of accentuated individuality and also overcome some of the problems relating to trust. With little secure knowledge of others' previous lives, knowledge of others is built up through word of mouth and reputation construction. And this concern with one's own and other's reputation both aids the construction of a safe and knowable community (as a 'good' reputation is earned through activities that help construct community) but also defines its values and limits. It is a subtle form of discipline, which maintains the egalitarian basis of society by exposing attempts at exclusivity using the threat of public opinion. As such, somewhat paradoxically, the emphasis on reputation — and the means of defining it through gossip — both diffuses the problems caused through the existence of an egalitarian community and yet helps to construct it. Indeed Spacks suggests it is the ambiguity of gossip which renders it so interesting, as it '...has good aspects and bad ones, it attests to community but can violate trust, it both helps and impedes group functioning' (1985: 258). In short, in Spain, gossip is both 'con-' and 'de'-structive of community, with the potential for both 'social unity *and* discord' (Percival 2000: 304). It is able to strengthen or limit bonds, shape consensus yet challenge it, and both build and diminish trust between individuals. These processes are so powerful because they appeal to the countervailing orientations of older migrants: to have a strong community, yet one in which their autonomy and past identities are respected.

7 Cultural Identities, Ageing and Death

Throughout the book, I have shown that moving to Spain engenders different imaginings of self and experiences achievable in retirement for British older migrants. Life in a new land however presents challenges of adjusting to linguistic and cultural difference at a later stage of life. This chapter focuses on how cultural identifications are experienced following this form of migration to Spain. It shows the multiplicity of post-migrant identities and shows how internal differentiation is used to narrate desired ageing identities.

In the first part of the chapter, I explore two broad orientations to national identity. On one hand, I consider how some people may be drawn to others of their own nationality and live according to age-influenced ideals of 'Britishness'. Many others, however, aspire to transcend these identity categorisations through claims of more 'cosmopolitan' or 'international' identifications. However, I show how these have symbolic associations, which support people's aspirations for certain classed and aged identities. In other words, the non-nationalist identity-claims and avoidance of group-membership are employed to narrate wider personal qualities of individualism and non-conformity as adventurous positive agers. These characteristics are contrasted to the putative restrictive and security-minded outlooks perceived in other people demonstrating more nationalist persuasions.

As in the other chapters, I explore the contradictions that influence migrants' identity aspirations, particularly around 'belonging' in Spain. In particular, the non-nationalist outlook adhered to by some people paradoxically rather subtly replays nationally-specific behaviour of class-distinction. Moreover, migrants' attempts to distinguish themselves from tourists (O'Reilly 2000a, Gustafson 2002, Oliver 2006) also ultimately limit the form of their relationships with Spanish people. Foreign residents' cultural fascination with Spain suggests their willingness to integrate, but yet it simultaneously reinforces a pseudo-touristic gaze that compounds mutually held perceptions of cultural difference. Moreover, whilst the excitement of a traveller existence is an ideal pursuit for healthy retirement, it is a risky endeavour, which may not, for a multitude of reasons, endure. The final part of the chapter shows how questions of belonging may be reassessed in relation to wider life course considerations, including the realities of ageing and death in a foreign land, particularly when it requires the negotiations of culturally different practices of disposal and memorialisation.

CULTURAL IDENTITY I — NATIONALITY, COSMOPOLITANISM AND LOCAL RELATIONS

A little Britain?

In Tocina, the receptionist of the *Pensionistas* observed, 'There are two classes of foreigner. A minority are interested in the culture...but the majority look for the sun'. Although speaking of foreigners in general, his observations echo a popular stereotype and 'thin description' of British migrants, depicting them as having limited engagement with locality and recreating a 'Little Britain' in Spain (O'Reilly 2000a: Chapter 1). However, according to O'Reilly, such collective representations do little to explain the phenomenon of the British in Spain. She shows in a Barthian analysis how British migrants attempt to integrate, but yet nevertheless construct a 'community' based on a British ethnic identity (2000a: Chapter 5 and see Rodriguez et al 1998). Others have shown this is not a process exclusive to British migrants; Gustafson (2001) documents how Swedish seasonal retirement migrants also may choose to orient themselves to a well-established Swedish infrastructure; they can listen to Swedish radio broadcasts, watch Swedish TV, speak little Spanish and use Swedish-speaking services (also see Huber and O'Reilly 2004 on Swiss migrants).

Such analyses support the notion that for some retired migrants at least, Spain is nothing more than a 'home plus sunshine' (Hannerz 1990: 241) which combines the advantages of the destination — such as the climate and the cost of living — with a recreation of migrants' familiar mode of existence. This was certainly the experience of Viv who lived in an urbanization on the outskirts of the town and explained that, 'it's just like being in England. I have a three-bedroomed house, just as I would in England. It's the same'. Viv spoke very little Spanish and socialised only with other English-speaking migrants from the International Club and American Club. Spain was purely a 'base' for her, and she still held strong feelings of attachment to Britain. She planned to return there eventually, particularly because when her husband had died, she had arranged for his body to be repatriated for burial at considerable cost. Viv's example suggests there is some truth behind the generalised observations of the limited engagement of older British migrants in Spain (Champion and King 1993).

The expatriate infrastructure is well developed in this area of Spain, including a number of national clubs, such as the British Legion, the French Club and the American Club, although some of these in this area have mixed national membership. Expatriate clubs rather cater to the general population of foreign residents, although, as is commonly found in international institutions (Zabusky 1995) English is the *lingua franca* (Rodrí-guez, Casado Díaz and Huber, 2000). These clubs are remarkably similar to other associations for expatriates worldwide (Forster, Hitchcock and Lyimo 2000 and see Verlot and Oliver 2005 for a comparison with EU civil servants in Brussels). Thompson and Tambyah refer to expatriate clubs in Singapore and explain they are often 'justified as temporary concessions to the difficulties of plugging into the local' (1999: 231) and certainly in Spain, the club infrastructure makes it easy for migrants like Viv, to engage in a lifestyle socially distant from local Spaniards. I rarely saw any Spanish visi-tors in the clubs, as Guillermo, a Spanish retired man who had attempted to join the expatriate's art club complained, 'it's a bit like a closed circle from my point of view, just the fact the meetings are in English, no? And they go to speak, to speak in English and if you only know a little of the lan-guage...'[1] Other clubs such as (ironically) 'the International club' in Tocina are run along the lines of a British social club; regular events there include darts evenings, based on the English TV show *Bullseye,* and monthly shop-ping and sight-seeing trips to Gibraltar. O'Reilly's (2000a) comprehensive account documents further examples of the ways Britishness is constructed amongst British residents in Spain.

However, one point, salient to the study of older migrants is impor-tant to consider. Much research on the recreations of cultural identities in migration tends to explore nationalisms as non-specific, but as I suggested in Chapter 1, it is also interesting to consider how post-migration identities are shaped by the characteristics of the particular migrants. In this context, the older age of the group inflects the nature of the recreation of national-ity, whilst reflections about nationality are equally used as an important resource to aid migrants' negotiations of ageing. In particular, O'Reilly's analysis of the essence of British nationality suggests that a key dimension of British national identity is the creation of a community spirit, 'reminis-cent of the rhetoric of war-time Britain and conjuring images of patriotism and unity' (O'Reilly 2000a: 92). This has resonance with themes found in generational identities in non-migrant contexts, where motifs of 'commu-nity' are important resources for older people's identity (Keith, 1980). Wil-liams' research on older Aberdonians from the interwar generation refers to how, for instance, 'fortitude and effort in confronting difficulties, domestic thrift in dealing with meagre rewards, a strongly sanctioned neighbourly ethic, and, for some, faithful religious belief, constituted the ideal identity of their generation'. (1990: 62). And Dawson's (1998, 2002) accounts of older people in a former mining community in the North East of Eng-land show that the 'community spirit' offers assurances of continuity that enable them to deal with change. This 'generational consciousness' (Wil-liams 1990: 60) when experienced with others living abroad, influences the construction of a specific national identity in the region, whose flavour is influenced by the life course stages of the migrants. And commentaries on the nation become ideal vehicles to express commentaries on generational difference (see Chapter 5), seen especially when positive visions of Spain are contrasted with an 'unidealised view of home' (O'Reilly 2000a: 98) in which Britain is a place where things are not as they 'used to be'. For example, Tony's positive reflections on the New Years' celebrations in Spain, where 'not one bottle in the morning was broken' was bolstered by his comparison with Britain, the homeland he had left because, 'I didn't like the way things are going. The younger generation are wrecking things'.

The intersection of generational and national identity is particularly shown in the activities of one association, the *Royal British Legion*, which has an important presence in the town. In their social gatherings and the more official ceremonies, the patriotic group prides itself on their ethos of staunch war-time loyalty. The Legion's formal meetings are held in a meeting place on the outskirts of town (also used by the Masonic Lodge) where the group's allegiance to the monarchy is displayed in a portrait of the Queen and a large Union Jack. Stories in the expatriate press also regularly feature the profiles of servicemen in the world wars; in this network, former military positions are regarded with awe, despite their apparent contradiction of the espoused egalitarian basis of the society (see Chapter 6). In fact, the group cherished the 'mascots' of the group, Roger and his wife, Pat. Roger was formerly a very high-ranking senior officer who worked with the Gurkhas in Burma, who was now in his nineties. His age and rank were the basis for continued respect by other members. He described how 'they'd lay down their lives for me if I asked them'.

Field (2000) argues that the experience of the Second World War significantly shapes participants' attitudes throughout their lives. Certainly in Spain, as in Britain, many of the Legion's social occasions are based on significant historical events from the Second World War. These can be particularly emotional moments as the collective group events provoke strong, personal memories. For example, at the British Legion one day, when planning the St George's Day lunch, the conversation turned to Victory in Japan day. Everyone there began to reminisce of where they were when it was announced. One man was in Bangladesh, Jan was a nurse in London and Tony recalled how he was on a ship when he heard Dutch people shouting the news. Sam said, 'you close your eyes and it's just like yesterday, so vivid', to which Judy added, 'and we all pulled together'. They wanted to include me in the conversation, and asked me out of interest what was the first thing I can remember. My description of a few childhood memories seemed bland in the absence of such definitive events. 'Not like the war' Judy said, at which Sam added, 'oh yes, it sticks there'.

The remembrance of war-time 'pulling together' amongst the British Legion is not purely reminiscence however, as it informs behaviours in the present. This is particularly evident in the sense of welfare responsibility to other ageing members (referred to in Chapter 5). Moreover, despite my age and lack of common experience, I was warmly welcomed by the tight-knit group, and this, I believe was informed by an emphasis on manners and respect. It was a principle also reflected in their attitudes to Spanish people. For example, following the hospitalisation of one of its key members, the group organised the presentation of some 'certificates of appreciation' (in both English and Spanish) to the local hospital (see Figure 7.1). Furthermore, when members died, their send-off was also treated with solemnity and respect, as the standard was paraded, a Union Jack draped over the coffin and other members of the military offered a salute.

Figure 7.1 Certificates of appreciation. Thanks to the committee of the local branch of the Royal British Legion for providing these copies.

Perhaps there is an element of these funerals which are resonant with the ideas of being buried in 'a corner of a foreign field', (from Rupert Brooke's poem *The Soldier*[2] [1915] 1999) as so vividly remembered during the Remembrance Service, the central point of the year for this association. The service is announced weeks in advance in the migrants' media and draws coachloads of pilgrims in the shape of older tourists from neighbouring resorts. On the occasions I attended, the standard bearer stood outside the church solemnly (see Figure. 7.2) and during the service, the money collectors marched in perfect unison in silence to offer the donations to the priest. The sound of the bugle moved some of the women with me to tears; The Remembrance Service was all the more intense because so many people in the Church had lived through the Second World War, and indeed for a few, the First World War. The commemoration had particular emotional meaning for the individuals, all growing older, and perhaps ultimately also dying, far from the homeland.

The example also highlights the place of religion in constructions of national belonging (Anderson 1983). Certainly in Catholic Spain, the Anglican church, and its outreach services, is a focal point of the British 'community' life for the mainly elderly congregation (see King et al 2000: 151–152). The position of the church is also emblematic of some of the difficulties facing British migrants, as the congregation has no premises of its own, and the services are held at a Catholic church. The parish also suffered problems of stability (see Chapter 6); during my fieldwork the priest died and Eddy, a popular priest who was there only on a temporary basis also returned back to Britain. Despite these upheavals, the church services invoke continuity through its unchanging rituals. This is similar to what Fortier (1999) observes in the use of Catholic rituals, including mass, as a means of sustaining collective identity amongst Italian migrants in Britain. Bell (1999: 3) summarises how, through embodied movements, the citations in mass operate, 'to recall and reconnect with places elsewhere that, through these very movements are remembered; at the same time, a site of diasporic belonging is created'. Amongst British migrants in Spain, services follow the same Anglican order of service used in Britain, whilst hymns with nationalist themes contribute to the maintenance of an English national identity (such as William Blake's *Jerusalem* with its reference to 'England's green and pleasant land'). When the hymn, 'I vow to thee my country' was sung at one service, the vicar said, 'let us move from thoughts of *our* country to the heavenly country'. It seemed unlikely that he was referring to Spain.

Avoiding 'the Brits': Internationalism and individualism

I swore that I would never ever ever set foot in an English bar. (Willie, village migrant)

Figure 7.2 The Remembrance Service. Photograph by author.

Whilst national identity and group membership are important resources for some British migrants, it has been shown how post-migration identities are heterogeneous and be displayed in a variety of different ways (Griswold 1994, Malkki 1995[3]). In Spain, Gustafson's (2001) study of seasonal Swedish migrants demonstrates the varying degrees of engagement of different people in both Spain and Sweden. This is equally true in the case of British migrants, where there were a surprising proportion of British migrants who, sometimes quite forcefully, rejected their national identifications. They claimed rather cosmopolitan, international or European identities, evidenced, they believed through their interactions with other nationalities and/or their cultural fascination with Spain. However, these intersect with aspirations for ageing experiences, because the identities are narrated as associated with qualities of mobility, individualism, stimulation, and education, which are the essential ingredients of a positively ageing existence.

In this case, when people assume international identities, they reiterate familiar distinctions of leisured 'traveller' and 'tourist' (Ryan 1991, Crick 1989, Jacobsen 2000) that help construct authentic retirement identities of activity, risk and authenticity as opposed to the safe comforts of home.

One of those claiming a 'cosmopolitan' identity was Barbara, a retired accountant originally from Britain, who settled in Southern Spain following periods working in Switzerland, Monaco, Geneva, California, London, Hong Kong, Iran and Belgium. She said, 'Nationality, or being English means nothing to me. I believe in Europe. Myself and my friends here', [referring to her German walking companions] we believe that we are the real Europeans'. And, Trisha, a former international banker who had moved to Freila to downgrade her life to run a bed and breakfast explained,

> I've absolutely always been fascinated with other cultures, other peoples...My first husband was a Russian, my second a Yugoslav, and well, what with my job [a banker]... I'm a linguist too, I always knew I'd come to a foreign country. It takes months and probably years to understand how and why people think the way that they do.

She saw her new role as to bring different people together: 'You share what you have, and you also learn from them', she explained.

Hannerz identifies cosmopolitans as those for whom 'entering other cultures is first and foremost a personal journey of discovery' (1992: 252). They adopt an open stance towards different cultural experiences, developing a competence in their dealings with others, and who may feel the homes of their precosmopolitan past hold 'some risk of boredom' (ibid.: 254). Zabusky's (1995) ethnography of national diversity in European co-operation in Space science shows how workers also extol the stimulation found in working with others of different backgrounds and contrast this with working within national industries, 'where work was perceived to be more "boring"' (ibid.: 162). As these descriptions show, cosmopolitan identifications are not neutral categories but are symbolic of other personal qualities. Thus when foreign residents in Spain commonly claimed a cosmopolitan or more international stance, it was often as a means of distinction against apparently restrictive, exclusivist nationalisms, evident in others' 'Little Britain' mentality. Rachel, for example, compared herself favourably to those in the town, pointing out, 'I live in an urbanization. It's very international...' and added disparingly, 'not like Tocina'. Many people also explained their choice to move to this part of the region for its 'authenticity' as more 'Spanish' and maintained that they avoided the British-run infrastructure. Joy pointed out, 'It's more Spanish here than you'd find on the Costa — you know it's all kiss-me-quick hats and fish and chips'. Here, the 'costa' and all its collective representations (see O'Reilly 2000a: 2–8) are located further down the coast. Joy was also a keen participant at the fine arts club, a group whose origins were English, but which had a cosmopolitan attendance, including some people who explicitly avoided other expatriate clubs. Monthly lectures were given by experts on topics including, 'the magnificent Medici', 'the Etruscans', or 'Vermeer: New Light on a master of mystery' in the exclusive Parador Hotel in the town. Joy referred jokingly to the cosmopolitan nature of the group by reinterpreting the society's acronym of DADFAS as 'Dutch and Danes, Finns and Swedes!'

In these discourses of internationalism, stereotypes of other British people as a collective category are articulated internally within the foreign residents' community. For instance, themes of colonialism were regularly employed by foreign residents to explain the behaviours of others, as Sharon referring to 'the International Club that is 99.9% English' disparagingly described as, 'the English colony implanted in the centre of Tocina'. And when Clare, Brian, Annie and Peter were discussing Peter's forthcoming eightieth birthday party, the topic got around to describing the behaviour of 'the Brits' who attended the expatriate clubs:

Caroline: Do you have much to do with the clubs?
Peter: No
Annie: We could have if we wanted to but...
Peter: ...but they're all so old aren't they when they're about 40? And they're British.
Annie: They're all Brits. British ankle socks and cardigans and sandals.
Brian: No we don't use British bars...
Annie: They're so 'king boring, British bars here they really are. Everyone has almost the same stool every day.
Peter: And they're double the price
Brian: And you get the same old questions, "how long have you lived here? how long have you been here? Do you like it?"
Annie: Do you like it!
Peter: After twenty years here, do you like it?!
Annie: I could hit them [laughing]

In these cases, national identity is associated with the qualities of being 'old', 'boring' and being 'stuck in the past' (utilising a common stereotype of older people, see Degnen 2007). Sarah, in her seventies, a former Women's Royal Air Force member explained, for instance, how she ventured down from the village to test out the British Legion and said, 'they seemed so *old*. I think, I can't be as old as them, but I suppose I am, it's just I don't feel it, and I did when I was there'. Mary also felt that being part of nationally-oriented groups encouraged a nostalgic outlook, explaining, 'of course, I could succumb to Fiona and the like and go to all those clubs. But that life is an English life, singing songs and hymns and things. I find it all too sentimental, like looking in a photo album'. And Elizabeth's disparaging comments on collective club life also portrays national orientations as constraining, restrictive and associated with oldness:

> the International Club! It's not international, it's English! I hate the way it's organised, it's like by going there you are wearing a tag, being labelled...I didn't come for that. It's cliquey, they get together for coffee to tell tales...There's lots of class struggles and struggles between the military. They are all very well off, very educated but so boring. For the same reasons I couldn't live in England...you just get together at parties for old people and it's boring. I can smell that sort a mile off, I'm not that way. I find it as objectionable here as I do in England. I've never felt that way, I can't be bothered with that national nonsense — I just want to 'be', mix with young, old, English, French, Spanish...I don't care as long as they are interesting.

Elizabeth's forceful articulations reveal how values of cultural identity intersect with multiple other identity associations and moralities. Attachment to former British lifestyles in Spain is judged by many as evidence of an unadventurous outlook, which does not correspond with other people's own narratives of stimulation and adventure. Thus, it was common for people to negatively comment on others who were perceived as recreating England in the sun. Indeed when Vera set up small café in Freila selling tea, coffee, and cakes and snacks, the venture was looked upon disapprovingly as evidence of an Anglicanisation of the village by some older migrants, who had assumed because Vera had lived in the *campo* for some time, she shared their non-nationalist 'cosmopolitan' outlook. One day, Vera moaned that she had to go to 'grotty' Gibraltar to buy raisins sold in the Safeway store there for her homemade cakes. This was ironic, because almost every other house in Freila had signs advertising the local speciality *pasas*, huge, juicy raisins of superior quality to the shrivelled, rabbit-dropping-like variety sold in Safeways. However, Vera maintained her cakes would not taste the same using those. Sharon complained one day whilst walking past the cafe disparagingly, 'she should know better' and complained, 'why do people do these things? Out of security I suppose'.

Sharon's evaluation of others' attachment to national goods as borne out of security corresponds with wider symbolic associations vested in places. O'Reilly identifies how for seasonal visitors to Spain, 'Britain signalled security and Spain the opposite' (2000a: 95) and Gustafson reports similarly how some seasonal migrants' journeys to Spain 'came to signify life and health' (2001: 377) whilst Sweden represented comfort and security. However, these symbolic associations also explain the lure of the familiar in Spain. Indeed, ironically, as time went by, many of the opponents to Vera's café who prided themselves on resisting living as 'Brits' in Spain, nevertheless guiltily 'gave in' to comforts offered from British products and bought Vera's cakes. Judy, a devoted hispanophile, also explained how she had 'succumbed' to buying satellite TV so that she could watch the BBC (and see Mary's fear of 'succumbing', p 139). I myself felt vulnerable to negative evaluations at the risk of being caught when I bought a particular British brand of tinned tomato soup when ill, rather than choosing to consume the delicious local gazpacho.

As such, when people assert their avoidance of the trappings of their own nationality, they also claim other personal desirable qualities of distinctiveness and freedom from the crowd. For instance, Elizabeth often commented on the imagined nationalist practices of other migrants living on the coast and said, 'I detest nationality. I flinch when they try and put me in a box'. Similarly, Jim, a seasonal migrant, responded to my query as to how I might describe British residents in Spain and wrote his email to me from 'a split-resident European'. He wrote, 'put me in a box but not one with a screwed down lid!' (Oliver 2006). For Jim, a 'British' label implied a categorical, restrictive group identity that contradicted his personal ethos of independence. Rather some people prided themselves on displaying individualistic or 'eccentric' identities; Chris Stewart, a 'good life abroad' novelist writes of inland Andalucía, 'There seems to be a preponderance of eccentric women among the foreigners here' (1999: 186) and Waldren (1997) notes how Deià, a village in Mallorca was valued as an attractive retreat for individualists and eccentrics. In Freila, Mary, a long term resident, relished her own eccentric reputation, describing with glee how she was known as, 'the batty old woman' on the hill. Mary regularly took in numerous stray cats and dogs, rarely socialised in group situations, and enjoyed her notoriety for speaking her mind. She had developed a friendship with another woman who also found it difficult to resist taking in abandoned cats and said, 'she's as mad as me, I know I'm a nut!'

Waldren notes that longer term foreign residents are protective of a particular way of life that they see themselves committed to, whereby, 'outside the mainstream or accepted norms of their own and the local culture, each was endeavouring to create an identity based on the criteria of activity, knowledge and freedom of choice in all aspects of their lives' (1997:67). The growing numbers of British migrants moving into the area disrupts these individualistic aims. In Freila, the presence of other 'bloody Brits' (see Chapter 2) was enough to make Derek move to a village inland in the hope of finding a more unspoilt site. Elizabeth also recounted the time many years ago when some other English people came to the village, built a house and invited her for drinks '...just because I was English. Well to hell with all that', she explained, 'just because they had a double-barrelled surname!' Ironically, however, these processes of distinction from other British people can also be understood as reflecting other expressions of British national identity, based on more middle class values of reserve and distance (see Strathern 1992 and Chapter 2). As Elizabeth's example showed, some migrants enact the practices of British travellers in the past who avoided others of their own nationality (Langford 2000). One expatriate writer explicitly describes how when moving to a white village in Andalucía, his family cultivated similar reserve to Victorian travellers by observing only a polite distance to others of the same nationality (Seymour-Davies 1996). Yet, in engaging in these practices, the articulations of 'cosmopolitanism' reflect simply a different style of national identity (see Oliver 2000) particularly when considering these articulations are sometimes made to an audience of a select group of friends of their own nationality.

The examples above demonstrate as such that the practice of distancing from other 'Brits' intersects with other mechanisms of class distinction. Sociological analysis, emerging from the work of Bourdieu, considers class not only as economic disparity, but as related to cultural forms or, 'the means by which people become judged as morally worthwhile, or as having the right kind of knowledge or 'taste'' (Lawler 2005: 797). In this part of Spain, evidence of national attachment is read by some retirees as poor taste, particularly revealed in longer term migrants' antipathy to the 'new lot' of (often lower class) 'Brits' arriving, who are conflated with mass tourists. Brian, in the company of four other British friends, said:

> the British tourists are embarrassing and I think a lot of the people who move out here now are a different breed....They come here and they only go for the Brits who want to be with Brits...what were they called today? "The Lottery Winners".

Brian was dismayed when the new people at the back of his house put up a sign to advertise their business. He said, 'they have no intention of integrating at all with the Spanish and they've done it exactly like *happy holiday sands: welcome to the caravan site!*...It's got a big sun in the corner, I cringe when I go past it, but they want this to be Britain'. As this demonstrates, those envisaged to represent the very worst of nationality are reprimanded by migrants utilising a class morality around taste and manners. Lily commented on Brian's story, 'It's disgraceful. It's insulting the country' whilst the inability to speak at least a smattering of Spanish she described, 'rudeness in another country'. This is often compared to migrants' own efforts to learn the language, which are 'a sign of courtesy to the host country', as Jenny explained.

Nowhere is this perceived insulting attitude manifested more strongly than in the epitome of the worst of the Brits: the tourists. Tourists are not only regular reminders of where migrants come from and what sorts of lives they have left, but through their presence have set in place a negative shift in migrants' status *vis à vis* locals (Waldren 1996). Their potential closeness however lays the grounds for the construction of firm distinctions by foreign residents[4] (Gustafson 2002 and O'Reilly 2000, 2003, Oliver 2006) through jokes, disparaging depictions (O'Reilly 2000a) and claims that they lead different sorts of lives (Gustafson 2002). I have argued elsewhere (Oliver 2006) that these commentaries on tourists reflect migrants' wider concerns about productivity and authenticity in ageing. For instance, migrants use narratives of strength and persistence to describe themselves, as Lilian commented, 'you have to be tough to survive it here'. By contrast, tourists, like other 'Brits', are shown as living in safely circumscribed worlds (Turner and Ash 1975, Urry 2002) run by hotel managers and travel agents who act as 'surrogate parents' to 'relieve the tourist of responsibility and protect him/her from harsh reality' (Urry 2002: 7). Foreign residents emphasise — as in the case of other 'Brits'— the putative unadventurous traits and lack of individuality shown by tourists. For example, they refer to tourists as 'herds' who follow a circuit through the main causeway of the village, going up and down certain steps. And some village migrants also referred to the main touristic urbanization in town as 'toy-town', 'that holiday camp' and like 'a rabbit hutch', extending themes of childhood dependency, overbearing security and containment to their depictions of tourism (Rojek 1985 and Oliver 2006).

Such distinctions however reflect class identities because antipathy is particularly felt towards *mass* tourists (Gustafson 2002). Lawler (2005) suggests that depicting working class people as a 'mob' or 'mass' has long been a cultural practice through which middle-class individuality can be asserted. Unsurprisingly, retirees' narratives of mass tourism regularly reveal themes of congestion and pollution, in which short-stay tourists are presented as clogging up the system and causing traffic jams through their force of number. Molly, a usually quiet woman, found herself flapping her arms and exploding, 'get out of my way' to the tourists wandering aimlessly in front of her when she wanted to get to a café to meet her friend. Moreover, tourists' imagined — and sometimes evident — inappropriate attitude and behaviour, such as heavy drinking and bad manners (Gustafson 2002) is seen as an embarrassing affront to migrants' reputations. Marjorie explained:

> I find it terrible in summer, I go back then. It's because there's all these people who let the side down. I was in Iceland [a shop selling frozen goods], and there was one woman, really large and all, wearing a Marks and Spencer's bra on top. I can understand Spanish and I heard the shopkeeper going on about how disgusting it was. It's the type of people who come, clogging up the road. It's a different place here then.

Marjorie's assertion that 'they let the side down' suggests a feeling of embarrassment at being perceived as part of the same group, and as with distinctions against 'the Brits', the theme of morality and manners is employed to mark the boundaries. Annie told me, 'I hate to see as much in the way of bad manners as I see the Brits towards Spanish waiters. There's never a please or thank you or...they're just pigs. It's really embarrassing'. The repulsion felt at Brits and tourists and the representations of their perceived grotesque behaviours suggest they are somewhat 'matter out of place' (Douglas 1966) in this case, disrupting the 'Spanishness' of the site through their rude reminders of nationality.

Belonging in Spain: The Lens of Cultural Fascination

Objections to tourists and other 'Brits' must also be understood in reference to some retirees' aspirations for retirement to integrate in 'real' Spain. Rodriguez et al (1998) show that whilst many retirement migrants live quite separate lives from Spanish people, they nonetheless attach a great deal of importance to a 'Spanish lifestyle'. O'Reilly (2002, 2004) also argues that many expatriates are motivated by an attraction to Spain and a Spanish way of life, despite their failure to integrate into Spanish society. Certainly it was common to find retirees — of both 'national' and more 'cosmopolitan' orientations — stressing authentic engagement and integration in Spain. This ranged from simply knowing which bars Spaniards use, having local knowledge (Gufstafson 2002), employing a Spanish gardener, or by pursuing fully-fledged studies of Spanish history and culture. However, as I show, there is a risk that this rearticulates a pseudo-touristic 'gaze' on Spanish people, who become falsely objectified as part of the attraction of the site. King, Warnes and Williams comment, 'the notion of the 'friendly local' is part of the imagination of a 'rural idyll' or arcadia that some retired British possess: evidence to confirm those notions may be unconsciously privileged over contrary indications' (2000: 120). This outlook, in consequence, limits real engagement.

Many retired migrants, particularly those claiming a more 'cosmopolitan' orientation, stressed their genuine cultural fascination with Spain and 'Spanishness'. In this region, it was common for migrants to write stories about their move to Spain (which are published in local magazines) that are similar to travel writing or 'expat abroad' accounts of adjustment to the challenges of life in Spain. Others wrote poetry and short stories, painted or drew 'traditional' Spanish scenes (see Brenda's Christmas card of sedentary older Spanish people in traditional attire knitting in Figure. 7.3). Kate also gave me a number of stories she had written based on anecdotes on, 'how life used to be' in Spain, which had been published in some of the free magazines. They focused on topics such as, 'the village blacksmith', 'the dignity of illiteracy' and 'courtship', which compared old courtship customs when she first came to those in the present. Within such accounts, the reading of the landscape and people is framed within a romantic and quasi-anthropological interest. For example, a poet in the village referred to how, 'it's funny to see how the men ride their *motos* [motorbikes] like mules'. Other migrants were almost amateur anthropologists, hypothesising their knowledge of Spanish characters gleaned from observations of life there. It is interesting to note representations often stressed an Andalucían non-conformism and willingness to bend the rules, which complement their own values, as Brian explained:

Brian: I was at the market one day on a Sunday and there was this Moroccan guy there with his car. You know how the Moroccans overload their cars and he'd got everything jammed inside so much so that he couldn't turn the wheel and he was like really struggling. And they told him to go and park his car somewhere. And the *guardia* (civil guard) was actually laughing. Instead of saying, 'we're going to prosecute you for overloading your vehicle, you can't drive it safely, duh duh duh,' he was not only laughing but he was pointing to people, 'come and have a look at this'. *[All laughing]*

Annie: Have you ever seen anything like it?

Brian: Absolute entertainment for five minutes whilst he's trying to turn the wheel.

Caroline: That sort of attitude attracts you?

Annie: Course it does!

Figure 7.3 A Christmas card drawn by Brenda, a British retired migrant, depicting an older Spanish couple. Thanks to Brenda Haddon.

Some migrants' activities are more specifically directed towards helping to preserve Spanish traditions against an encroaching modernity. A report in *the Observer* outlines the role of expatriates in fighting against new building developments ('British import Nimbyism to save Spanish retreats', Fuchs, 19 June 2005). In the village, Elizabeth felt concern that the *ayuntamiento* (municipal government) planned to illuminate her house, the old tower, and she was concerned that this would remove the 'mystical' atmosphere of the site. In the village, a number of foreign residents also established and participated in a mixed nationality voluntary group to report upon the traditions, customs, style and architecture of the village in the face of progress and change (Oliver 2002). Others living in the village or *campo* have restored their old houses in a 'gentrified Mediterranean' style, using original materials for doors and window-frames, old tiles and rustic beams inside. One observer in another inland village mirthfully pointed out how house decoration was as she described, *rustico-Monopoly*, a competition through which the more rustic the house, the more kudos can be gained in the foreign community. These practices of showing cultural interest in Spain, not only support personal authentic identities, but are cited as evidence of integrating in Spain. Thus although Tony, the chairman of one of the associations admitted he did not speak as much Spanish as he liked, he described himself as 'well integrated', qualifying this with, 'I came here for Spain. We've just been to Toledo, it was remarkable, it's real Spain, with real history'. He loved this part of the region because, again, it was 'real Spain'.

There is indeed a moral esteem levelled at those who show evidence of engagement with 'local culture' and attempt to learn the language. This interest is a source of distinction against the 'new foreigners' (Waldren 1997:67) who are deemed to show less interest in the locality. Many of the leisure clubs stage opportunities to learn more about the region, running visits to sites such as the Alhambra or Phoenician and Roman ruins. Whilst these may regularly also feature in tourist itineraries, the tours for migrants differ in that they are opportunities for people to demonstrate their knowledge from reading and studying. Judy's oversubscribed history club runs guided tours to destinations such as Jaen, 'Garcia Lorca's Granada' and Córdoba, with lectures and reading lists accompanying them. Such practices blur the boundaries of work, education and tourism and are congruent with the time of the third age as one of learning. As such, they bolster retirees' narratives of autonomy and moral betterment through travel (see Chapter 3); by engaging in these processes, retirees, like cultural tourists, 'accept the invitation to become a better person' (Rojek and Urry 1997: 4). This cultural interest is also welcomed from some Spaniards; for instance, Jorge, a man on the committee in the *pensionistas* in Tocina explained that he would like more foreigners to participate in the centre: 'because they would teach us. For example, Judy: a very intelligent lady, we like her because she teaches us things [about] Spain's history that we don't know'.[5]

However, a stance of cultural fascination, although well-intentioned would permit integration only in some sectors of Spanish society, and for most, restricts the nature of integration that can occur. For instance, taking part in religious rituals is considered a key means of participation in the *pueblos* (see Figure 7.4), but the majority of foreign residents, as non-Catholics attend the ritual occasions only as spectators. One example is the *día de la cruz* (the day of the cross) in May, when people make flower crosses to decorate the village. Yet as María commented, 'locals make the crosses and they're [foreigners] like, watching, not participating. It's rare to find people participating'.[6] Indeed, when I attended the communal meal after one procession, I was the only foreigner attending. This, of course, depends on the nature of events; some (often younger) foreign migrants participated in their children's first communion and a few migrants, such as Judy, attended Catholic services regularly. However, John explained how he had attempted to attend mass in the village, but found the formal nature of the services — and particularly the lack of songs — unappealing. And even Elizabeth, a Catholic, explained with regard to the ritual festivities, 'once you've seen one procession, you've seen them all'.

The social distance also has practical and political implications. In the last few years, voting rights for municipal elections have been granted to EU residents, which at the outset provoked some speculation that foreigners could potentially install foreign mayors (Marina ABC 1 January 1994). As it has transpired, there is general disinterest, the uptake of voting rights

Figure 7.4 San Antonio. Photograph by author.

is low (Rodríguez, Casado Díaz and Huber, 2000, O'Reilly 2004) and foreign candidates have not achieved highly (*El País* 27 June 1999). In Tocina,
there is a German Town Councillor, but in the village, as Jesús and María
discussed, it was difficult to attract interest from foreign residents:

Jesús: Freila has a large census of foreigners. And there should be a
           foreigner involved on the list, but there aren't many.
María: Last year... one...
Jesús: One?
María: Well, one on the PA [Partido Andalucista] list.
Jesús: But at the bottom, nearly the last one. And then in the 'Greens',
           when they didn't find people for the lists they got more foreigners.
           But only because they didn't find anyone (laughs). I was involved
           in making the list for the party I belong to and there was just one
           foreigner but...
María: It took effort.
Jesús: ...Tocina has a German Town Councillor and the man works
           hard and does things...but not here; here everything's laid on for
           them. And they don't get involved in the festivities, either.[7]

The foreign residents' interest in Spain is limited to more cultural matters, which sustains notions of cultural difference. However, these are met
by similar perceptions held by Spanish people, who regard the foreigners
as distinct from local people; having different habits, outlooks and roles
in local life. Spaniards' comments on the presence of foreigners was overwhelmingly positive (although this was undoubtedly influenced by my own
position as a foreigner), but people often qualified their responses with
reference to the economic benefits associated with foreigners in general,
whether tourists or residents (see also Rodríguez et al 2000). Álvaro, a businessman answered my enquiries into relationships with foreign migrants
with the response that the only negative issue associated with the foreigners' presence was rising prices. Failing to distinguish between migrants and
tourists he maintained, 'we're lucky to have tourism, it's a privilege that
other villages wish to have'.[8] Foreign residents are particularly viewed as
important to the local economy because their consumption helps overcome
the seasonality of the tourist industry; they eat in the restaurants all year
round, their visitors spend money in the handicraft shops and tradesmen
find regular employment through working on their properties.

Indeed, despite the positive reception, Spaniards nevertheless see the
foreigners in their midst as distinct, as evidenced through various linguistic references as '*extranjero*' (foreigner) or '*forastero*' (outsider) or sometimes in slang as '*guiris*'[9] (referring to Northern European foreigners and
tourists). Thus although many Spaniards had foreign residents as friends,
when pressed about the nature and degree of relationships, they nevertheless discussed the multiple differences that set them apart from foreigners.

As referred to in Chapter 1, this can be explained through the problems of limited communication; many interactions are constrained by the use of an elementary sign-language and physical gestures.[10] My Spanish landlady, María, explained how she related with her retired British neighbours who seasonally inhabit the house next to their rural *cortijo* (farmhouse) and said, 'we speak 'red Indian' (*'Hablamos como los indios'*) and 'through signs' (*'por señas'*). And Guillermo commented, 'I've got some neighbors and there's no way...they say to you "bye" in Spanish and "very thanks" and we have to communicate through sign language'.[11] And distance also arose out of wider perceptions of cultural difference. Whether it was different meal times or a different manner of alcohol consumption, many foreigners had, as María explained, *'otra forma de ver la vida distinta'* — a different way of seeing life. A number of Spanish people suggested that foreigners 'make their own circles' through going to particular bars and clubs where other foreigners congregate. But this distance was felt both ways, as other British migrants, such as Ed, explained, 'you'll always be a foreigner here'. David, a qualified Spanish teacher, fluent in Spanish, also observed, 'there is a mutual drawing back'.

CULTURAL IDENTITY II: ASSESSING LIFESTYLES IN AGEING AND DEATH

I have shown that although many people express attachment to living in Spain, their aspirations for belonging are somewhat restricted by the very motivations which draw them there. However, it is important also to acknowledge how the aspiration itself is also subject to change, and liable to become more or less salient at different points in time. O'Reilly (2000a) observes that full residents in Spain often hold a myth of (no) return, in which migrants rarely see themselves returning to Britain, and possess a wider sense of ambivalence about their nationality (ibid. 2002). Indeed, many migrants feel strong attachments to Spain and intend never to return (Warnes 2004), a feeling reflected in Lynn's statement that, 'I'd never go back, never!' However, as Ackers and Dwyer (2002) point out, migrants' trajectories shift between different forms of migration (from holidays, to renting, to permanent living and returning home), which demonstrates how attachments to place regularly come under revision. In the final section of this chapter, I consider how lifestyles may be particularly reviewed when aspects of ageing intervene. I also explore briefly how differences in death and disposal are negotiated in the ultimate sedentarisation of these older age travellers.

First, the reluctance to return to Britain, commonly expressed by many older people, must be considered within a framework of cultural references about aspirations for good ageing and the associations with 'home'. As I showed in Chapter 4, assertions of staying 'forever' in Spain are made in a temporal framework geared towards the present. Furthermore, throughout the book I have shown that many associations of the homeland, particularly those to do with the experience of ageing, are negative, especially when compared to the enjoyable experiences of life in Spain. These images however are undoubtedly confirmed by the fact that when people do move back to the UK, it is often because of painful circumstances. In the course of my fieldwork, when people returned, it was often because of their deteriorating health, the fact that they had insufficient resources to finance private care, or was prompted by the death of a partner, which rendered it difficult to continue living in Spain (see Linda, Chapter 4, and Monica, John, Jan, Bob, Rose, Josie and Jane, Chapter 5). For those left behind, it is unsurprising that movement back to the homeland can therefore come to signify an 'end' of sorts (see the justification of Roger's reluctance to leave in Chapter 5, 'to move back would be like giving up wouldn't it? Like admitting, well that's it, that's your life gone'). This informs many people's stated reluctance to move; Hilda was fending off her family's requests that she returned to Britain, because she explained, 'If I go back, I'll have to go in a home'.

However, although most migrants expressed the desire to remain in Spain and certainly many did, a significant proportion face returning at some point. For seasonal migrants engaging in a peripatetic lifestyle, this eventual return is planned; for instance, Gustafson (2001) shows that Swedish seasonal migrants expected to remain in Sweden rather than Spain in the event of ill-health or death of a spouse. However, it may also be considered at some point for 'permanent' migrants. In a financial advice supplement in a newspaper, an advisor wrote:

> Many [expatriates] will say that Spain is now their permanent home and they will stay here for the rest of their lives or, as one client told me, 'until hell freezes over'. However, they, like most others, then admitted that they would probably return home if one or other or both became ill or one of them had died — note the use of the word 'home' even though they had no house in Britain. (Floodgate 1999: xiv)

There is little data on the extent of return migration, although in the course of my fieldwork, I observed that despite assertions to the contrary, over time, many people's previously strongly held attachments to location of residence and associated lifestyles were often rethought when their experiences of ageing necessitated. This is not only evident in returns to the homeland, but as King, Warnes and Williams' (2000) survey showed, nearly half of retired migrants in their study moved at least once within the destination region, for varying reasons including a change in household makeup, decreased income, personal mobility and changes in the neighbourhood. Indeed Derek who had moved to an inland village to 'escape the bloody Brits', moved down to the coast to safer bungalow accommodation when he was diagnosed with cancer, much to the surprise of Elizabeth. During the course of my fieldwork, both Sarah and Dorte also reluctantly moved for health reasons from Freila to the urbanizations in town, despite Sarah's former observation a year or two before that 'I couldn't stand the urbanization life — no way!' Joy's move back to Britain was also preceded by a number of steps; she moved away from a hill village down to an urbanization in the town because the dampness in her house aggravated her arthritis. She eventually moved back to Britain, although she still returned to Spain for visits.

Decisions to move back to Britain permanently are often made on the basis of more practical than aspirational reasons, and certainly a significant factor for most is public healthcare (Dwyer 2000) and comfort in old age. Elizabeth's friend, who had lived in Spain for thirty years grew increasingly deaf and moved back to Britain so he could benefit from small comforts including reading subtitles on the television in his care home. For those who retain their domiciliary in England[12] (see King, Warnes and Williams 2000: 109-110) the move is relatively easy. Yet the examples of Bob, Jean and Rose in Chapter 5 demonstrate how return movement may be complicated by difficulties in selling houses, arranging the removal of belongings and the transportation of beloved pets at vulnerable times.

When circumstances change to the extent that moving 'home' is likely, I found amongst some people a tendency to reinterpret and invert former values associated with place. As permanent migrants prepared to move, the freedom of Spain or lifestyles inland were sometimes rather presented as risky and dangerous rather than exciting, with the security and comfort of the homeland, desired (although see the exception of Doreen, Chapter 5, who despite moving back was keen to 'inject' her life in Britain with the spirit of life in Spain). When Josie was planning to go back to the United States after twelve years in Spain, her depiction of Spain therefore became deeply unflattering, as she repeated stories of older people in difficulty, how her friends were mugged, the increasing cost of living there and a perceived rudeness of Spanish people. Bob and Jan moved back to Britain and on a visit back to Spain they emphasised the home-comforts (such as central heating and soft carpets on the floor) of life in Britain, and maintained that they had made the right decision.

Despite the lure of the comforts of the homeland when suffering ill health, nevertheless, there were plenty of people in my study who were adamant that they would remain in Spain until death. Certainly, death occurs in the foreign residents' community on a fairly regular basis; Marjorie, for instance, tallied one death that occurred as, 'the third one this year' and in my second year of fieldwork four of her close friends died, as another woman put it, 'one after the other'. At the annual meeting of the British Legion, the meeting began with an exhortation and tribute to eight members that had died that year. From a sociological point of view, these occurrences of death in migration raise interesting questions. It is an occasion when beliefs about collective identities are made visible (Jonker 1997, Reimers 1999) whilst memories of how death is treated in the homeland may influence how the receiving country's customs are judged (Jonker 1997).

In Andalucía, the systems of administration, disposal and memorial are distinct from those in Britain (see Oliver 2004 for a fuller account). First, death and disposal is dealt with more rapidly in Spain, usually within a day or forty-eight hours. In the village, usually a public Catholic *misa* (mass) is followed by immediate interment and a memorial service is held some weeks later. Moreover, in Mediterranean Spain, 'burial', as is known in Britain rarely occurs, and interment is instead practiced in above-ground 'niches'. These are concrete structures, arranged in long rows and built up to six or seven niches high (see Figure. 7.5). Instead of burial, coffins are simply placed inside the niche and sealed up by concrete, which are later covered by memorial plaques. The ledges of the niches are commonly decorated with flowers (artificial or real) and figurines and votive candles are often placed in a glass display case over the plaque. What is starkly different to UK practices is that niches are not necessarily for permanent use; they can be reused after a time-period that is decided by the municipality (in this area, after a minimum of five years). People must pay to continue the use of the niche, otherwise a sticker is placed on the grave from the *ayuntamiento* (municipality) to give notice of the removal of remains, which are then placed in a common ossuary. For those foreign residents who face dealing with a death in Spain, they must generally adhere to the shorter timescale of the process, although some choose to extend the short period between death and disposal through use of cold storage in Málaga, 50kms away. They may also avoid niche interment by choosing cremation or underground burial (again in Málaga), or they can opt for the expensive process of repatriating the body for burial in Britain, as Viv's earlier example shows.

Adjustment to these practices of death and disposal is however informed by cultural beliefs, and significant differences emerge between retired migrants and Spanish people. Ariès' well-known treatise, *Western attitudes toward death* (1976) documents attitudes to death in North-West Europe and North America. He shows how the public acknowledgement and simple ritual management of death in the Middle Ages shifted to death as a romanticised process (ibid.: 56). Yet by the middle of the twentieth century, death occurred rather as a sequestered, private and individualised occurrence, as, 'a technical phenomenon, obtained by a cessation of care' (ibid.: 88). The custom of treating death as a private event amongst North-Western Europeans was reflected upon by a Spanish friend, who explained to me how she had felt puzzled when her neighbour, a foreign woman died, and 'we found out three days later that she had died'. She mused, 'No, they see it [death] in a different way'.[13] Conversely, the less private treatment of death observed in Spain[14] provided a source of amusement for foreign residents, as a discussion with Annie, Peter, Brian and Claire shows:

Figure 7.5 A local cemetery with niche interment.Photograph by author.

Annie: Well next door when her husband died, a very charming man, he was from Argentina actually, shades above this lot here and I knew he'd died, so I went next door the following day to pay my respects and say how sorry I was. To my horror, I went in and not being *au fait* with Spanish funerals, her whole sitting room — which is big, lined with chairs — and the coffin was there

Caroline: Yes

Annie: And it was open and his head was there and I couldn't believe this.

Peter: And she [the spouse] was wailing and...

Annie: She was howling, howling like a banshee.
          [Everyone laughs.]

Annie: What will I do? So I sat on a chair [more laughs] and I thought well I can't sit here all day like this. So I just got up and zoomed across to her, gave her a big hug and a kiss and said, you know *lo siento* [I'm sorry] and ran. I didn't know what else to do, it was

> so unexpected to see him there, you know I didn't know he was going to be there all day.

Annie considered this another reason for her cultural admiration of Spanish life and attitudes. She said, 'they love it. It's drama. Whether it's fun or whatever it is, it's a *wonderful* reaction. It's not this grey scene in England, no, no...sensible'. However other foreign residents referred to the differences in less positive terms. Some found the mode of burial/interment particularly disquietening, reading the Spanish cemeteries as 'spooky', or 'macabre' because they so explicitly contain the dead. They commented on the rapidity of disposal and its manner in niche interment, considering it 'cold' or at least less reverent (Oliver 2004). One woman, for example, referred to the funeral of her gardener as a process of 'bung[ing] him in a hole' (Oliver 2004) whilst Judy recounted how her friend objected when Judy's husband's coffin was placed in the top niche, stating how she couldn't look because it was 'too macabre'. The means of disposal is read as 'cold', modernist and expedient, and vastly different from burial in a cemetery in Britain. Most importantly, it disrupts a key association held in Britain that the body merges with nature through burial (Francis, Kellaher and Neophytou, 2001). Ackers and Dwyer (2002) report how, for one of their interviewees, the intense distress felt at this possible mode of disposal was strong enough to make them move back.

Further study would be required to explore in more detail how and why disposal choices vary, and what this tells us about cultural belonging. But it is clear that in migration, deaths are complicated by the consideration of where the remains should be, particularly as Francis, Kellaher and Neophytou (2000) show, place of burial may reveal attachments to locality and people. Bloch shows that for the Merina of Malagasy, kinship relations are fixed only following the sedentarisation of the dead (Hallam and Hockey 2001). When the dead fuse with the physical space of the tomb, they become part of the ancestral stone of localised Merina territory (ibid.). I observed for some foreign residents who felt they belonged in Spain, the possibility of interment in Spain was less the obstacle it was understood by others who saw themselves as temporary guests in Spain (see Oliver 2004). Therefore, for long-term migrants such as Mary, Elizabeth (who had her own niche reserved in Freila's cemetery) as well as Judy, there was no debate about their future interment in the Spanish cemeteries, where their relatives were also interred. Nevertheless, choices of memorials still projected elements of the mourner's own self identity (Francis et al: 2001) because the memorial plates on British residents' niches' generally were engraved in English, but often included a phrase in Spanish, and were often less ostentatious in design. The few exceptions were of niches maintained by some long-term migrants. These memorials were completely in Spanish, although the plaques were still simpler than those on surrounding Spanish niches. In fact, Mary explicitly rejected the 'big show' she maintained the

Spanish made of death; during the Catholic All Saints' Ritual in which Spaniards decorate niches lavishly with flowers and attend the cemetery until the early hours of the morning, she showed her objection by putting 'ugly old pot plants up there!' on her husband's niche, much to the dismay of her Spanish housekeeper.

For migrants in Spain, interment is a choice available to all those registered in the locality as a *padrón,* whether Catholic or not. However, as I have suggested, other options include underground burial in the English cemetery in Málaga, which is an expensive choice.[15] This is equally true for repatriating a body back to Britain for burial, whose cost, in the region of £4000 is not within everybody's means (expatica.com: September 2004). Cremation is by far the cheapest option and also allows for mobility of the remains, including the possible return back to the homeland. In this case, however, as Kellaher, Prendergast and Hockey's (2005) analysis of cremation in Britain shows, the location of ashes remains significant. Doreen explained, for example, that when her husband died on a visit back to Britain, her children requested she kept her husband's ashes there rather than taking them back to Spain. She insisted, however, on playing the song *Viva España* at her husband's cremation explicitly because it had the words, 'take me back to sunny Spain'. Doreen did not take her husband's ashes back to Spain, but found the idea of post-mortem travel of others' ashes amusing. She explained her decision:

> ....they didn't want anything like that [taking ashes back to Spain], no, the family didn't want anything like that. Because I've heard these stories about people sitting on a plane and if you see someone sitting besides you with a black plastic bag you know that the ashes are in there. Yeah, so I thought to myself no way, and now I always look around myself to see [laughing] that they've got a black bag [laughs]'

Doreen's humorous account was typical of other public reflections on deaths amongst migrants, which employed the customary joking style of migrants' interactions (see Chapter 5). Deaths are socially significant events where people feel their common humanity (Young and Cullen 1996) but also become occasions in which the 'community' draws together and asserts its values. In Spain, foreign residents often told me how there is more help and support than one would expect elsewhere, as Reg pointed out, 'When a spouse dies, there's more camaraderie, more so than at home'. Surviving relatives are given much well-meant advice on coping, and this is often informed by others' personal experience. One man pointed out that when his wife died four years ago, he got 'so much attention it was embarrassing!' This concurs with how, as Hockey considers, rituals have either a protective function for society, or as emphasised by Bloch and Parry (1982) can rather have a transformative function in which society is created as 'an *outcome* of ritual practices' (Hockey 2002b: 217, original emphasis). In Spain, migrants' funerals and memorial services are occasions in which members of the community come together, express solidarity and give a 'good send-off' to one of their travellers, thereby reaffirming the values of the community to everyone around. Thus in the village, when a German man, known as somewhat of a loner, died, I was struck by the way people pulled together to help his son after the death. When the son arrived from Germany, he was warmly embraced in the village by foreign residents (see Chapter 6). People drove him to Málaga to sort out the practicalities of the death, a memorial drink was arranged, and he was cooked for, invited along to events and fussed over for the week he was there. In return, he donated many of his father's belongings, including an expensive car, to individual foreign residents. Furthermore, when Charlotte died and her ashes were scattered in the sea, her husband Gerald could not afford to pay for a wake. A local English bar-owner rallied round, laying on wine, cheese and biscuits, and once Gerald had left, those attending donated contributions to cover the costs. One person attending with us had not even known Charlotte but had simply followed other people on to the occasion from another club's social meeting.

These 'good send-offs' demonstrate also how death is treated as an expected aspect of life given the average older age of the migrant community. Yet simultaneously, the constant arrival of new members of the community ensures that deaths are not too disruptive to its overall continuity. Newcomers do not remember those who have died before their arrival and beyond the foreigners' niches in the cemeteries, there are no material reminders of previous characters who have lived there before. Moreover, to minimise the immediate impact of any individual's death in the community, vacant roles are quickly taken. Reg told me that following a recent funeral, he was immediately given the deceased man's 'job' at the urbanization's community office. He explained, 'I thought I'd got rid of my job at last, then I went down to the community office for the Annual General Meeting to be told, 'you are now the community secretary'.

Such practices ensure that life continues 'in the here and now', although this stance can be more difficult to bear for bereaved spouses. Mullan points out (1993) that for some couples, migration to Spain makes people more dependent on their partners when they live together as a couple away from Britain. Dealing with grief when a partner dies is not easy in the transient and sociable community. Others are informed of deaths through word of mouth but due to the regular comings and goings, not everyone in the social network can be sure of finding out. Spouses who distance themselves from socialising to grieve find that others are unaware of their bereavement and fail to modify their behaviour when they return. On one occasion, when an English man died, his Swedish friend, arriving back from a visit to Sweden had rung up to ask the couple out to dinner. It was only then that they found out that their good friend had died. The widow involved told me later, 'that's what's so difficult...nobody knows'. As such, dealing with grief may be particularly hard to deal with in a context of sociability, where people may only have a relatively small shared past with other migrants (Jonker 1997). This is exemplified by the response when I asked after a club member whose husband had recently died, and another member said,

> Well I asked her if she was coping and she said she's fine. But then I suppose what else would you say? You know I don't know her that well really, only on a social level. I think she's going away somewhere soon...But that's the thing here, it keeps changing all the time. There are always different people to talk to...

SUMMARY

This chapter explores the multiple ways in which cultural identities are manifested in Spain. Many retired migrants view Spain merely as a 'home-plus' and do little to change their ways of life in the new context, particularly as they are supported by a thriving infrastructure catering to their needs. However, others express a more 'cosmopolitan' identity and pursue feelings of deeper belonging to Spain by gaining knowledge of the new destination. However, both perspectives have particular consequences for integration as the analysis shows how in addition to structural impediments, wider cultural factors, of aspirations and values, influence the means, shape and form of relationships with the Spanish people that take place. The chapter also considers that although cultural difference may be part of the fascination that comes with living in Spain, their outlooks may change over time as they age. In particular, the fascination may not extend to embracing the distinct cultural approaches to death and disposal, of which reactions range from amusement to admiration to disgust. The range of responses only briefly explored here requires further investigation, although it is clear that the death of a migrant is nevertheless a moment of immense importance; an occasion in which, despite their many internal differences, the foreign residents come together as a community to mark the loss of one of their own.

8 Conclusion
Paradoxes of Ageing in Retirement Migration

The ethnographic exploration of retirement abroad by British and other Northern European people offered in this book shows how the movement is associated with a re-evaluation of what retirement is about. Crucially, retirees' migration experiences inform their resistance to paths of ageing imagined to be expected of people 'back home'. Moving away involves numerous new challenges: of selling, buying or renting houses, sifting through possessions, sorting out tax and social security arrangements to live in another country, attempting to learn a new language and sometimes struggling to overcome the emotional ties of the home left behind. Yet rather than the discontinuity from previous lives being disruptive (Phillipson 2002 in Torres 2004, Daatland and Biggs 2004), migration is narrated as a catalyst for creativity in identity, in which changes forced by retirement become prompts to redefine what lives retirees hope to have. In this way, the study stresses how ageing is a cultural process dealt with imaginatively as well as practically, involving hopes and new aspirations for retirement. The book has examined the experiences behind some of the common aspirations articulated in movement to Spain, through four themes: temporality, ageing (space, place and body) sociability and cultural identities. Through these arenas, older people recast their expectations of older age, although as I have also shown, contemplation of their new lifestyle simultaneously invites processes of temporal, spatial and social displacement of other less desired experiences of ageing.

In summary, the book has shown first how movement abroad is associated with the adoption of qualitatively different experiences of time. Spain is a place in which people express they have 'more' time and 'free' time to be spent at no-one else's bidding but their own. Time-use is judged according to a powerful imperative to 'live for today', which is easily achieved given the positive advantages of living in Spain afforded by the climate, cheaper cost of living, perceived slower way of life and notions of 'traditional' community. These make for a positive experience of old age, far from the invisibility and marginality often assumed to be the fate of those at home. The exposure to different cultural ways of ageing also provides a useful benchmark for Northern European retirees' to reflect on their own ageing experiences. Living in a likeminded community, migrants share an intragenerational sociability where 'age doesn't matter' or is certainly not an impediment to experimentation with new activities. There is much evidence of practical and emotional support between individuals, and the wide and varied social life helps foster friendships which fill the void left by absent kin. Finally, moving to Spain is presented as offering lifestyles that could never be lived back home, and despite much evidence of an attachment to a British way of life, there are also aspirations for belonging in Spain. Experiences of living away from home are often used to positively recast narratives of self, in which a zest for discovery of the 'real' Spain, however limited in practice, contributes to an authentically ageing self.

Certainly, retired migrants' views considered in the book show that people evaluate their adopted home and lifestyle very highly on these bases; retirees put great stock by the autonomy experienced in ageing and the new opportunities to do things in life they have never done before. Of course, as King et al point out, it is worth bearing in mind that the sample in aspirational migration is probably skewed, as those 'who have become unhappy, disenchanted, frail or sick will have returned to Britain' (2000: 117). There may also be elements of posthoc rationalisation or 'burnt bridges syndrome' (ibid.) as Keith Ross (1977) points out in her study of *Les Floralies*, a retirement community in France, where satisfaction following movement may be understood through the psychological theory of cognitive dissonance. In other words, 'making a substantial investment, especially if it is irreversible, stimulates commitment to the community as a means of justifying the investment' (1977: 9). However, as I suggested from the outset, the book's aim was to sidestep evaluation of their decision, and rather to provide a more complex picture and deeper understanding of people's experiences of desirable ageing lifestyles.

In doing so, the ethnographic study explores consequences of the aspirations as they are lived in practice and reveals that retirees' lifestyles require constant negotiation of contradictions that their desires bring. It shows that the achievement of their aspirations are complicated by the often paradoxical desires they articulate, which reflect wider ambiguities inherent in Western contemporary experiences of old age. Perhaps this is unsurprising; the liminality of retiree's life course stage and the marginality of the geographic space provokes a bounding of aspects of culture and social structure into 'complex semantic systems of pivotal, multivocal symbols and myths which achieve great conjunctive power', as Turner (1974: 259) identifies in liminality. In retirement migration in Spain, the myths or aspirations associated with retirement migration in general — certain experiences of time, ageing, sociability and identities — are replete with contradiction and are inherently paradoxical and ambiguous, as I recapitulate here.

In Chapter 4, I explore the paradoxical nature of migrants' experiences of time, as in Spain, retirees enjoy both a sense of having both 'more' time, but 'less' time. Thus on one hand, people can enjoy free time to slow down, relax and savour life without care for where it goes. Yet as a period of time both 'earned' by migrants and finite but indeterminate in duration, it is nevertheless important that it is utilised wisely and not wasted away in unproductive activities. As such, time-structured activities and routines are reintroduced by the retirees to the point in which, whilst there is 'more' time in Spain, it is also best used when provoking a sense of there being 'less' time, where it is difficult to fit everything in. Second, in Chapter 5, I examined the ambiguity of space, place and body, showing how amongst foreign retirees in Spain, age does not matter, but paradoxically it absolutely does. The subjective interpretation of old age has limits, because the activity — on one hand a measure of good ageing — can be tiring and the socialising, exhausting. Ageing is also made salient through the fragmentation into cohorts of retirees, and people engage in social reflections on ways of ageing. This means that whilst there are loosened constraints around ageing, nevertheless vigilance is required to manage retiree's ageing processes 'well', to keep up certain bodily appearances and to take individual responsibility to plan for their own future.

Third, in the sphere of social relationships explored in Chapter 6, I showed how the freedoms of personality of 'being what one wants to be' (O'Reilly 2000a) is a maxim that is easier to assert than experience in practice. This is especially felt to be the case by some people at an age where they are less comfortable leaving behind the certainties on which their lives had been constructed. Moreover, they may dislike the trust issues raised by having to rely on new relationships which have not yet 'stood the test of time'. As such, the acceptance of the egalitarian bunch of friends is matched by subtle power struggles, new hierarchies, word-of-mouth information sharing and emphasis on reputations, which help to discipline and make more knowable other individuals around. Finally, as I show in Chapter 7, there are strong internal distinctions made within the community, which reassert style and taste distinctions, whilst affirming positively ageing identities through practices of cultural tourism in Spain. I showed, however, how many people's attraction to Spain rests on a stance of cultural fascination, which perpetuates mutual perceptions of cultural 'difference' with Spanish people, and affects the nature of the relationships that take place. And, whilst narratives of retirement abroad stress excitement and risk, ultimately the security of shared language, familiar cultural practices and home-comforts hold a considerable pull, particularly when facing questions of deep old age and death. In facing these myriad contradictions, far from an unproblematic period of pure leisure, the account shows how post-retirement lifestyles require careful and ongoing vigilance; the aspirations lived in practice reflecting a kind of tempered 'flirting' with the freedoms associated with life in Spain, rather than outright plunging into the unknown.

CHALLENGE OR CONFIRMATION?

As the summary shows, life in Spain requires considerable self-management to negotiate the dilemmas inherent in retirees' aspirations towards positive ageing in Spain. Old habits of work-orientation, productivity, time organisation and previous values still struggle against the alternative drives encouraging relaxation, rest, hedonism and reinvention. Such fractures in the myths of retirement in Spain concur with other observations of liminal experiences, in which the transgressive potential to liberate individuals from old ways and communal norms are shown as far from simple in practice (Dentith 1995). Turner himself observes that where liminality is less a *moment* of aberrance than enduring over time, a group's need to create social control requires that, 'the existential communitas is organised into a perduring social system' (Turner 1969: 132). Yet even when this is not the case, such as in instances of tourism, Crick argues nevertheless that 'one does not find neat reversals from ordinary time to structureless communitas' (1989: 334). Hetherington considers the sphere of new-age traveller festivals as a form of cultural resistance and again also finds that scholars 'often miss how disorder also performs order as part of an on-going process' (2000: 57).

Certainly in this particular circumstance, the degree to which migrants' lifestyles challenge the marginalisation associated with ageing in the homeland is questionable. This is particularly because retirees contrast their aspirations with a temporal, social and spatial displacement of less desirable ways of life and experiences of ageing. Their positive lives are claimed as much through processes of distancing and relocating negative pictures of ageing — commonly stressing monotony, security and control by other people — onto others, rather than necessarily challenging the negative evaluations of slowing down and dependency associated with old age. In the site, retirees' own authenticity is contrasted with the lesser desirable lifestyles of other older people, 'the Brits', or tourists; they resist putative 'boring' and dependent lifestyles through displacement onto others. Thus Belle and Doreen impute images of sedentarism and lack of verve to those in the homeland. For Mary and Elizabeth, the same negative qualities are associated with the recently arriving migrants living on the coast, whose experiences of retirement, as Mary described of, 'playing scrabble and old time dancing' is judged as dull, and associated with oldness (Chapter 7). This social and spatial displacement, which operates on a number of levels, echoes observations made by McHugh that older people in winter retirement communities in the United States contrast their difference to 'old folks who while away their lives in rocking chairs back home' (2000: 112).

This begs a wider cultural question raised in Chapter 2, whether such experiences of 'alternative' or indeed 'positive' ageing are simply reiterations of existing ageist stereotypes (Andrews 1999). In projecting oldness — and its feared stereotypical associations — as the province of other times, other people and other places, is it not the case that the stereotypes remain unchallenged and are simply just not applied to the migrants themselves (ibid.)? As Gibson argues, this commonly seen resistance to oldness occurs as an understandable refusal to 'identify with the false stereotype of what an 'old person' is commonly supposed to be' (Gibson 2000: 775). Yet the process demonstrates a wider cultural dilemma, as Andrews explains:

> It's a Catch 22 situation: depressed, disengaged old people are described as old, while those who defy this stereotype, who retain a passion for life are considered young, if only in spirit. (1999: 305)

The lifestyles of the people in this book exemplify this predicament, which exemplify the contradictions at the heart of the wider cultural imperative towards 'successful ageing', as discussed in Chapter 2. As I explored, the powerful movement towards positive ageing is underpinned by an optimism about the increasing life expectancy and advances in physical and mental fitness of many older people today (Baltes and Smith 2006). It is, no doubt, a welcome move that challenges some of the negative and incorrect associations of ageing in the contemporary period. However, it has also been subject to pertinent critiques on the basis of the exclusionary consequences of the motif. As I explored in more detail earlier in the book, it encourages the individualistic management of ageing which is met by an expanding commercial sector keen to exploit the moralities constructed about the self-management of ageing.

In exploring some of the experiences of those seeking new positively ageing experiences through retirement migration, the book exposes how individuals negotiate the recent changing expectations of the life course, and shows that the contradictions in wider cultural messages of ageing do not disappear. Thus on the one hand, the people in this book mount a powerful challenge against ageist stereotypes of dependency and ill health. Their lifestyles are based on upbeat and anti-ageist conceptions of old age as a period of life presenting new opportunities. On the other hand, their lifestyles and values do not alter the negative ways in which ageing is perceived and, as Katz (2005) points out, such positivity thereby risks ironically being anti-*ageing*, encouraging a denial or shrouding of the realities and inevitable challenges of old age. It enables the extension of certain cultural values to old age, whether or not they are appropriate, as evident in retirees' importation of concerns about productivity, work and self-reliance (Cruikshank 2003, Blaikie 1999). The ultimate paradox of retirees' lifestyle is therefore that the articulations of good ageing both powerfully challenge stereotypes of ageing but simultaneously risk imparting new, equally unrealistic expectations of autonomy and productivity in old age. And, as Andrews argues, the fact remains that 'success' is not evaluated for other age-periods of life. As she describes, the pursuit is 'mission amorphous, mission impossible' (1999: 304).

This book offers no simple solution to these dilemmas. However, in showing the complexity in experiences through grounded empirical study, it rather draws attention to the variety of individual attempts to negotiate the paradoxical and contradictory currents that are integral to ageing in the contemporary period. Those seeking out positive retirement experiences abroad must manage contradictory imperatives in their everyday negotiations. They find the adoption of a laid back approach to time chafing against a countervailing pull to be busy and their freedoms from societal marginalisation requiring yet new vigilance for ageing well. The friendly faces of the welcoming community must be sifted for trustworthy and not dependent companions, allowing both the experience of communal unity but simultaneously allowing them the space to pursue their own desires. And the exciting, but ultimately risky possibilities of living abroad, are tempered with concerns for security and comfort as they grow older and more frail.

The book shows that although the saturation of images of 'good' ageing form the basis of new cultural expectation of ageing, the way this is lived is personally variable and subject to re-evaluation. Therefore although certain ideals of autonomy and activity are central to most people's understandings of good ageing, the personal interpretations of these benchmarks vary widely. So, although Belle's club-oriented lifestyle is viewed with dismay by Mary (and likely vice-versa) Belle and Mary each, in their own way believe themselves to be ageing well, and these self-beliefs are important resources in their ability to negotiate some of the struggles they face as they grow older. Furthermore, as much as there is individual variety in beliefs about ageing 'well', the book confirms how identities are not static but subject to transformation. As the people I met grew older, as new physical challenges and experiences of ill-health limited their abilities to engage in certain pursuits, they reinterpreted their original ideals to recast the limitation not as failure, but as offering new possibilities. This corresponds with Jerrome's notion of 'personal ecology' (1992: 144) where individuals change strategies to conserve energy, by refocusing on another activity. So when Les (Chapter 5) suffered his consecutive heart attacks and his former pursuit of swimming in the sea for a mile a day became impossible, he re-evaluated the extent of his activities. He reflected instead on how this simply gave him more time to pursue his new hobby of painting model aeroplanes, a pursuit which he had always wanted to do, but had never found the time for. And when Jack could no longer do karate, he still went out daily for his beer, and focused instead on a more limited and realistic intention to return to the gym to do upper body exercises (Chapter 5). And at these points, as individuals deal with the bigger questions of ageing, their re-evaluation may expand to include possibilities prohibited before, but that nevertheless continue to be cast within positive narratives. So, when it seemed sensible for Doreen, now in her eighties, to return to Britain to be near her children, she stressed how she simply hoped to export the benefits of her lifestyle in

Spain to the UK. Gradually, albeit sometimes reluctantly, the materiality of bodily change is adjusted to as what constitutes 'good' ageing is reviewed and open to change. And this contextual reinterpretation of good ageing or 'self-plasticity' (Baltes and Smith 2006) allows individuals to confront their limits and experience decline, but nevertheless recast their more limited opportunities in a positive light.

On the other hand, the continuation of a narrative of success helps the individuals maintain distance from the ultimate fear and dread of abject physical or mental impairment (Featherstone and Hepworth, 1990). This is a very important point, because whilst this book has explored aspirations around ageing, nevertheless a subtext remains that these attitudes are driven as much by *fears* around the process of deep ageing. As Sheila summed up when talking of Roger's health difficulties, 'nobody wants to get like that'. Spending time with the people in this study showed quite clearly to me how, for them, ageing was undoubtedly one of the most difficult and hazardous processes that they, as individuals faced. Any unconscious agenda on my part to support challenges to ageism through a 'positive' portrayal of age-ing were soberly brought into perspective by bearing witness to people's feelings of sadness and readjustment when having to move from beloved houses or having to deal with betrayals in bodily and mental functioning. Their fears of the losses associated with the fourth age present existential challenges that individuals must personally contemplate. Yet, migrants' fears also reveal much about the continued place of the old in contempo-rary society, reflecting as they do concerns about how their own bodily and mental weaknesses will be treated by others in society.

These fears inform some retirees' conceptions of ageing as a process to be combated and managed. This is captured in Mary's explanation of her unconventional lifestyle. On the verge of leaving Spain in December 1999, I called at Mary's house to say my goodbyes and we had, as usual, a long chat over two cups of tea. Mary's practice of making us each two cups of tea at the same time was a strategy she used so that she could rest for a while and avoid having to get up again and make more during our long discussions. When I left, she took the time to write me a four-page handwritten letter, dated and timed as 5.45 p.m., shortly after the time I left. Her letter was a personal reflection on her ageing experiences written, 'from this age when I fear all the batty things I do are the disintegration of my personality'. Her written account featured a harrowing story of the marginalisation she felt she had been subject to at hospital when recently ill. She expressed her struggle at 'refusing to be browbeaten' and attempts to resist being treated 'like idiot zombies [by those who] destroy the free spirit of each and every person'. Her impassioned response expressed the personal difficulties she felt in adjusting to the transformation of her personal and physical capabili-ties as she grew older and less self-sufficient. She wrote:

In the past I always felt in charge. Everyone asked *me* what to do. 'Help, help' they said, I replied, 'OK, coming!' But suddenly no one asks. No cries. It's only my own voice in the night crying, 'help, help' and no-one replies, 'coming'. So it seems to me when we cut down as we get older — smaller house, one dog, one cat then no dog, no cat, two or three visitors, no visitors! Get the pattern?... All these people should be given more and more things they have to do, not relieved of the will to fight the onslaught of old age.

She signed off: 'Now — 6.45. Dogs and cats calling', referring to her self-imposed responsibilities in caring for numerous stray cats and dogs. Mary's account articulated what drove the lifestyle she set for herself and it is clear that this is fuelled by her angry reaction to what she feels is a prevailing marginality and invisibility that comes with dependence in Western societies. Like Mary, the other retirees' lifestyles I have explored in this book are narrated as the process of meeting aspirations that aim to free them from negative associations that continue to plague old age. Maybe the pendulum swings too far in their attempts to live 'positively' ageing lifestyles; as the account has shown, the contradictions that they bring are difficult to negotiate, and are done so in a consumer society where agencies exploit, for financial gain, the insecurities of this period of life. However, they are ways of living, for individuals facing growing older in contemporary Western societies, which are, nonetheless understandable.

Notes

CHAPTER 1

1. Work is referred to as comprising both paid employment (as a majority of the people in this study participated in the labour market) but also unpaid work, such as family care, which may continue or change in retirement.
2. Hockey and James (2003), for example, refer to how women must negotiate social trends for delayed motherhood in the face of widespread concerns about the ticking biological clock.
3. Indeed, there has been controversy recently amongst British pensioners who live in countries outside the EU, including Canada and South Africa, who rather than receiving annual uprating of their pensions, receive a pension frozen to the rate received when they left the country.
4. However, figures widely quoted in expatriate publications cite the Office of National Statistics as suggesting that 74,433 UK pensioners have moved to Spain since 1996 (http://www.costa-action.co.uk, 2003 and www.fxproperty.co.uk, 2006). However, it is not clear as to what period these figures refer to, and the Department for Work and Pensions was unable to provide clarification.
5. Tulle-Winton comments how, 'Becoming a successful ager does not come cheap and ageing now represents an expanding field of industrial and money-making activity' (1999: 290).
6. Other areas studied in King et al's (2000) study are the Algarve, Malta and Tuscany.
7. O'Reilly (2004) states that the population of foreign residents might be underestimated by as much as two-thirds.
8. Some anthropologists have problematised the culture concept on the basis that it falsely depicts an inherent discreteness of cultures which helps to 'freeze differences' (Abu-Lughod 1991: 146) but 'inevitably carry a sense of hierarchy'. Culture therefore is a 'tool for making "other"' (ibid.: 147) which helps sustain the place-contingent depiction of separated 'cultures'.
9. Certainly studies of immigration in Spain favour the documentation of economic labour migration (Rodríguez Rodríguez, Casado Díaz and Huber 2000).
10. This demonstrates Hannerz's position which presents globalization as fostering processes of unequal exchange, through which, 'creolisation ...increasingly allows the periphery to talk back' (1992: 265).
11. A reference to Bronislaw Malinowski, who is credited with establishing participant observation as the dominant mode of ethnographic inquiry.

12. My approach corresponds with Hockey's argument that anthropologists now focus not purely on 'groups', but on 'categories' 'whether social, experiential or cognitive' (2002: 221).

13. The research was funded through employment as a Graduate Teaching Assistant at Hull University, which involved the fulfilment of teaching duties at regular intervals.

14. Insights from Spanish participants have been translated into English to aid the readability and cohesion of the book, although readers can consult the original Spanish in endnotes. Although I conducted the tape-recorded interviews in Spanish, transcription and translation were completed from Spanish to English by Esther Jimenez, a qualified Spanish teacher native to Málaga. Her work, combined with my own perspective, ensured appropriate linguistic interpretation, although the provision of the original verbatim quotations enables readers' own interpretations if required.

15. Williams and Hall (2002) have noted that retirement occurs on a continuum, in which retirement can also involve informal or part-time flexible work arrangements.

16. I refer to people on first name terms, as this is customary in the social context.

CHAPTER 2

1. Other factors identified by King et al (2000: 93–96) include the social advantages of moving to a place where there is an established British community, opportunities for socialising, an admiration of the destination country's way of life and antipathy to Britain. In addition, some practical benefits may influence the decision, including the existence of family links, the presence of good transport links, the fact that English is spoken or that migrants already own a second home. Finally, some migration is undertaken to build on previous work links.

2. The recent legislation in the UK introduces a duty on employers to consider any employee's request to continue working beyond retirement if they wish.

3. Originally identified to account for ritual processes, the schema of the rites of passage have been extended to account for other marginal identities, explaining phenomena as diverse as tourism, disability, and so-called 'new-age' alternative identities (see Graburn [1978]1989, Shakespeare 1994, Hetherington 2000).

4. The 2005 *Road to Nowhere* tour was staged by the *Young at Heart* chorus as taking place in a day-centre, complete with janitor and piano. The older people slowly shuffled on stage one by one, before the performers suddenly and dramatically turned around and began to sing loudly. Their renditions of the songs were accompanied by projected photographs of the singers as younger adults, this placing the older people before the audience within the contexts of their previous lives (cf. Hazan 1994).

5. The reference 'saga-louts' plays on the term, 'lager louts' through reference to SAGA, a company that caters to over-fifties.

6. The area of this study could be defined, at least seasonally, as a de facto retirement community, as particularly in the winter, the foreign community is overwhelmingly comprised of older people. Moreover, some urbanizations in the area were specifically designed to be retirement complexes and 'community' activities are overwhelmingly run for and by older people.

7. This may not necessarily always be the case. Law and Warnes' (1982) study reveals less salience of negative push factors away from former homes.
8. Biggs et al's (2000) study of a retirement community in Birmingham shows that residents felt it offered protection, security and a close-knit community.
9. There are parallels with Malkki's observation of Hutu refugees in Tanzania, who also remain beyond categorisation in the hegemonic system of nation-states. She states, 'they are an "abomination" (Douglas 1966) produced and made meaningful by the categorical order itself, even as they are excluded from it' (1995: 6).
10. For instance, foreign children who have attended or are attending the local school are from my observations much more likely to be fluent in Spanish.
11. These factors are taken into account as significant in other research accounts from the subaltern point of view. For example, in Ganguly's study of middle-class Indian migrants in New Jersey, she points out, 'I emphasise the post-colonial aspect of this particular community's constitution because I think the history of a colonial past substantially inflects the ways in which this community's members imagine and represent themselves' (1992: 27–28).
12. Early anthropological works have explored the 'Mediterranean' character-istics of the region and its people (Schneider 1981). In particular, accounts elaborated on the honour and shame complex (see, for instance, Pitt Rivers 1971, Gilmore 1987a) whilst the remote villages of the region were shown to be governed by strict social stratification, corporate village organisation and apparent rigid and unchanging axioms of division by class and gender (Brandes 1980, Gilmore 1987b, although see Corbin and Corbin 1986).
13. This reflects Ennew's (1980) observation that some 'remote' areas (in her case in the Western Isles of Scotland) have been wrongly defined as non-capital-ist/traditional, despite being locked into capitalism.
14. According to the 2001 census of the town, 4479 people worked in services and 1043 people worked in construction, compared to 308 in farming and fishing, and 238 in industry. In the village, 403 people worked in services, 179 in construction, 29 in industry and 24 in farming and fishing (*Instituto de Estadística de Andalucía* 2001).

CHAPTER 3

1. Alicia said: '*porque ella ya para mí también es como algo, como si fuera o madre o abuela. Aquí mucha gente también me dice "bájate a tu abuela!... Y mucha gente me pregunta "¿cómo está tu abuela?"*'
2. Alicia said '*Pero no es como antes. Antes, yo te digo que conocía muchos y eran todos un círculo que era un amigo de Elizabeth aquí, otro aquí, otro más allá, y luego todos fiestas juntos y... pero ahora no*'.
3. Alicia commented: '*Y sus cosas me impresionaban a mi mucho porque era zapatos...yo tenía unos y cuando "me se" rompían me compraba otros. Pero ella tenía unos, otros, otros... y más y más... claro. Pues entonces eso te impresionaba mucho. Y lo he vivido desde dentro, desde que ella me traía amigas, de que yo estaba con ella, de todo... la forma de comer... las cosas tan raras, como decían "¡uy, qué raro comen los extranjeros!"*'
4. Quote by Alicia: '*Y yo con mucha gente también me decía: "Alicia cuando Doña Elizabeth se harte de tí, se va a ir mi niña"*'.
5. Dolores said: '*yo pienso que mucha gente querría imitar algunas cosas... La libertad, estábamos demasiado protegidos....Porque veían "esta chica extranjera es más libre que yo, yo quiero ser como ella"*'.

6. Bakhtin notes that within carnival settings, it is common to find a fantastic accumulation of superlatives (Morris 1994).

CHAPTER 4

1. Ideas such as these have been criticised; see Fabian (1983), Gell (1992: 23–29) and Adam (1995: 34–36).
2. Although the analysis is not levelled at seasonal migrants, it is no less applicable because the break is less clearly defined. Indeed, the association of temporary stays with 'holidays' heightens the conception of a liminal and qualitatively different experience of time (see Graburn [1978] 1989).
3. The woman said, '*Los amigos que yo tengo les gustan preguntarme nuestras costumbres, para la fiesta o para horarios y eso... intentan adaptarse a España. Pero, vamos, ellos siempre tendrán sus costumbres a la hora de su comida y cosas así*'.

CHAPTER 5

1. Longino acknowledges that the interviews conducted may have measured people's subjective desires for independence rather than the actual freedom experienced.
2. Alicia commented: '*los jubilados extranjeros piensan de una manera y viven de otra. Y los españoles tienen una vida más sedentaria. Más aquí me siento, veo el que pasa y luego voy a mi casa, comen y se van, por ejemplo: al hogar del pensionista. Viven distinto, y hasta pueden casi apenas andar. Van a comer con amigos, salen, entran y los españoles no. Al menos en Freila no. Hay un día con los hijos a comer por algo pero que no es una... no es tan constante como los extranjeros...*'
3. María said, '*los extranjeros se jubilan con 65 años y no hacen nada más. Y aquí no se jubila nadie. Aquí el hombre que pueda estar yendo al campo esta yendo al campo hasta los 80 años. No se jubila*', and '*.. los extranjeros se jubilan, vienen a la playa tranquilamente a pasear, su casa también, pero siempre tienen a alguien que les ayuda. No es como aquí. Aquí ¡ahora esta empezando la tercera edad a empezar a salir de viaje! Algunos, no todos. Aquí no, aquí no se jubila nadie. Porque todos tienen el trozo de tierra, tienen la mijilla de algo, la mijilla de negocio... y todos están trabajando hasta él ultimo día*'.
4. María said, '*no se como decirle lo que es. Es como una obligación o un deber, un deber de que nosotros los cuidemos a ellos, de que no les falten nada. De que cuando estén ya ellos mal en la cama ayudarles. Es como una obligación, no es una responsabilidad. No pensamos tanto en un hogar o en una residencia de ancianos, no. Pensamos mas que estén en su casa, tranquilos, y los hijos ayudarles*'.
5. Alicia commented: '*y nosotros nos ponemos, como se dice aquí "a morirnos". Ya nos echamos, nos da igual todo, si el aspecto y, te digo que con los años eso ha cambiado....es decir, que ahora ya eso ha cambiado, ahora ya las mujeres con 80 años tú las ves y están todas de color y entran y salen más que antes*'.
6. Alicia stated, '*Elizabeth... se moriría si va al hogar del pensionista*'.

7. A useful comparison is Shields' analysis of the carnivalesque at Brighton. He points out for example how lewd innuendo found in seaside postcards transgresses social codes, yet simultaneously encourages self-regulation by people through emphasising the embarrassment of being 'caught-out' (Shields 1991).
8. O'Reilly suggests that there is little evidence that people return home on a large scale (2000a: 97). See also Chapter 7 for further discussion.
9. Mullan (1993) and Dwyer (2000) point out that some people can be reliant on friends for care.
10. The reference is to niche interment that is practiced in the local cemeteries, as discussed in Chapter 7.

CHAPTER 6

1. María argued, '*ellos mismos se molestan con ellos. Ellos se estorban, ellos quisieran venirse a España y ser únicos. Tener una Inglaterra o una Alemania aquí para ellos con sus leyes aquí...con sus leyes aquí pero vivir...en su.. sus leyes.... en su finca y luego todo lo demás España. Pero lo mío es mío y no lo pisa nadie, y no te conozco de nada y... todo es mío. Y me molesta que haya otro extranjero al lado. Ellos quisieran tener todo para ellos... Aunque vivan puerta con puerta están peleados. Siempre por algo, por una linde, por el ruido, por alguna siesta. Por lo que sea siempre terminan... Yo tengo el ejemplo de ahí, Jenny e Isabel: peleadas. Ruth y Frida peleadas*'.
2. The description corresponds with Turner's observation that 'despotism, over-bureaucratisation, or other modes of structural rigidification' (1969: 129) may follow from exaggerated communitas.
3. The situation calls to mind the oscillation of gumsa and gumlao in Leach's (1954) study of the Kachin in Highland Burma. Social organization rests on a dynamic series of change. Over time, *gumlao*, a republican system of equality between individuals, yields to *gumsa*, based on the hierarchy of ranked lineages and back again.
4. See Pink (1997: 37) and Mintz (1997) on the continued social salience of gossip in Andalucían life and Zinovieff's (1991) study of Greek hospitality.
5. These statements echo the antipathy displayed by individualistic middle class inhabitants of suburbia towards those living in the collectivities of council estates in Britain as detailed by Oliver, Davis and Bentley (1994).
6. Many thanks to John Roche, a former student who lived part of the year in Almería province in Spain, for this information.
7. The consequences of this are identified by Brison's (1992) study of a community in Papua New Guinea. There, any attempts to assert control and enforce one's opinion are potentially open to attack. Small communities such as these, 'create a situation in which almost anything anybody does provokes a negative reaction' (1992: 31).

CHAPTER 7

1. Guillermo said, '*Naturalmente es un poco coto cerrado, desde mi punto de vista, por aquello de que precisa que las reuniones sean en inglés, ¿no? Que van a disertar, diserta en inglés y a menos que conozca un poco el idioma*'.

2. The poem includes the lines:
   'If I should die, think only this of me;
   That there's some corner of a foreign field
   That is for ever England' (Brooke [1915] 1999).
3. Malkki's (1995) ethnography was based in a refugee camp and a township
   in Tanzania. Refugees in the camp stress a collective Hutu identity, imagined
   through mythico-histories, whilst those living in the township negate collective identifications as 'Hutu' or refugee, in favour of more cosmopolitan and
   fluid identities.
4. For example, Harrison (1999: 23) argues of the strength of antagonism
   between Serbs and Croats in the Balkans that, 'it is the perceived similarities of the ethnic Other that are experienced as threatening, rather than the
   differences'.
5. Jorge said, *'ellos nos enseñarían, por ejemplo Judy, una mujer muy inteli-
   gente, y a nosotros nos gusta porque nos enseña cosas, historia de España
   que no conocemos. Esto si nos gusta, que vengan personas para enseñarnos
   cosas nuevas que no conocemos'.*
6. María said, *'la gente del pueblo y ellos están, pero como viendo, no partici-
   pando. Para encontrar gente que participe es muy raro'.*
7. The discussion between Jesús and María:

Jesús:	*...Freila ya tiene un censo bastante grande de extranjeros. Y tenía que haber ya un extranjero implicado en las listas y se ven pocos.*
María:	*El año pasado uno..*
Jesús:	*¿Uno?*
María:	*Bueno, uno en la lista del PA [partido Andalucista].*
Jesús:	*Pero en la cola, casi el ultimo. Y luego en los verdes, como no encontraban gente para las listas, tenían muchos extranjeros. Pero porque no encontraban a gente. Yo estuve en la confección de la lista – al partido al cual pertenezco, y había un extranjero pero...*
María:	*Con trabajo.*
Jesús:	*Tocina tiene un concejal alemán y el tío trabaja mucho y hace sus cosas... pero aquí no, aquí que me las preparen todas. Y luego no se meten tampoco en las fiestas.*

8. Quote by Álvaro: *'mira, subidas de precios donde tenemos la suerte que
   tenemos turismo para mí es una suerte y es un privilegio que otros pueblos
   no tienen quisieran tener'.*
9. Various theories of the origin of the term exist, including speculation that
   it derived from the Initials G.R.I. on Carlistas uniforms in the nineteenth
   century civil wars. In recent usage it is a term to describe Northern European
   mass tourists and visitors. The significance of the word varies contextually;
   my Spanish friends described it as a harmless generic description to refer to a
   foreigner, but in some usages, it is an insult.
10. This is particularly problematic in medical consultations; the diagnosis of a
    condition may be misunderstood when communication is through hand ges-
    tures and language from phrase books (Stevens, *the Observer* 2006).
11. Guillermo said, *'Yo tengo unos vecinos y no hay manera de... y luego esos
    te dicen "adiós", "gracias muy" [risas] y nos tenemos que comunicar con el
    idioma universal del lenguaje de los gestos'.*
12. This is a common practice to avoid inheritance tax between spouses, as in
    Spain there is no spouse exemption.
13. María said, *'se murió una vecina y yo me entere a los 3 días. Murió una
    extranjera y aquí nos enteramos a los 3 días que había muerto y... no, lo ven
    de otra manera'.*

14. The strong engagement of the local Spanish community when individuals die is depicted, for example, in the film *Volver* (2006) by Pedro Almodóvar.
15. There is also an International cemetery at Benalmádena, approximately seventy kms away, offering both burial and niche-interment, although this was not considered (or even known about) by the informants I knew.

Bibliography

Abu-Lughod, J. (1991) 'Writing against culture', in Fox, R.G. (ed.) *Recapturing Anthropology. Working in the Present*, Santa Fe, NM: School of American Research press, pp. 137–162.

Ackers, L. and Dwyer, P. (2002) *Senior Citizenship? Retirement, Migration and Welfare in the European Union*, Bristol: The Policy Press.

—— (2004) 'Fixed laws, fluid lives: the citizenship status of post-retirement migrants in the European Union', *Ageing and Society*, 24: 451–475.

Adam, B. (1990) *Time and Social Theory*, Cambridge: Polity Press.

—— (1995) *Timewatch. The Social Analysis of Time*, Cambridge: Polity Press.

Age Concern España. (2003) 'Information and advice: Health care for EC pensioners living in Spain or visiting another EEA country'. Available at: http://www.acespana.org/acespana/info_572.htm (accessed 30 July 2006).

Allan, A. (1979) *A Sociology of Friendship and Kinship*, London: George Allen and Unwin.

Amit, V. (2002) 'Reconceptualizing community', in V. Amit (ed.) *Realizing Community. Concepts, Social Relationships and Sentiments*, London: Routledge, pp. 1–20.

—— (ed.) (2007) *Going First Class? New Approaches Towards Privileged Movement and Travel*, Oxford: Berghahn.

Amit, V. and Rapport, N. (2002) *The Trouble with Community. Anthropological Reflections on Movement, Identity and Collectivity*, London: Pluto.

Anderson, B. (1983) *Imagined Communities. Reflections on the Origin and Spread of Nationalism*, London: Verso.

Andersson, L. and Öberg, P. (2004) 'Diversity, health and ageing', in S.O. Daatland and S. Biggs (eds.) *Ageing and Diversity. Multiple Pathways and Cultural Migrations*, Bristol: The Policy Press, pp. 45–60.

Andrews, M. (1999) 'The seductiveness of agelessness', *Ageing and Society*, 19: 301–318.

Anthias, F. (1992) *Ethnicity, Class, Gender and Migration: Greek Cypriots in Britain*, Aldershot: Avebury.

Anthias, F. and Lazaridis, G. (2000) *Gender and Migration in Southern Europe*, Oxford: Berg.

Appadurai, A. (1991) 'Global ethnoscapes. Notes and queries for a transnational anthropology', in R.G. Fox (ed.) *Recapturing Anthropology. Working in the Present*, Santa Fe, NM: School of American Research Press, pp. 191–210.

Arber, S. and Ginn, J. (1991) *Gender and Later Life. A Sociological Analysis of Resources and Constraints*, London: Sage.

—— (eds.) (1995) *Connecting Gender and Ageing. A Sociological Approach*, Buckingham: Open University Press.

Aries, P. (1976) *Western Attitudes Toward Death from the Middle Ages to the Present*, trans. Patricia M. Ranum, London: Marion Boyars.

Atkinson, R. and Flint, J. (2001) 'Accessing hidden and hard to reach populations: Snowball research strategies', *Social Research Update*, 33: 1–4.

Bailey, F.G. (1971) *Gifts and Poison. The Politics of Reputation*, Oxford: Basil Blackwell.

Baird, D. (2004) *Sunny Side Up. The 21st Century hits a Spanish Village*, Fuengirola: Santana.

Ballard, J.G. (1997) *Cocaine Nights*. London: Flamingo.

Baltes, P.B. and Baltes, M.M. (eds.) (1990) *Successful Ageing: Perspectives form the Behavioural Sciences*, New York: Cambridge University Press.

Baltes, P.B. and Smith, J. (2002) 'New frontiers in the future of aging: From successful aging of the young old to the dilemmas of the Fourth Age', Keynote paper presented at the Valencia Forum, April 2002.

Barke, M. and Towner, J. (2003) 'Learning from experience? Progress towards a sustainable future for tourism in the central and eastern Andalucían littoral', *Journal of Sustainable Tourism*, 11 (2 &3): 162–180.

Baudrillard, J. (1998) *The Consumer Society: Myth and Structures*, London: Sage.

Bedell, G. (2005) 'The third agers', *The Guardian Review*, 30 October: 1–3.

Bell, S. and Coleman, S. (1999) 'The anthropology of friendship: enduring themes and future possibilities', in S. Bell and S. Coleman (eds.) *The Anthropology of Friendship*, Oxford: Berg, pp. 1–20.

Bell, V. (1999) 'Performativity and belonging: An introduction', in V. Bell (ed.) *Performativity and Belonging*, London: Sage, pp. 1–10.

Bellah, R.N., Madsen, R., Sullivan, W.M., Swidler, A. and Tipton, S.M. (1984) *Habits of the Hearth: Individualism and Commitment in American Life*, Berkeley: University of California Press.

Bergmann, J.R. (1993) *Discreet Indiscretions. The Social Organisation of Gossip*, New York: Aldine de Gruyter.

Betty, C. (1997) 'Language problems of older British migrants on the Costa del Sol', *Generations Review. Journal of the British Society of Gerontology*, 7 (2):10–11.

—— (2001) 'Why don't you ask me whether I have a better quality of life?' *Generations Review. Journal of the British Society of Gerontology*, 11 (2): 7–9.

Betty, C. and Cahill, M. (1999) 'British expatriates' experience of health and social services on the Costa del Sol', in F. Anthias and G. Lazaridis (eds.) *Into the margins. Migration and Social Exclusion in Southern Europe*, Aldershot: Ashgate, pp. 83–113.

Biggs, S. (1999) *The Mature Imagination: Dynamics of Identity in Midlife and Beyond*, Bucks: Open University Press.

Biggs, S., Bernard, M., Kingston, P. and Nettleton, H. (2000) 'Lifestyles of belief: Narrative and culture in a retirement community', *Ageing and Society*, 20, 649–672.

Blaikie, A. (1999) *Ageing and Popular Culture*, Cambridge: Cambridge University Press.

Blakemore, K. (1999) 'International migration in later life: social care and policy implications', *Ageing and Society*, 19, 761–774.

Bloch, M. and Parry, J. (1982) *Death and the Regeneration of Life,* Cambridge: University of Cambridge Press.

Bok, S. (1984) *Secrets. On the Ethics of Concealment and Revelation*, Oxford: Oxford University Press.

Borrow, G. 1843. *The Bible in Spain*, London: John Murray.

Bourdieu, P. (1984) *Distinction. A Social Critique of the Judgement of Taste*, London: Routledge and Kegan Paul.

Bower, B. (2001) 'Croning, crones, ceremonies', *Croning. Resources for Wise Women of All Ages*. Online. Available at: http://www.croning.org/pages/534083/index.htm (accessed 5 September 2005).

Brandes, S. (1975) *Migration, Kinship and Community. Tradition and Transition in a Spanish Village*, New York: Academic Press.

—— (1980) *Metaphors of Masculinity. Sex and Status in Andalusian Folklore*, Philadelphia: University of Pennsylvania Press.

Brenan, G. (1980) *South from Granada*, Cambridge: Cambridge University Press.

Brettel, C.B. (2000) 'Theorizing migration in anthropology. The social construction of networks, identities, communities, and globalscapes', in C.B. Brettel and J.F. Hollifield (eds.) *Migration Theory. Talking Across Disciplines*, New York: Routledge, pp. 97–135.

Brewer, J. (2007) 'Entry on 'Ethnography', in Robertson, R. and Scholte, J.A. (eds.) *Encyclopaedia of Globalization*. New York: MTM/Routledge, pp. 408–410.

Brison, K.J. (1992) *Just Talk. Gossip, Meetings and Power in a Papua New Guinea Village*, Berkeley: University of California Press.

British Sociological Association (2002) 'Statement of Ethical Practice for the British Sociological Association'. Available at: http://www.britsoc.co.uk/user_doc/Statement%20of%20Ethical%20Practice.pdf (accessed 10 June 2006).

Brody, H. (1973) *Inishkillane. Change and Decline in the West of Ireland*, London: Faber and Faber.

Brooke, R. [1915] (1999) 'The soldier', in Untermeyer, L. (ed.) Modern British Poetry, New York. Online. Available at: http://www.bartleby.com/103/149.html (accessed 9 May 2006).

Brooks, G. (1997) 'District South-Spain. Provision of welfare and residential accommodation for elderly ex-service pensioners resident in Spain. A discussion paper'. Unpublished paper.

Bury, M. (1995) 'Ageing, gender and sociological theory', in S. Arber and J. Ginn (eds.) *Connecting Gender and Ageing. A Sociological Approach*, Buckingham: Open University Press. pp. 15–29.

Bytheway, B. (1995) *Ageism*, Buckingham: Open University Press.

Campbell, C. (1987) *The Romantic Ethic and the Spirit of Modern Consumerism*, Oxford: Basil Blackwell.

Castles, S. and Miller, M.J. (1998) *The Age of Migration. International Population Movements in the Modern World*, London: Palgrave Macmillan.

Chambers, I. (1994) *Migrancy, Culture, Identity*, London: Routledge.

Champion, T. and King, R. (1993) 'New trends in international migration in Europe', *Geographical Viewpoint*, 21: 45–57.

Chaney, D. (1995) 'Creating memories. Some images of aging in mass tourism', in M. Featherstone and A. Wernick (eds.) *Images of Ageing. Cultural Representations of Later Life*, London: Routledge, pp. 209–24.

Christensen, P., James, A. and Jenks, C. (2001) 'All we needed to do was blow the whistle: children's embodiment of time', in S. Cunningham-Burley and K. Backett-Milburn (eds.) *Exploring the Body*, Hampshire: Palgrave, pp. 201–222.

Clarke, J. and Critcher, C. (1985) *The Devil Makes Work. Leisure in Capitalist Britain*, Basingstoke: Macmillan.

Clifford, J. (1992) 'Travelling cultures', in L. Grossberg, C. Nelson and P. Treichler (eds.) *Cultural Studies*, London: Routledge, pp. 96–116.

Clifford, J. and Marcus, G. (eds.) (1986) *Writing Culture. The Poetics and Politics of Ethnography*, Berkeley: University of California Press.

Cohen, A.P. (1978) 'The same-but different': The allocation of identity in Whalsay, Shetland', *Sociological Review*, 26, (3): 449–470.

—— (1994) *Self Consciousness. An Alternative Anthropology of Identity*, London: Routledge.

—— (2002) 'Epilogue', in V. Amit (ed.) *Realizing Community. Concepts, Social Relations and Sentiments*, London: Routledge, pp. 165–170.

Conde, P. and Pelaez, A. (1999) 'Language difficulties mean that foreigners lead separate lives', in *Sur in English*, 9 –15 April: 27.

Corbin, J. and Corbin, M. (1986) *Urbane Thought: Culture and Class in an Andalusian City*, Hampshire: Gower Publishing Company.

Costa-action.co.uk (2003) 'Overseas property professional. British retirees in Spain are "living in squalor" says Foreign Office'. Available at: http://www.costa-action.co.uk/index.asp?file=Retiring_in_Spain (accessed 5 September 2006).

Counts, D.A. and Counts, D.R. (1996) *Over the Next Hill. An Ethnography of Rving Seniors in North America*, Ontario: Broadview Press.

Cribier, F. (1982) 'Aspects of retired migration from Paris: An essay in social and cultural geography', in A.M. Warnes (ed.) *Geographical Perspectives on the Elderly*, Chichester: John Wiley and Sons, pp. 111–137.

Crick, M. (1989) 'Representations of international tourism in the social sciences: Sun, sex, sights, savings and servility', *Annual Review of Anthropology*, 18, 307–344.

Cruikshank, M. (2003) *Learning to be Old. Gender, Culture and Aging*, Lanham, MD: Rowman and Littlefield.

Daatland, S.O. and Biggs, S. (2004) 'Ageing and diversity: A critical introduction', in S.O. Daatland and S. Biggs (eds.) *Ageing and Diversity. Multiple Pathways and Cultural Migrations*, Bristol: Policy Press, pp. 1–9.

Dawson, A. (1990) 'Ageing and change in pit villages of North East England', Unpublished thesis, University of Essex.

—— (1998) 'The dislocation of identity: Contestations of 'home community' in Northern England', in N. Rapport and A. Dawson (eds.) *Migrants of Identity. Perceptions of Home in a World of Movement*, Oxford: Berg, pp. 207–221.

—— (2002) 'The mining community and the ageing body: towards a phenomenology of community?', in V. Amit (ed.) *Realizing Community. Concepts, Social Relationships and Sentiments*, London: Routledge, pp. 21–37.

Deem, R. (1987) '"My husband says I'm too old for dancing": Women, leisure and life cycles', in P. Allatt, T. Keil, A. Bryman and B. Bytheway (eds.) *Women and the Life Cycle. Transitions and Turning Points*, Basingstoke: Palgrave Macmillan, pp. 106–116.

Degnen, C. (2007) 'Back to the future: temporality, narrative and the ageing self' in E. Hallam and T. Ingold (eds.) *Creativity and Cultural Improvisation*, London: Berg, unpaginated.

Dentith, S. (1995) *Bakhtinian Thought. An Introductory Reader*, London: Routledge.

Denzin, N.K. (1997) *Interpretive Ethnography. Ethnographic Practices for the 21st Century*, Thousand Oaks, CA: Sage.

Department for Work and Pensions (2005) Opportunity Age. Opportunity and Security Throughout Life, London: DWP. Available at: http://www.dwp.gov.uk/opportunity_age/first_report.asp (accessed 1 March 2006).

Dixey, R. (1988) '"Eyes down": A study of bingo', in E. Wimbush and M. Talbot (eds.) *Relative Freedoms. Women and Leisure*, Milton Keynes: Open University Press, pp. 91–101.

Douglas, M. (1966) *Purity and Danger. An Analysis of the Concepts of Pollution and Taboo*, London: Routledge and Kegan Paul.

Dunphy, R. (1995) 'Escaping from the jackboots: Spain, Portugal, Greece', in D. Gowland, B. O'Neill, and A. Reid (eds.) *The European Mosaic. Contemporary Politics, Economics and Culture*, Harlow: Longman, pp.127–145.

Dwyer, P. (2000) 'Movements to some purpose? An exploration of international retirement migration in the European Union', *Education and Ageing*, 15 (3): 353–377.

Echezarreta Ferrer, M. (2005) *El Lugar Europeo de Retiro*, Granada: Biblioteca Comares de Ciencia Jurídica.

Ekerdt, D. (1986) 'The Busy Ethic: Moral Continuity between Work and Retirement', *The Gerontologist*, 26(3): 239–244.

Elder, G.H.J. (1978) 'Family history and the life course', in T.K. Hareven (ed.) *Transitions. The Family and Life Course in Historical Perspective*, New York: Academic Press, pp. 17–64.

Ennew, J. (1980) *The Western Isles Today*, Cambridge: Cambridge University Press.

Eriksen, T.H. (2003) 'Introduction', in T.H. Eriksen (ed.) *Globalisation. Studies in Anthropology*, London: Pluto, pp.1–17.

Evandrou, M. (1997) *Baby Boomers. Ageing in the 21st Century*, London: Help the Aged.

Evans-Pritchard, E.E. (1940) *The Nuer: A Description of the Modes of Livelihood and Political Institutions of a Nilotic People*, Oxford: Oxford University Press.

Expatica.com. (2004) 'The Spanish way of dying'. Available at: http://www.expatica.com/source/site_article.asp?subchannel_id=86&story_id=12236&name=The+Spanish+way+of+dying (accessed 5 October 2005).

Fabian, J. (1983) *Time and the Other. How Anthropology makes its Object*, New York: Columbia University Press.

Featherstone, M. (1995) *Undoing Culture. Globalization, Postmodernism and Identity*, London: Sage.

Featherstone, M. and Hepworth, M. (1990) 'Images of ageing', in J. Bond and P.G. Coleman (eds.) *Ageing in Society. An Introduction to Social Gerontology*, London: Sage, pp.304–332.

—— (1991) 'The mask of ageing and the postmodern life course', in M. Featherstone, M. Hepworth and B. Turner (eds.) *The Body. Social Process and Cultural Theory*, London: Sage, pp. 371–389.

—— (1995) 'Images of positive aging: A case-study of Retirement Choice magazine', in M. Featherstone and A. Wernick (eds.) *Images of Aging: Cultural Representations of Later Life*, London: Routledge, pp. 29–47.

Fernandez, J. (1988) 'Andalusia on our minds: Two contrasting places in Spain as seen in a vernacular poetic duel of the late 19th century', *Cultural Anthropology*, 3 (1): 21–35.

Field, D. (2000) 'Older people's attitudes towards death in England', *Mortality*, 5 (3): 277–297.

Fisher, B.J. and Specht, D.K. (1999) 'Successful Aging and Creativity in Later Life', *Journal of Aging Studies*, 13 (4): 457–472.

Fitzgerald, F. (1986) *Cities on a Hill. A Journey through Contemporary American Cultures*, New York: Simon and Schusser.

Fixsen, R. (1999) 'Personal finance: Pensions in peril', *The Independent*, August 7.

Floodgate, P. (1999) 'Inheritance taxes: Nothing to do with me', *Sur in English, Finance and Gibraltar Special*, 29 October–4 November: xiv.

Ford, R. (1845) *A Handbook for Travellers in Spain*, London: John Murray.

Forster, P., Hitchcock, M. and Lyimo, F. (2000) *Race and Ethnicity in East Africa*, Basingstoke: Macmillan.

Fortier, A.M. (1999) 'Re-membering places and the performance of belonging', in V. Bell (ed.) *Performativity and Belonging*, London: Sage, pp. 41–64.

Foucault, M. (1977) *Discipline and Punish: The Birth of the Prison*, London: Penguin.

Francis, D., Kellaher, L. and Neophytou, G. (2000) 'Sustaining cemeteries: the user perspective', *Mortality*, 5 (1): 34–52.

—— (2001) 'The cemetery: the evidence of continuing bonds' in J. Hockey, J. Katz and N. Small (eds.) *Grief, Mourning and Death Ritual*, Buckingham and Philadelphia: Open University Press, pp. 226–236.

Friedman, J. (ed.) (1994) *Consumption and Identity*, London: Harwood Academic Publishers.

Fuchs, D. (2005) 'British import nimbyism to save Spanish retreats', *The Observer*, 19 June: 19.

Fxproperty.co.uk (2006) 'Poor pension planning costs UK retirees' dream of new life abroad'. Global Property News, 21 August 2006. Available at: http://www.fxproperty.co.uk/article2.aspx?article=news210806 (accessed 10 November 2006).

Ganguly, K. (1992) 'Migrant identities: Personal memory and the construction of selfhood', *Cultural Studies*, 6 (1): 27–50.

Gardner, K. (2002) *Age, Narrative and Migration. The Life Course and Life Histories of Bengali Elders in London*, London: Berg.

Geertz, C. (1973) *The Interpretation of Cultures*, New York: Basic books Inc.

—— (1988) *Works and Lives. the Anthropologist as Author*, Stanford, CA: Stanford University Press.

Gelfand, D. E. (1994) *Ageing and Ethnicity*, New York: Springer.

Gell, A. (1992) *The Anthropology of Time. Cultural Constructions of Temporal Maps and Images*, Oxford: Berg.

Giarchi, G.G. (1996) *Caring for Older Europeans. Comparative Studies in 29 Countries*, Aldershot: Arena.

Gibson, H. B. (2000) 'It keeps us young', *Ageing and Society*, 20: 773–779.

Giddens, A. (1990) *The Consequence of Modernity*, Oxford: Polity Press.

—— (1991) *Modernity and Self-Identity*, London: Polity Press.

Gilmore, D. (1987a) *Aggression and Community: Paradoxes of Andalusian Culture*, New Haven, CT: Yale University Press.

Gilmore, D. (ed.) (1987b) 'Honor and shame and the unity of the Mediterranean', *American Anthropological Association* special publication, 22.

Ginn, J. and Arber, S. (1999) 'Changing patterns of pension inequality: the shift from state to private sources', *Ageing and Society*, 19, (3): 319–342.

Gluckman, M. (1963) 'Gossip and scandal', *Current Anthropology*, 4 (3): 307–316.

Golander, H. (1995) 'Rituals of temporality. The social construction of time on a nursing ward', *Journal of Aging Studies*, 9 (2): 119–135.

Graburn, N. H. H. [1978] (1989) 'Tourism. The sacred journey' in V. Smith (ed.) *Hosts and Guests. The Anthropology of Tourism*, Philadelphia: University of Pennsylvania Press, pp. 21–36.

Grayson, S. (2001) *The Spanish Attraction. The British Presence in Spain from 1830 to 1965*, Fuengirola: Ediciones Santana S.L.

Grice-Hutchinson, M. (1964) *The English Cemetery at Málaga*, Granada: Gráfico ARTE.

Griswold, W. (1994) *Cultures and Societies in a Changing World*, Thousand Oaks, CA: Sage.

Gupta, A. and Ferguson, J. (1997a). 'Culture, power, place: ethnography at the end of an era', in A. Gupta and J. Ferguson (eds.) *Culture, Power, Place: Explorations in Critical Anthropology*, Durham, NC: Duke University Press, pp.1–46.

—— (1997b). 'Discipline and practice: 'the field' as site, method and location in anthropology', in A. Gupta and J. Ferguson (eds.) _Anthropological Locations: Boundaries and Grounds of a Field Science_, Berkeley: University of California Press, pp.1–29.

Gustafson, P. (2001) 'Retirement migration and transnational lifestyles', _Ageing and Society_, 21: 371–394.

Gustafson, P. (2002) 'Tourism and seasonal retirement migration', _Annals of Tourism Research_, 29, (4): 899–918.

Hallam, E. and Hockey, J. (2001) _Death, Memory and Material Culture_, Oxford: Berg.

Hammersley, M. and Atkinson, P. [1983] (1995) _Ethnography. Principles in Practice_, London: Routledge.

Hannerz, U. (1990) 'Cosmopolitans and locals in world culture', in M. Featherstone (ed.) _Global Culture. Nationalism, Globalization and Modernity_, London: Sage, pp. 237–51.

—— (1992) _Cultural Complexity. Studies in the Social Organization of Meaning_, New York: Columbia University Press.

—— (1996) _Transnational Connections. Culture, People, Places_, London: Routledge.

—— (2003) 'Several sites in one', in T.H. Eriksen (ed.) _Globalization. Studies in Anthropology_, London: Pluto, pp.18–38.

—— (2004) _Foreign News. Exploring the World of Foreign Correspondents_, Chicago: University of Chicago Press.

Hardill, I., Spradbery, J., Arnold-Boakes, J. and Marrugat, M. L. (2005) 'Severe health and social care issues among British migrants who retire to Spain', _Ageing and Society_, 25 (5): 769–783.

Hareven, T. K. (1982) 'The life course and ageing in historical perspective', in T.K. Hareven and K.J. Adams (eds.) _Ageing and Life Course Transitions. An Interdisciplinary Perspective_, London: Tavistock, pp. 1–26.

Harrison, S. (1999) 'Identity as a scarce resource', _Social Anthropology_, 7 (3): 239–251.

Harvey, P. (1994) 'Gender, community and confrontation: Power relations in drunkenness in Ocongate (Southern Peru)', in M. McDonald (ed.) _Gender, Drink and Drugs_, Oxford: Berg, pp.209–234.

Hastrup, K. (1992) 'Writing ethnography. State of the art', in J. Okely and H. Callaway (eds.) _Anthropology and Autobiography_, London: Routledge, pp. 116–133.

Haviland, J. (1977) _Gossip, Reputation and Knowledge in Zinacantan_, Chicago: University of Chicago Press.

Hawkin, N. and Rouse, H. (1999) 'Learning Spanish. Start off on the right foot', _The Marketplace_, September: 12.

Haworth, J.T. (1997) _Work, Leisure and Well Being_, London: Routledge.

Hazan, H. (1980) _The Limbo People. A Study of the Constitution of the Time Universe Among the Aged_, London: Routledge.

—— (1994) _Old Age. Constructions and Deconstructions_, Cambridge: Cambridge University Press.

Hellum, M. (1998) _Foreign Wives in the Wake of Tourism. Creating Identity on an Island in the Greek Archipelago_, working paper no. 31, Mannheim: Mannheim Centre for European Social Research.

—— (2000) _Have You Heard About......? Gendered Discourses in Gossip among Foreign Wives Living on an Island in the Greek Archipelago_, Athens. EKKE Working Papers, National Centre for Social Research.

182 *Bibliography*

Hemingway, E. (1932) *Death in the Afternoon*, New York: Scribner.
——— (1940) *For Whom the Bell Tolls*, New York: Scribner.
Hen Co-op. (1993) *Growing Old Disgracefully. New Ideas for Getting the Most out of Life*, London: Piatkus.
Hepworth, M. (1998) 'Ageing and the emotions', in G. Bendelow and S.J. Williams (eds.) *Emotions in Social Life. Critical Themes and Contemporary Issues*, London: Routledge, pp.173–189.
Hetherington, K. (1998) *Expressions of Identity. Space, Performance, Politics*, London: Sage.
——— (2000) *New Age Travellers. Van loads of Uproarious Humanity*, London: Casell.
Hockey, J. (1990) *Experiences of Death. An Anthropological Account*, Edinburgh: Edinburgh University Press.
——— (2002a) 'Interviews as ethnography? Disembodied social interaction in Britain' in N. Rapport (ed.) *British Subjects. An Anthropology of Britain*, Oxford: Berg, pp. 209–222.
——— (2002b) 'The importance of being intuitive: Arnold Van Gennep's rites of passage', *Mortality*, 7 (2): 210–219.
Hockey, J. and James, A. (1993) *Growing up and Growing Old. Ageing and Dependency in the Life Course*, London: Sage.
——— (2003) *Social Identities Across the Life Course*, Hampshire: Palgrave Macmillan.
Huber, A. and O'Reilly, K. (2004) 'The construction of *Heimat* under conditions of individualised modernity: Swiss and British elderly migrants in Spain', *Ageing and Society*, 24: 327–351.
Huby, G. (1992) 'Trapped in the present: The past, present and future of a group of old people in east London' in S. Wallman, S. (ed.) *Contemporary Futures. Perspectives from Social Anthropology*, London: Routledge, pp. 36–50.
Humphrey, R. (1993) 'Life stories and social careers: Ageing and social life in an ex-mining town', *Sociology*, 27 (1): 166–178.
Hurd, L.C. (1999) '"We're not old!": Older women's negotiation of aging and old-ness', *Journal of Aging Studies*, 13 (4): 419–439.
Hurtado Garcia, I. (2006) 'Desires, changes and uncertainties. European retired women on the Costa Blanca', paper presented at the European Association of Social Anthropologists, Bristol, UK, September.
Inglis, D. (2000) *The Delicious History of the Holiday*, London: Routledge.
Ingrisch, D. (1995) 'Conformity and resistance as women age', in Arber, S. and Ginn, J. (eds.) *Connecting Gender and Ageing. A Sociological Approach*, Buckingham: Open University Press, pp.42–55.
Instituto de Estadística de Andalucía. (2001) *Censo de Poblacíon y Viviendas* (2001) Online. Available at: http://www.juntadeandalucia.es/institutodeestadistica/censo2001 (accessed 30 July 2006).
——— (2002) *Inmigración extranjera en Andalucía*, Sevilla: Instituto de Estadística de Andalucía.
International Labour Organisation (2002) 'Facing the ageing gap: New-age solutions to old age problems', press communication from the UN Forum on Ageing. 2nd World Assembly on Ageing, Madrid. Online. Available at: http://www.ilo.org/public/english/bureau/inf/pkits/2002/ageing.htm (accessed 10 December 2004)
Jacobsen, J.K.S. (2000) 'Anti-tourist attitudes: Mediterranean charter tourism', *Annals of Tourism Research*, 27 (2): 284–300.
Jahoda, M. (1982) *Employment and Unemployment. A Social-psychological Analysis*, Cambridge: Cambridge University Press.

James, W. and Mills, D. (2005) *The Qualities of Time. Anthropological Approaches*, Oxford: Berg.

Jeffrys, M. (Ed.) (1989) *Growing Old in the Twentieth Century*, London: Routledge.

Jerrome, D. (1989) 'Virtue and vicissitude. the role of old people's clubs', in M. Jeffrys (ed.) *Growing Old in the Twentieth Century*, London: Routledge, pp. 151–165.

—— (1990) 'Intimate relations', in J. Bond and P. Coleman (eds.) *Ageing in Society*, London: Sage, pp. 181–208.

—— (1992) *Good Company. An Anthropological Study of Old People in Groups*, Edinburgh: Edinburgh University Press.

Jonker, G. (1997) 'Death, gender and memory. Remembering loss and burial as a migrant', in D. Field, J. Hockey and N. Small (eds.) *Death, Gender and Ethnicity*, London: Routledge.

Joseph, A.E. and Hallman, B.C. (1998) 'Over the hill and far away: Distance as a barrier to the provision of assistance to elderly relatives', *Social Science and Medicine*, 46 (6): 631–639.

Jurdao Arrones, F. (1990) *España en Venta*, Madrid: Endymion.

Jurdao Arrones, F. and Sánchez, M. (1990) *España, Asilo de Europa*, Barcelona: Planeta.

Kahn, J. (1989) 'Culture. Demise or resurrection?' *Critique of Anthropology*, 9 (2): 5–25.

Kastenbaum, R. (1993) 'Encrusted elders: Arizona and the political spirit of postmodern aging', in T.R. Cole, A. Achenbaum, P. Jakobi, and R. Kastenbaum (eds.) *Voices and Visions of Aging: Toward a Critical Gerontology*, New York: Springer, pp.160–183.

Katz, S. (2005) *Cultural Aging: Life Course, Lifestyle, and Senior Worlds*, Ontario: Broadview Press.

Katz, S. and Laliberte-Rudman, D. (2005) 'Exemplars of retirement: Identity and agency between lifestyle and social movement', in S. Katz (ed.) *Cultural Aging. Life Course, Lifestyle and Senior Worlds*, Ontario: Broadview Press, pp. 140–160.

Keith, J. (1980) 'Old age and community creation', in C.L. Fry (ed.) *Aging in Culture and Society*, New York: J.F. Bergin Inc.

Keith, J., Fry, C.L. and Glascock, A.P. (1994) *The Aging Experience: Diversity and Commonality Across Cultures*, London: Sage.

Keith-Ross, J. (1977) *Old People, New Lives. Community Creation in a Retirement Residence*, Chicago: The University of Chicago Press.

Kellaher, L. Prendergast, D. and Hockey, J. (2005) 'In the shadow of the traditional grave', *Mortality*, 10 (4): 237–250.

King, R. (2001) 'The troubled passage: migration and cultural encounters in southern Europe', in King, R. (ed.) *The Mediterranean Passage. Migration and New Cultural Encounters in Southern Europe*, Liverpool: Liverpool University Press, pp. 1–21.

King, R., Warnes, A. M. and Williams, A. M. (1998) 'Editorial introduction', *International Journal of Population Geography*, 4: 87–89.

—— (2000) *Sunset Lives. British Retirement Migration to the Mediterranean*, Oxford: Berg.

Kinoshita, Y. and Kiefer, C. W. (1992) *Refuge of the Honored. Social Organization in a Japanese Retirement Community*, Berkeley: University of California Press.

Kofman, E., Phizacklea, A., Raghuram, P. and Sales, R. (eds.) (2000) *Gender and International Migration in Europe: Employment, Welfare and Politics*, New York and London: Routledge.

Lakoff, G. and Johnson, M. (1980) *Metaphors We Live By*, Chicago: University of Chicago Press.

Langford, P. (2000) *Englishness Identified. Manners and Character: 1650–1850*, Oxford: Oxford University Press.

Laslett, P. (1989) *A Fresh Map of Life: The Emergence of the Third Age*, London: Weidenfeld and Nicolson.

Law, C.M. and Warnes, A.M. (1982) 'The destination decision in retirement migration', in A.M. Warnes (ed.) *Geographical Perspectives on the Elderly*, Chichester: John Wiley and Sons, pp. 53–81.

Lawler, S. (2005) 'Introduction: Class, culture and identity', *Sociology*, 39 (5): 797–806.

Leach, E.R. (1954) *Political Systems of Highland Burma: A Study of Kachin Social Structure*, Cambridge, MA: Harvard University Press.

—— (1966) *Rethinking Anthropology*, London: The Athlone Press.

Lee, L. (1955) *A Rose for Winter. Travels in Andalusia*, London: Hogarth Press.

—— (1970) *As I Walked Out One Midsummer Morning*, London: World Books.

Llobera, J. (1986) 'Fieldwork in Southwestern Europe: Anthropological panacea or epistemological straitjacket?' *Critique of Anthropology*, 6 (2): 25–31.

Long, J. (1989) 'A part to play: Men experiencing leisure through retirement', in B. Bytheway, T. Keil, P. Allatt, P. and A. Bryman (eds.) *Becoming and Being Old. Sociological Approaches to Later Life*, London: Sage.

Longino Jnr, C.F. (1982) 'American retirement communities and residential relocation', in A.M. Warnes (ed.) *Geographical Perspectives on the Elderly*, Chichester: John Wiley and Sons, pp. 239–262.

Luhmann, N. (1979) *Trust and Power*, New York: Wiley.

Lund, K. (2005) 'Finding place in nature: 'Intellectual' and local knowledge in a Spanish natural park', *Conservation and Society*, Special edition: B. Campbell (ed.) *Re-placing Nature* 3 (2): 371–387.

—— (2007). 'Walking and viewing: narratives of belonging in Southern Spain' in S. Coleman and P. Collins (eds.) Dislocating the field (provisional title)., Newcastle: Cambridge Scholars Press, unpaginated.

Macdonald, S. (1994) 'Whisky, women and the Scottish drink problem. A view from the Highlands', in M. McDonald (ed.) *Gender, Drink and Drugs*, Oxford: Berg, pp. 125–142.

Macfarlane, A. (1978) *The Origins of English Individualism. The Family, Property and Social Transition*, Oxford: Blackwell.

Malkki, L. H. (1995) *Purity and Exile: Violence, Memory and National Cosmology Among Hutu Refugees in Tanzania*. Chicago: University of Chicago Press.

—— (1997) 'National geographic: The rooting of peoples and the territorialization of national identity among scholars and refugees', in A. Gupta and J. Ferguson (eds.) *Culture, Power, Place: Explorations in Critical Anthropology*, Durham, NC: Duke University Press, pp. 52–74.

Marcus, G. E. (1995) 'Ethnography in/of the world system: the emergence of multi-sited ethnography', *Annual Review of Anthropology*, 24: 95–117.

Marcus, G. and Fischer, M. (1986) *Anthropology as Cultural Critique: An Experimental Moment in the Human Sciences*, Chicago: University of Chicago Press.

The Marketplace, (1998) 'The liturgy of the drunkards', poem in *The Marketplace*, October.

—— (1999) 'Dream houses', in *The Marketplace*, August.

Mason, J. (1988) 'No peace for the wicked: Older married women and leisure', in E. Wimbush and M. Talbot (eds.) *Relative Freedoms. Women and Leisure*, Milton Keynes: Open University Press, pp. 75–86.

Mason, J. (1996) *Qualitative Researching*, London: Sage.

McDonald, M. (1994) 'Drinking and social identity in the west of France', in M. McDonald (ed.) *Gender, Drink and Drugs*, Oxford: Berg, pp.99–124.

McHugh, K. E. (2000) 'The 'ageless self'? Emplacement of identities in sun belt retirement communities', *Journal of Aging Studies*, 14 (1): 103–115.

—— (2003) 'Three faces of ageism: society, image and place', *Ageing and Society*, 23: 165–185.

Miller, D. and Slater, D. (2000) *The Internet: An Ethnographic Approach*, Oxford: Berg.

Mintz, S. (1997) *Carnival, Song and Society. Gossip, Sexuality and Creativity in Andalusia*, Oxford: Berg.

Misztal, B. (1996) *Trust in Modern Societies. The Search for the Bases of Social Order*, Cambridge: Polity Press.

Moore, S. F. (1978) *Law as Process. An Anthropological Approach*, London: Routledge and Kegan Paul.

Morgan, C. (2006) 'Gran tours. The market for exciting breaks that won't blow the pension is maturing nicely', *The Mirror*, 9 March.

Morgan, D. H. J. (1985) *The Family, Politics and Social Theory*, London: Routledge and Kegan Paul.

Mullan, C. (1993) 'Growing old in Spain — the problems of the elderly British expatriate community in Spain', *International Journal of Geriatric Psychiatry*, 8: 1015–1017.

Myerhoff, B. (1978) *Number our Days*, New York: Simon and Schuster.

—— (1984) 'Rites and signs of ripening: the intertwining of ritual time and growing older', in D.I. Kertzer and J. Keith (eds.) *Age and Anthropological Theory*, Ithaca: Cornell University Press. pp. 305–330.

—— (1986) "Life not death in Venice': It's second life', in V. Turner and E.M. Bruner (eds.) *The Anthropology of Experience,* Urbana and Chicago: University of Illinois Press, pp. 261–287.

Nettleton, S. and Watson, J. (1998) 'The body in everyday life. An introduction', in S. Nettleton, S. and J. Watson (eds.) *The Body in Everyday Life*. London: Routledge, pp. 1–24.

Neugarten, B. L. (1974) 'Age groups in American society and the rise of the young old', *Annals of the Academy of Social and Political Science*, 415: 187–198.

Nowotny, H. (1994) *Time. The Modern and Postmodern Experience,* trans. Neville Plaice, Cambridge: Polity Press.

Okely, J. (1990) 'Clubs for the troisième age? 'Communitas' or conflict?' in P. Spencer (ed.) *Anthropology and the Riddle of the Sphinx. Paradoxes of Change in the Life Course,* London: Routledge, pp. 194–210.

Okely, J. and Callaway, H. (eds.) (1992) *Anthropology and Autobiography*, London: Routledge.

Oliver, C. (1999) 'Ordering the disorderly', *Education and Ageing*, 14, (2): 171–185.

—— (2000) 'We've got the style it takes. British national identities in Andalucía', *Intergraph. Journal of Dialogic Anthropology*, 1 (3). Available at http://www.intergraphjournal.com (accessed January 2002).

—— (2002) 'Killing the golden goose? Debates about tradition in an Andalucían village', *Journal of Mediterranean Studies*, 12 (1): 169–189.

—— (2004) 'Cultural influence in migrants' negotiations of death. The case of retired migrants in Spain', *Mortality*, 9 (3), 235–253.

———— (2005) 'El consumo de patrimonio cultural: Migración norte europea en Andalucía' in Carrera, G. and Dietz, G. (eds.) *Patrimonio Inmaterial, Multiculturalidad y Gestion de la Diversidad*, Sevilla: Instituto Andaluz del Patrimonio Histórico, Junta de Andalucía, Consejería de Cultura.

———— (2006) 'More than a tourist: Distinction, old age and the selective consumption of tourist-space', in K. Meethan, A. Anderson and S. Miles (eds.) *Narratives of Place and Self: Consumption and Representation in Tourism*, Wallingford, Oxfordshire: CAB International, pp. 196–216.

———— (2007, forthcoming). 'Imagined communitas: older migrants and aspirational mobility', in V. Amit (eds.) *Going First Class? New Approaches to Privileged Travel and Movement*, Oxford: Berghahn, unpaginated.

Oliver, C., Jansen, S. and Heller, D. (2000) 'Up-routings: a critical engagement with identity and/in movement', *Anthropology in Action*, 7 (1-2): 2–10.

Oliver, P., Davis, I. and Bentley, I. (1994) *Dunroamin. The Suburban Semi and its Enemies*, London: Pimlico.

Olwig, K. F. (1993) *Global Culture, Island Identity, Continuity and Change in the Afro-Caribbean Community of Nevis*, Reading: Harwood Academic Publishers.

Ong, A. (1995) 'Women out of China: traveling tales and traveling theories in postcolonial feminism', in R. Behar and D. Gordon (eds.) *Women Writing Culture*, Berkeley: University of California Press, pp. 350–372.

O'Reilly, K. (2000a) *The British on the Costa-del-Sol. Transnational Identities and Local Communities*, London: Routledge.

———— (2000b) 'Trading intimacy for liberty: women on the Costa-del-Sol', in F. Anthias and G. Lazaridis (eds.) *Gender and Migration in Southern Europe*, Oxford: Berg, pp. 227–248.

———— (2002) 'Britain in Europe/The British in Spain. Exploring Britain's changing relationship to the other', *Nations and Nationalism*, 8 (2): 179–194.

———— (2003) 'When is a tourist? The articulation of tourism and migration in Spain's Costa del Sol', *Tourist Studies*, 3 (3): 301–317.

———— (2004) The Extent and Nature of Integration of European Migrants in Spanish Society. With Special Reference to the British Case, Online. Available at: http://www.abdn.ac.uk/socsci/documents/staff/report%20for%20councils1.doc (accessed August 2006).

Paerregaard, K. (1997) *Linking Separate Worlds. Urban Migrants and Rural Lives in Peru*, Oxford: Berg.

Paine, R. (1967) 'What is gossip about? An alternative hypothesis', *Man*, 2: 278–285.

Percival, J. (2000) 'Gossip in sheltered housing: Its cultural importance and social implications', *Ageing and Society*, 20: 303–325.

Phillips, A. (1996) *On Flirtation*, Cambridge, MA: Harvard University Press.

Phillimore, P. and Bell, P. (2005) 'Trust and risk in a German chemical town', *Ethnos*, 70 (3): 311–334.

Phillipson, C. (1982) *Capitalism and the Construction of Old Age*, London and Basingstoke: Macmillan.

———— (1990) 'The sociology of retirement' in J. Bond and P. Coleman (eds.) *Ageing in Society. An Introduction to Social Gerontology*, London: Sage, pp. 144–167.

Phillipson, C. and Ahmed, N. (2004) 'Transnational communities, migration and changing identities in later life: a new research agenda', in S.O. Daatland and S. Biggs (eds.) *Ageing and Diversity. Multiple Pathways and Cultural Migrations*, Bristol: Policy Press, pp. 157–173.

Pina-Cabral, J. de (1989) 'The Mediterranean as a category of regional comparison: A critical view', *Current Anthropology*, 30 (3): 399–406.

Pink, S. (1997) *Women and Bullfighting. Gender, Sex and the Consumption of Tradition*, Oxford: Berg.

Pitt-Rivers, J. A. (1971) *The People of the Sierra*, Chicago: University of Chicago Press.

Price, D. (1992) 'Retirement abroad. The pastoral care of English-speaking Catholics in Spain'. Unpublished paper.

Rapport, N. (1993) Diverse *World Views in an English Village*, Edinburgh: Edinburgh University Press.

—— (1998) 'Coming home to a dream: A study of the immigrant discourse of 'Anglo-Saxons' in Israel', in N. Rapport and A. Dawson (eds.) *Migrants of Identity. Perceptions of Home in a World of Movement*, London: Berg, pp. 61–83.

Rapport, N. and Dawson, A. (eds.) (1998) *Migrants of Identity. Perceptions of Home in a World of Movement*, Oxford: Berg.

Rapport, N. and Overing, J. (2000) *Social and Cultural Anthropology. The Key Concepts*, London and New York: Routledge.

Reimers, E. (1999) 'Death and identity: Graves and funerals as cultural communication', *Mortality*, 4 (2): 147–166.

Rodríguez, V. (2001) 'Tourism as a recruiting post for retirement migration', *Tourism Geographies*, 3 (1): 52–63.

Rodríguez, V., Fernández-Mayoralas, G. and Rojo, F. (1998) 'European retirees on the Costa del Sol: A cross-national comparison', *International Journal of Population Geography*, 4: 183–200.

Rodríguez, V., Casado Díaz, M.A., and Huber, A. (2000) 'Impactos de los retirados Europeos en la costa española', *Ofrim Suplementos*, 7: 117–138.

Rojek, C. (1985) *Capitalism and Leisure Theory*, London and New York: Tavistock.

—— (1993) *Ways of Escape. Modern Transformations in Leisure and Travel*, London: Macmillan.

Rojek, C. and Urry, J. (1997) 'Transformations of travel and theory', in C. Rojek and J. Urry (eds.) *Touring Cultures. Transformation of Travel and Theory*, London: Routledge, pp. 1–19.

Rosaldo, R. (1993) *Culture and Truth. The Remaking of Social Analysis*, Boston: Beacon Press.

Rossman, G. B. and Rallis, S. F. (1998) *Learning in the Field. An Introduction to Qualitative Research*, Thousand Oaks, CA: Sage.

Rouse, R. (1991) 'Mexican migration and the social space of postmodernism', *Diaspora*, 1 (1): 8–23.

Rowe, J. W. and Kahn, R. L. (1998) *Successful Aging*, New York: Dell.

Rozenberg, D. (1995) 'International tourism and utopia: the Balearic Islands', in M.F. Lanfant, J.B. Allcock and E.M. Bruner (eds.) *International Tourism: Identity and Change*, London: Sage, pp. 159–176.

Ryan, C. (1991) *Recreational Tourism. A Social Science Perspective*, London: Routledge.

Sallnow, M.J. (1981) 'Communitas reconsidered: The sociology of Andean pilgrimage', *Man*, 16: 163–182.

Salmon, K. (1991) *The Modern Spanish Economy: Transformation and Integration into Europe*, London: Pinta.

Sartre, J.P. (1947) *No Exit and the Flies*, New York: Knopf.

Savidge, V.E. (1999) 'Long-term care — is it an issue? The expatriates' guide to long-term care', *Streetwise Magazine*, 12 November.

Sawchuk, K.A. (1995) 'From gloom to boom: Age, identity and target marketing', in M. Featherstone and A. Wernick (eds.) *Images of Aging. Cultural Representations of Later Life*, London and New York: Routledge, pp. 173–187.

Scheper-Hughes, N. (1992) *Death Without Weeping: The Violence of Everyday Life in Brazil*, Berkeley: University of California Press.

Schneider, J. (1981) 'Of vigilance and virgins: Honor, shame and access to resources in Mediterranean societies', *Ethnology*, 10: 1–24.

Schuller, T. (1989) 'Work-ending: employment and ambiguity in later life', in Bytheway, B. (ed.) *Becoming and Being Old: Sociological Approaches to Later Life*, London: Sage, pp. 41–54.

Seligman, A.B. (1997) *The Problem of Trust*, Princeton, NJ: Princeton University Press.

Senior Journal.com. (2005) 'World's oldest marathon runner leads team of seniors in Scotland'. Online. Available at: http://www.seniorjournal.com/NEWS/Sports/5-06-13OldesMarathoner.htm (accessed 5 July 2006)

Seymour-Davies, H. (1996) *The Bottlebrush Tree: A Village in Andalusia*, London: Blackswan.

Shakespeare, T. (1994) 'Cultural representations of disabled people: dustbin for disavowal', *Disability and Society*, 9 (3): 283–299.

Shields, R. (1991) *Places on the Margin: Alternative Geographies of Modernity*, London: Routledge.

Shilling, C. (1993) *The Body and Social Theory*, London: Sage.

—— (2005) *The Body in Culture, Technology and Society*, London: Sage.

Sibley, D. (1995) *Geographies of Exclusion*, London: Routledge.

Škrbiš, Z. (1999) *Long Distance Nationalism. Diasporas, Homelands and Identities*, Hants: Ashgate.

Spacks, P.M. (1985) *Gossip*, Chicago: University of Chicago Press.

Spencer, P. (ed.) (1990) *Anthropology and the Riddle of the Sphinx. Paradoxes of Change in the Life Course*, London: Routledge.

Stephens, J. (1976) *Loners, Losers and Lovers: Elderly Tenants in a Slum Hotel*, Seattle: University of Washington Press.

Stevens, J. (2006) 'Dark side of sunny Spain for Britain's elderly expatriates', *The Observer*, July 9.

Stewart, C. (1999) *Driving over Lemons. An Optimist in Andalucía*, London: Sort of books.

Strathern, M. (1992) *After Nature: English Kinship in the Late Twentieth Century*, Cambridge: Cambridge University Press.

Suárez-Navaz, L. (2004) *Rebordering the Mediterranean. Boundaries and Citizenship in Southern Europe*, New York and Oxford: Berghahn.

Szwed, J.F. (1966) 'Gossip, drinking and social control: Consensus and communication in a Newfoundland parish', *Ethnology*, 5: 434–441.

Tebbutt, M. (1995) *Women's Talk? A Social History of Gossip in Working Class Neighborhoods, 1880–1960*, Brookfield, VT: Scolar Press.

Thompson, C.J. and Tambyah, S.K. (1999) 'Trying to be cosmopolitan', *Journal of Consumer Research*, 26 (3): 214–241.

Thompson, E.P. (1967) 'Time, work discipline and industrial capitalism', *Past and Present*, 38: 56–97.

Thompson, P.R., Itzin, C. and Abendstern, M. (1991) *I Don't Feel Old. The Experience of Later Life*, Oxford: Oxford University Press.

Thrift, N. (1996) *Spatial Formations*, London: Sage.

Tinker, A. (1992) *Elderly People in Modern Society*, London: Longman.

Torres, S. (1999) 'A culturally relevant theoretical framework for the study of successful ageing', *Ageing and Society*, 19: 33–51.

—— (2001) 'Understandings of successful ageing in the context of migration: the case of Iranian immigrants to Sweden', *Ageing and Society*, 21 (3): 333–355.

―――― (2004) 'Making sense of the construct of successful ageing: the migrant experience' in S.O. Daatland and S. Biggs (eds.) *Ageing and Diversity. Multiple Pathways and Cultural Migrations*, Bristol: Policy Press, pp. 125–139.

Townsend, P. (1986) 'Ageism and social policy', in C. Phillipson and A. Walker (eds.) *Ageing and Social Policy. A Critical Assessment*, Aldershot: Gower, pp. 15–44.

Tulle-Winton, E. (1999) 'Growing old and resistance: Towards a new cultural economy of old age?' *Ageing and Society*, 19: 281–299.

Turner, B. (1996) *The Body and Society*, Sage: London.

Turner, V. (1967) *The Forest of Symbols: Aspects of Ndembu Ritual*, Ithaca, NY: Cornell University Press.

―――― (1969) *The Ritual Process. Structure and Anti-Structure*, London: Routledge and Kegan Paul.

―――― (1974) *Dramas, Fields and Metaphors: Symbolic Action in Human Society*, Ithaca, NY: Cornell University Press.

Turner, L. and Ash, J. (1975) *The Golden Hordes: International Tourism and the Pleasure Periphery*, London: Constable.

Tyler, S.A. (1986) 'Post-modern ethnography. From document of the occult to occult document', in J. Clifford and G.E. Marcus (eds.) *Writing Culture. The Poetics and Politics of Ethnography*, Berkeley: University of California Press.

Urry, J. (2002) *The Tourist Gaze. Leisure and Travel in Contemporary Societies*, 2nd edition, London: Sage.

Valenzuela, M. (1988) 'Spain: The phenomenon of mass tourism', in G. Shaw and A.M. Williams (eds.) *Tourism and Economic Development. Western European Experiences*, London: Belhaven, pp. 40–60.

van den Hoonard, D.K. (1994) 'Paradise lost: Widowhood in a Florida retirement community', *Journal of Aging Studies*, 8 (2): 121–132.

Van Gennep, A. [1909] (1960) *The Rites of Passage*, London: Routledge and Kegan Paul.

Veblen, T. [1899] (1967) *The Theory of the Leisure Class*, New York: Penguin.

Verlot, M. and Oliver, C. (2005) 'European consciousness amongst expatriates in Belgium and Spain', in D. Wildemeersch, M. Bron and V. Stroobants (eds.) *Active Citizenship and Multiple Identities in Europe*, Frankfurt: Peter Lang Verlag, pp. 259–277.

Vincent, J. (1995) *Inequality and Old Age*, London: UCL Press.

Waldren, J. (1996) *Insiders and Outsiders. Paradise and Reality in Mallorca*, Oxford: Berghahn.

―――― (1997) 'We are not tourists. We live here', S. Abram, J.D. Waldren and D. Macleod (eds.) in *Tourists and Tourism. Identifying with People and Places*, Oxford: Berg, pp 51–70.

Walker, A. and Maltby, T. (1997) *Ageing Europe*, Buckingham: Open University Press.

Walker, A. and Phillipson, C. (eds.) (1986) *Ageing and Social Policy. A Critical Assessment*, Aldershot: Gower.

Warnes, A.M. (1982) 'Geographical perspectives on ageing', in Warnes, A.M. (ed.) *Geographical Perspectives on the Elderly*, Chichester: John Wiley and Sons.

―――― (1991) 'Migration to and seasonal residence in Spain of Northern European elderly people', *European Journal of Gerontology*, 1: 53–60.

―――― (2004) 'Older foreign migrants in Europe: multiple pathways and welfare positions' in S.O. Daatland and S. Biggs (eds.) *Ageing and Diversity. Multiple Pathways and Cultural Migrations*, Bristol: Policy Press, pp. 141–155.

Warnes, A.M. and Williams, A. (2006) 'Older migrants in Europe: A new focus for migration studies', *Journal of Ethnic and Migration Studies*, 32 (8): 1257–1281.

Warnes, A.M., Friedrich, K., Kellaher, L. and Torres, S. (2004) 'The diversity and welfare of older migrants in Europe', *Ageing and Society*, 24: 307–326.

Werbner, P. (1999) 'Global pathways. Working class cosmopolitans and the creation of transnational ethnic worlds', *Social Anthropology*, 7 (1): 17–35.

Williams, A.M. and Hall, C.M. (2002) 'Tourism, migration, circulation and mobility: The contingencies of time and place', in A.M. Williams and C.M. Hall (eds.) *Tourism and Migration: New Relationships Between Production and Consumption*, London: Kluwer Academic Publishers, pp. 1–52.

Williams, A.M., King, R. and Warnes, T. (1997) 'A place in the sun. International retirement migration from northern to southern Europe', *European Urban and Regional Studies*, 4 (2): 115–134.

Williams, R. (1990) *A Protestant Legacy. Attitudes to Death and Illness among Older Aberdonians*, Oxford: Clarendon.

Woodward, K. (1991) *Aging and its Discontents. Freud and Other Fictions*, Bloomington: Indiana University Press.

Wray, S. (2003) 'Women growing older: Agency, ethnicity and culture', *Sociology*, 37 (3): 511–527.

Xavier, Inda, J. and Rosaldo, R. (eds.) (2002) *The Anthropology of Globalization. A Reader*, Oxford: Blackwell.

Young, E., Seale, C. and Bury, M. (1998) '"It's not like family going is it?" Negotiating friendship boundaries towards the end of life', *Mortality*, 3 (1): 27–43.

Young, M. and Cullen, L. (1996) *A Good Death. Conversations with East Londoners*, London: Routledge.

Zabusky, S. E. (1995) *Launching Europe*, Princeton, NJ: Princeton University Press.

Zinovieff, S. (1991) 'Inside out and outside in: Gossip, hospitality and the Greek character', *Journal of Mediterranean Studies*, 1 (1): 120–134.

Index